PENGUIN CANADA

BUILDING CANADA

JONATHAN F. VANCE is a professor of
history and the Canada Research Chair
in Conflict and Culture at The University
of Western Ontario, London, and the
author of *High Flight*.

Also by Jonathan F. Vance

A Gallant Company:
The True Story of "The Great Escape"

High Flight:
Aviation and the Canadian Imagination

Encyclopedia of Prisoners of War and Internment (editor)

Death So Noble:
Memory, Meaning, and the First World War

Objects of Concern:
Canadian Prisoners of War Through the Twentieth Century

BUILDING
CANADA

PEOPLE AND PROJECTS THAT SHAPED THE NATION

JONATHAN F. VANCE

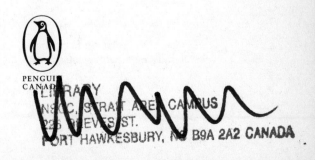

PENGUIN
CANADA

PENGUIN CANADA

Published by the Penguin Group

Penguin Group (Canada), 90 Eglinton Avenue East, Suite 700, Toronto, Ontario, Canada
M4P 2Y3 (a division of Pearson Penguin Canada Inc.)

Penguin Group (USA) Inc., 375 Hudson Street, New York, New York 10014, U.S.A.
Penguin Books Ltd, 80 Strand, London WC2R 0RL, England
Penguin Ireland, 25 St Stephen's Green, Dublin 2, Ireland (a division of Penguin Books Ltd)
Penguin Group (Australia), 250 Camberwell Road, Camberwell, Victoria 3124, Australia
(a division of Pearson Australia Group Pty Ltd)
Penguin Books India Pvt Ltd, 11 Community Centre, Panchsheel Park, New Delhi – 110 017, India
Penguin Group (NZ), cnr Airborne and Rosedale Roads, Albany, Auckland 1310, New Zealand
(a division of Pearson New Zealand Ltd)
Penguin Books (South Africa) (Pty) Ltd, 24 Sturdee Avenue, Rosebank, Johannesburg 2196,
South Africa

Penguin Books Ltd, Registered Offices: 80 Strand, London WC2R 0RL, England

First published 2006

1 2 3 4 5 6 7 8 9 10   (WEB)

Copyright © Jonathan F. Vance, 2006

Page 310 constitutes an extension of this copyright page.

Manufactured in Canada.

ISBN 0-14-305528-1

Library and Archives Canada Cataloguing in Publication data available upon request

Visit the Penguin Group (Canada) website at **www.penguin.ca**

Special and corporate bulk purchase rates available; please see
www.penguin.ca/corporatesales or call 1-800-399-6858, ext. 477 or 474.

*This book is dedicated, not to the architects, designers,
and politicians who gathered public acclaim for these projects,
but to the numberless workers who actually built them,
and especially to those who lost their lives in the endeavours.*

CONTENTS

ACKNOWLEDGMENTS

My first debt goes to Cynthia Good, who brought this project to me nearly four years ago under what I thought then was the mistaken impression that I was the right person for it. It has turned out to be a great joy to research and write, as has working with Cynthia on it through the early stages. I hope that the finished product hasn't disappointed her. I'm also very grateful to Jonathan Webb, whose sage advice and clear thinking made this a much better book than it was when he first laid eyes on it, to Allyson Latta, for her sensitive editing and genuine enthusiasm for the project, and to everyone at Penguin, especially Tracy Bordian and Diane Turbide.

I would also like to thank the many friends and colleagues who have offered assistance, advice, and wise counsel as the book was taking shape: Mike Bartlett, David Bentley, Claire Campbell, Michael Dove, James Flath, Keith Fleming, Alan MacEachern, Linda McKnight, Vern Shute, Neville Thompson, John Willis, and Christine Wright. My gratitude also goes to the research assistants who worked with me on various parts of the project: Kara Brown, Erin Dunham, and Lisa Huynh.

Many other people went above and beyond the call of duty in digging out obscure information to fill the holes that opened up in the narrative as I wrote it: Sarah Kalnay, of the Legislative Assembly of the Northwest Territories; Francis Mansbridge at the North Vancouver Museum and Archives; Patrick Michael Clark of the Legislative Assembly of the Yukon Territory; Michael Pennock of the Fernie and District Historical Society; architect Gino Pin; Richard Stoker at the Arts and Culture Centre in St. John's; Tory Tronrud of the Thunder Bay Museum; and Jill MacMicken Wilson of the Prince Edward Island Archives and Records Office. I am especially grateful to Qennefer Brown, for her generosity in giving me a glimpse inside the life of her parents, Emanuel Hahn and Elizabeth Wyn Wood. Finally, and as always, I am grateful to my family for their patience and good humour, particularly in putting up with my excitement as we crossed the Quebec Bridge by train in the summer of 2005.

INTRODUCTION

Some countries have too much history, former prime minister Mackenzie King once quipped, but Canada has too much geography. He was probably thinking in political terms—certain regions remained a mystery to our longest-serving and most politically astute national leader—but there was a deeper truth to his words. The challenge of geography has loomed over much of our history, the sheer size of the country being at once its greatest strength and a source of weakness. When one end of the country is separated from the other by thousands of miles of land and water, people and governments face a host of difficulties unknown to smaller nations.

The indigenous peoples of North America, of course, would never have thought in these terms. For them, the land was not something to be overcome but rather something to be used, albeit through toil, to their advantage. The innumerable rivers and streams cutting into the interior of the continent gave them a ready-made transportation system, and over the centuries, Aboriginal communities established a vast network of interlocking trade routes, using waterways where they could, portaging where they had to, and pushing trails through the bush only where the river system failed them.

The first Europeans to establish a foothold in North America were quick to graft their own trade networks onto the centuries-old Aboriginal routes, but, for them, the rivers alone weren't enough. They soon realized that they could exploit the fur economy efficiently only by erecting small trading posts at key points along the waterways. Rough log huts and stockades thus formed the basis of an expanding infrastructure for transportation and trade in North America.

The fur barons, of course, wouldn't have known it as an *infrastructure*— a term that came out of the industrial age and was first used in the British magazine *Chamber's Journal* in 1927 to refer to the bridges, tunnels, and culverts that had to be constructed before a railway line could be built. Still, it *was* in fact an infrastructure that began to take shape as the European presence expanded. Merchants, politicians, and settlers looked for ways to reshape nature, even to conquer it, in order to overcome its obstacles. Where there were portages, they began to develop canals. As settlement expanded, the native trails gradually became roads; when those roads became inadequate for the quickening pace of trade, Europeans built small local railways, first between cities and eventually linking provinces.

When the continent reached that point of development, another consideration came into play. Anyone who imagined a British North America that would be more than just a scattered collection of colonies began to see that an infrastructure, in addition to its immense practical value, had psychological value. This important realization links the twelve projects explored in *Building Canada.* If the projects were about building a nation in a physical sense, they also sought to build one in an emotional sense.

One of the first discoveries was that no matter how important they remained as a means of communication, Canada's rivers could stand in the way of progress: as society expanded and technology improved, the waterways that had once been the most efficient means of transportation increasingly became obstacles to moving people and goods, especially where thriving communities grew on either side of a river. From Canada's first major bridge, across the Ottawa River, to its longest, between Prince Edward Island and New Brunswick, building materials changed—from wood to iron to steel to concrete—but the underlying goal remained the same: to unite a country by defeating geography. The transcontinental railways and their successor, the Trans-Canada Highway, were certainly dependent on bridges, but one of Canada's least heralded transportation projects, the trans-Canada airway, was not. That it has largely been forgotten is ironic, for the airplane was the first technology that allowed Canadians not to overcome the land, but to escape it. Yet, just as with the bridges and the highway, the airway's practical impact led seamlessly to a psychological one. The easier it was to travel, the more likely people were to travel; and the more people travelled, the better they would get to know other regions. The result, politicians and entrepreneurs argued, would be a stronger, more unified nation.

Unity depended, however, on more than just the physical links provided by bridges, highways, and air routes. It could also be fostered by buildings that expressed national cohesion, either through form or function. The British politician and novelist Benjamin Disraeli once remarked that nothing so completely represents a nation as a public building—an idea that was writ large in the provincial legislatures erected in the late nineteenth and early twentieth centuries. Those legislatures, as well as the ones that came before and after them, didn't represent a single building campaign, but they might as well have, for they shared common principles: to express the province's sense of itself, its dreams for the future, and its understanding of the relationship between the people and their government. Underlying all of that was a strong spirit of competition, a kind of sibling rivalry that was, in most cases, healthy. In trying to outdo one another, the provinces all got to know each other a little better.

And Disraeli's comments went far beyond public buildings. If we are looking for a national style of architecture, one that evolved into a sort of Canadian brand, we need to look to the railways that built stations and hotels in what became known as the château style, and to the architects who adapted that style for other types of buildings. Only after it had been widely embraced as an expression of our nation in architecture was the château style adopted for government buildings. In this case, public architecture followed where private architecture had led.

The performing arts centres built as memorials to Canada's one hundredth birthday in 1967 represent the other end of the spectrum in that they were connected not by their form but by their function. It wasn't what they looked like that was important, but what went on inside them. They represented a cultural infrastructure, something that was as essential as the infrastructure for transportation or governance. After all, many people believed that without adequate facilities, the performing arts in Canada would wither and die, with disastrous consequences for our identity. The resulting Confederation Memorial Program, then, was also implicitly about nation-building.

The transportation and architectural projects were all about overcoming regional divisions, but in the late nineteenth century another kind of division emerged. Canada had always been a nation of country dwellers, but in the decades after Confederation, there were growing worries about the youth of the countryside deserting their farms for the cities. The term *rural depopulation* was uttered more and more frequently, and politicians soon discovered that they had better have an opinion, and preferably a policy, on the issue. The First World War made things even worse—what appeal would the family farm have for the soldier who had sampled the pleasures of Europe's great cities? Then, to confirm their worst fears, came the results of the 1921 federal census: for the first time in Canada's history, more people lived in urban areas than in rural. As far as the Toronto *Globe* was concerned, the exodus from the country districts had become a "national menace."

The dangers of rural depopulation were primarily practical. In the days before farm mechanization, agriculture depended on human labour, not just the children of the farmer but the itinerant labourers hired by the week or the season. If they were drawn away to the cities, who would plant, tend, and harvest the crops? Looming over Canada was the spectre of a country that couldn't feed itself, simply for want of labour. But there was also the psychological element. Canadians had long embraced an identity rooted in the rural ethos. Turning prairie grassland or wooded valley into a productive farm was part of what made us Canadian; the national spirit was forged in a struggle between the human and the natural environment, not by the struggle to catch a streetcar or see through the foul smoke belching from factory chimneys. These worries were even greater in French Canada. The lifeblood of the French Canadians, argued *nationalistes,* was drawn from the rural parish, where the traditional family worked the land under the watchful yet benevolent eye of the *curé.* Since the conquest of 1759, the French Canadians had succeeded in preserving their language, culture, and religion against just about everything English Canada could throw at them. Was it all to be lost just because the next generation of French Canadians couldn't resist the lure of the factories of Montreal or New Hampshire? In short, wrote everyone from politicians to poets to priests, the national character would not, could not, flower in an urban setting.

What could be done to stem the flood to the cities? The most obvious answer was to make rural living more attractive by extending to the countryside the infrastructure that was commonplace in the cities. Three great modern conveniences came into use at the very time that concerns over rural depopulation were growing: mail delivery, the telephone, and electrification. But they came first to the cities. For years, the majority of Canadians could only dream of the conveniences that urbanites took for granted. If such services could be extended to rural areas, life on the farm would be more comfortable, less arduous, and less isolating; once that was achieved, so the thinking went, rural depopulation would end. Once inequalities between life in the city and in the country were eliminated, why would people want to leave the farm?

Yet nations are also built on less tangible foundations than highways and telephone lines. Every society has its icons, objects whose practical utility as infrastructure, if it ever existed, is superseded by an inspirational value. By common if unconscious consent, such objects become symbols of the nation; in various ways, they provide us with recognizable forms that are understood to be distinctly Canadian. The grain elevator is a perfect example of a structure whose iconic value emerged only as it began to disappear from the landscape. Once the most common commercial building in the Canadian West, the elevator had, according to almost everyone involved in the wheat economy, no purpose beyond the practical. The notion that it would one day be considered a national icon would have seemed absurd to the men who built them, and to the first generation of farmers who used them. As their practical value diminished, however, their symbolic worth grew enormously. They couldn't be used to store wheat anymore, but they could stand for other things—the heritage of the rural way of life, the history of the wheat economy that built the country, the memories of countless Canadians whose entire lives were spent in the shadow of these sentinels of the plains.

The great towers of the nineteenth and twentieth centuries, from Nelson's Monument in Montreal to the CN Tower in Toronto, were different, for they were constructed specifically to *become* icons. They had practical value on a variety of levels, but above all else, they symbolized what mattered to Canadians at various stages in their history. In the nineteenth century, it was the military heroes on whom their fate hung; in the twentieth, it was the commercial might of a modern nation celebrating its centenary. The monument to Isaac Brock may seem insignificant when compared with the CN Tower, but both were built on the same assumption: that a tower's meaning transcended the obvious, and that it stood for values that should be embraced by all.

Set against the soaring CN Tower in Toronto or even Brock's Monument in Queenston, the widely seen war memorials of Toronto sculptor Emanuel Hahn seem small and insignificant. They shared the commemorative function that was explicit in the nineteenth-century towers, but they weren't about building economic might, as were the grain elevators, or celebrating it, as were the twentieth-century towers. They didn't try to use transportation or architecture as a unifying force, either practically or emotionally, and they didn't represent an effort to foster a national culture. In a way, though, they are much more than any of that, a fact that makes them powerful and meaningful elements of our landscape. They stand as mute testimony to the need of communities to come to terms with the losses suffered in the most devastating war Canada has ever fought. In this way, unlike everything else in this book, they were local: each individual monument belonged to one community alone. But the ubiquity of Hahn's pensive soldier was, in some ways, more unifying than a grain elevator or a great tower could ever be. It reminded Canadians that they didn't mourn alone, and that the pain they experienced was also felt by others they would likely never meet. And that's a kind of nation-building we should never ignore.

These days, we are often preoccupied by the practical dimension of our infrastructure—especially when we're confronted with massive highway potholes, overburdened public transit systems, or power outages as utilities struggle to keep up with the demands of an energy-greedy society— but we tend to forget about its collective psychological dimension. Perhaps this is because it's now unfashionable to talk about nation-building in anything but an economic sense. Canada is many nations, we are constantly reminded, and their goals and aspirations are not always parallel, or even compatible. One of the luxuries of the historian, however, is the ability to fall back into the rhetoric of earlier times as a way to help understand the past. And so while some of the rhetoric that surrounded these projects may seem laughable to our jaded, postmodern sensibilities, the sentiment behind it at the time was authentic and heartfelt. The men and women who drift in and out of these pages believed passionately in the importance of building a nation with a strong sense of itself; they also believed that highways, telephone lines, and concert halls could help achieve that end.

None of these projects was entirely free from controversy, and there are lots of tawdry stories of mismanagement, skullduggery, and corruption. Ultimately, though, they are all success stories. We hear enough about what does not work in the Canadian nation; there should always be room to celebrate what did work.

Within each theme in *Building Canada,* I had to make difficult choices about what to include. The nation's best-known and most significant transportation project, the Canadian Pacific Railway and the other transcontinental lines that followed, is absent, mainly because its story has been told so many times by capable storytellers. An indication of the importance of the railway in the nation's history, however, is that it is used frequently, often incongruously, as an exemplar. If there was one thing that surprised me in researching the subject, it's how many other projects were compared, in terms of emotional impact, to the railway.

Readers will doubtless think of many other building projects that might have been included: the St. Lawrence Seaway, the national microwave network, the building of small-town banks, the pipeline projects, and dozens of others. The fact that there are so many possibilities for a book such as this suggests how significant has been the challenge of geography in creating this country, and how important have been these ambitious projects, both practically and in terms of the national consciousness, in meeting that challenge.

THE WAYS
MOST TRAVELLED

HANDSHAKES ACROSS THE WATER

Almost every transportation project undertaken in this country has had to deal with the fact that Canada has an awful lot of water. Indeed, crossing the countless rivers, streams, creeks, and lakes that make up nearly a sixth of some provinces' surface area proved to be one of the biggest challenges in transportation. Settlers tended to follow the waterways and established fledgling communities along rivers and streams. But settlement was rarely confined to one bank of a waterway, and as communities grew, the split became more problematic; the very waterways that provided the only access to the interior often separated two communities on opposite sides of a river.

This was certainly the case with Quebec City, separated from the growing town of Lévis, on the south shore, by the St. Lawrence River, and Montreal, which sat on an island in the middle of the river. Boats of all shapes and sizes crossed regularly in the summer, but winter made the trip much more perilous. Passengers sat or lay in the bottom of an immense dugout canoe, which was pushed out into the river by ten or twelve paddlers. They looked for open water, zigzagging or circling around when ice blocked the path. If there was no way past, all of the men got out and hauled the canoe to the next patch of water. It could take hours to cross the river, and travellers rarely landed exactly where they wanted to on the opposite shore. It was such an ordeal that contemporary accounts tell of passengers who died of fright during the crossing.

Canada's first major bridge project, however, had more to do with politics than the safety of residents. In the early nineteenth century, Upper and Lower Canada were entirely separated by the St. Lawrence and Ottawa rivers—without a fixed link, could there be any prospect for unity between the Canadas? In May 1824, the surveyor-general of Lower Canada, Joseph Bouchette, toured the colony and returned to Quebec with a recommendation that a bridge be constructed across the Ottawa River. The importance of such a project, he reported, could scarcely be overstated: "[T]he communication between this Province and Upper-Canada would, thereby, become uninterrupted, certain, and secure; and must, necessarily, consolidate and strengthen the Canadas." Fortunately, another major project would give added weight to Bouchette's recommendation. The British government had decided to build a string of locks along the Rideau River, to make it navigable between Wright's Town, on the Ottawa River, and Kingston, the main British military base on eastern Lake Ontario. Wright's Town (renamed Hull in 1875) was a bustling community of eight hundred souls on the north bank of the Ottawa River, across from the proposed north end of the canal, with all the necessary mills, smithies, stores, and workers' accommodation. But to raft supplies and labourers across the river every day was a time-consuming and expensive operation. It made much more sense to take up Bouchette's suggestion and build a bridge.

Compared with almost every other Canadian infrastructure project, this one was decided in the blink of an eye. On 26 September 1826, the governor of Lower Canada came to Bytown (then little more than an encampment on the south side of the Ottawa River) to turn the first sod for the Rideau Canal Waterway. After the ceremony, engineers raised the bridge idea with him; he approved the plan and ordered work to begin on the 28th. The key men on the job were three: Colonel John By, the British engineer in charge of the canal project; John Mactaggart, who was both an engineer and an antiquarian with an interest in the bizarre; and Montreal stonemason Thomas McKay, whose Ottawa mansion, Rideau Hall, later became the residence of Canada's governor general. The designer, the engineer, and the stonemason got along well together and held each other in high regard. (Mactaggart later confessed to being particularly impressed with By's ability to eat raw pork.)

After a single day of surveys, By picked a spot near the Chaudière Falls, where the river was dotted with islands and rocky outcrops. There they could build a series of seven short bridges from island to island, rather than a single long span. The first was a stone arch from the north shore to the first island. It was finished in just three weeks, and on 31 October 1826, the workers gathered to witness its completion. In a structure like this, the stonework was built around a wooden frame arch; when everything was in place, the wooden frame was to be removed in a process called striking the centre, and the stones would settle firmly into place. But when workers struck the centre, the span promptly collapsed. Clearly, speed in construction hadn't been a virtue. By mid-January 1827, the bridge had been rebuilt, and the next span was completed in the summer of 1827. The four bridges from the south bank were constructed of wooden trusses; simply engineered and rapidly built, they were also in place by that summer.

That just left the biggest gap, some 212 feet long, over a treacherous stretch of water called the Big Kettle, at the foot of the falls. A rope suspension footbridge would be used as a platform from which to build the permanent bridge, an elegant truss frame that By had modelled on a design by the great Italian architect Andrea Paladdio. But how to get the ropes across in the first place? Mactaggart recruited a local artillery captain, who hauled a bronze cannon to the riverbank, lashed a rope to a cannon ball, and then fired the ball across the river. On the first two tries, the force of the detonation broke the rope, but the third attempt was a success. Workers used the first rope to pull across two heavier ropes, each of which was attached to trestles on either side of the Big Kettle. They laid down planks crosswise and anchored them to the ropes, and then nailed boards lengthwise on the planks. With ropes on either side to serve as handrails, the temporary bridge was ready for use.

The next step was to reinforce the footbridge with chains, a process that led to tragedy when one of the chains snapped, hurling a work crew into the river. Three men were swept to their deaths. John By then decided to anchor two large scows in the Big Kettle under the bridge site; these would act as supports while the wooden trusses were assembled. But after some weeks of work, another chain snapped, and then a third. This final mishap was fatal to the structure, and the half-completed truss bridge plummeted into the river. The colonel was not easily put off, and he ordered immense chains with 10-inch links from the naval stores in Kingston. Within five weeks, the operation was complete: by October 1828, the Ottawa River was bridged by a series of spans that could support 6 tons. Because it had been built with government money, By declared that it should be a toll bridge—one penny for every person or animal, two pennies for every vehicle. The real profit, however, was made by the toll collector, who regarded himself as a border official outside the jurisdiction of either colony: his shaky grasp of constitutional law didn't stop him from operating a kind of duty-free shop that sold cheap liquor to anyone who passed by.

The Union Bridge was on the cutting edge of the science of bridge building, or perhaps it was just *over* the cutting edge. Mactaggart's assessment—"There it stands, and likely will for a length of time"—was hardly a ringing endorsement, and within a few years of its completion, the bridge over the Big Kettle had started to deteriorate. In 1834, military engineers installed heavy chain cables for added support, but on 5 May 1836 the bridge had to be closed to vehicles. Just thirteen days later, it collapsed into the river. A new Union Suspension Bridge was built within a few years and it stood the test of time better, though it lacked the charm of By's elegant if unstable design. The important thing was that the gulf between Upper and Lower Canada had been bridged, at least in a physical sense, by what one traveller called "a *solid* step to the union of the Provinces." The process of building a nation with bridges had begun.

AS A RESULT of its versatility and availability, wood had been the material of choice for the majority of bridges in Canada for decades, but, to many forward-thinking engineers, it was fast becoming a thing of the past. In 1779, architect T.M. Pritchard and iron-founder Abraham Darby had constructed the first iron bridge at Coalbrookdale, England, setting in motion a revolution in bridge building. By the 1850s, structural iron had arrived in Canada and was ready to cross gaps that would make the Big Kettle seem little more than a puddle.

Montreal in the mid-nineteenth century was the largest and wealthiest city in British North America, home to fabulously rich entrepreneurs who dominated Canada's financial, industrial, and transportation sectors. But by the 1840s, the city's location was becoming its Achilles heel. Situated on an island in the middle of a river that was frozen for part of the year, it was losing ground as the U.S. canals and railways that spread through New England and siphoned off trade wherever they appeared.

This fact was painfully clear to the Grand Trunk Railway. Running from Portland, Maine, to Sarnia, Canada West, the Grand Trunk aspired to be one of the world's great railways, but a bottleneck at Montreal stood in its way. There, goods had to be transferred across the river by ferry, a process that the railway found inconvenient and that shippers hated. But bridging the St. Lawrence was a different proposition entirely from the one that had faced John By in Ottawa. The Big Kettle was a little over 200 feet wide; the St. Lawrence was over 8600 feet wide at Montreal, had a current running to 7 miles per hour, and frequently saw ice jams that reached the height of the houses on either side of the river. Any bridge would need piers strong enough to withstand the force of the shifting ice, and it had to be high enough to allow sailing ships to pass underneath and have spans long enough that huge timber rafts could pass between the piers. It was the kind of challenge that Victorian engineers relished.

They submitted design after design for consideration, and in 1852 the government of the Canadas asked a British engineering firm, Peto, Brassey, and Betts, to examine the plans and come up with a recommendation. They gave the file to engineer Alexander Ross, who eventually produced a design with the help of Thomas Keefer and Robert Stephenson, the son of George Stephenson, builder of the world's first steam-powered railway engine, The Rocket. The three men envisioned a bridge, to be located above the entrance to the Lachine Canal, that would be over 6000 feet long and consist of twenty-five spans resting on piers spaced across the river. Each pier would be flared outward on the upstream side, so that sheets of ice drifting downriver would be forced up the piers and break under their own weight. Because the distance between piers was nearly 250 feet, close to the tolerance of the structural iron available at the time, the designers decided to use a square tube, to give each span greater stability and strength. All of the wrought-iron plates to make up the tubes were imported from Birkenhead, England, and assembled at the river's edge like a giant child's toy. The central span alone consisted of 10,309 pieces held together by nearly half a million rivets. Remarkably, the pieces were so well made that they fit together without a single alteration or new rivet hole being necessary.

Not that the project was easy. According to supervising engineer James Hodges, the first construction season in 1854 was "a period of disaster, difficulty, and trouble." The English engineers had little experience in the Canadian climate, and didn't cope well with the short working season. Nor were the labourers, more than three thousand of them over the life of the project, happy. Brief strikes happened regularly—"it is almost a custom in Canada for mechanics and labourers to strike twice a year," wrote Hodges—and cholera swept through the living quarters that had been built near the site (one such building is now the groundsman's hut at the Beaconsfield Golf Club), sometimes felling up to a third of a two-hundred-man work gang at a time. The English labourers, imported at great expense, were rarely willing to work more than four days a week, when they bothered to stick around at all, and managers from other projects frequently visited the bridge to poach workers with offers of better wages.

The first winter, engineers surveyed a path across the frozen river that corresponded exactly to the course of the bridge. The approximate pier sites were marked, and holes were drilled through the ice so surveyors could take depth soundings to determine exactly where a pier should be sited—a flat slab of rock on the river bottom was ideal. For each pier, a wooden cofferdam had to be built; it was anchored at the pier site, the water pumped out, and the masonry put in place. Building, sinking, and pumping out the cofferdams was such a long process that it was usually August before the masons could begin on the stonework. Because freeze-up started in November, they had to work at a feverish pace.

As the piers were being built, ironworkers were assembling the bridge tubes, which were put in place and riveted together as each pier was completed. The final pier was finished on 26 September 1859, and the final tube installed shortly after. The last thing to be erected was the sloping wooden roof, covered with tin so that snow and ice would slide off. Hodges even finished ahead of schedule—but would it stand the test of use? To gauge its strength, engineers lined up a 520-foot-long string of railway flatcars, long enough to extend over two tubes of the bridge, and loaded them with boulders. When they were pushed across the span, the first tube deflected less than an inch, well within the safety margin. With that, the bridge was declared open for traffic.

On a cold afternoon in December 1859, nearly a thousand passengers boarded a Grand Trunk Railway train in Montreal. There was the usual noisy hubbub—the scramble for seats, shouts of recognition as old friends spotted each other, a temporarily misplaced child, the piercing whistle of the conductor—and then the train was on its way. The journey took them south, and as they reached the St. Lawrence River, the passengers were suddenly plunged into darkness. Soon, black smoke from the engine began to filter into the compartments; a few of the passengers lifted handkerchiefs to cover their mouths. The minutes ticked by—two, three, four, five—and still they were in darkness, the smoke in the carriages growing ever thicker. A child began to wail, and one woman announced that she felt faint. Then, just as suddenly, the train emerged into the light again after nearly eight minutes in the gloom. The travellers could barely contain their excitement and amazement: they were the first members of the public to travel through the great Victoria Bridge, already dubbed the Eighth Wonder of the World.

Its official opening, however, would have to wait until 25 August 1860, when the Prince of Wales and future King Edward VII would drive in the last rivet to finish the bridge that was to be named after his mother, Queen Victoria. It was an occasion like nothing the city had ever seen. Eight

triumphal arches, made of wood, canvas, and stucco and ornately decorated with flags, gilding, painted paper and cloth, and gaslights, marked
the route of the royal procession to the bridge site. Souvenir sellers had a
field day, hawking special flags, the Victoria Bridge Medal, Victoria Bridge
perfume, the Victoria Bridge pipe. The ceremony itself was followed by
a grand ball featuring some specially commissioned tunes, such as "The
St. Lawrence Tubular Bridge Mazurka Polka," "The Victoria Bridge
Gallop," and "The Grand Trunk Celebration Waltz."

Even with the abundance of local luminaries and foreign dignitaries
on hand, the bridge itself was the star of the show. There were a few
grumbles about the $7-million price tag, but as the longest bridge ever
built, it enchanted journalists: "one of the noblest works of engineering
in the world and in its way perfectly unique," "the greatest example of
engineering at present extant," "the most magnificent work of its kind
in existence." It soon became a magnet for curious visitors, who were
keen to see for themselves the structure that resembled, as travel writer
W.H. Withrow put it, "a gigantic centipede creeping across the flood."

In the wake of the grand opening, much was made of the amount of
freight carried over the bridge in its first five nights of operation—
11,723 barrels of flour, 1552 barrels of pork, 170 tons of iron, 39,000 feet
of lumber, 140 bales of cotton, and 644 tons of general goods—but the
bridge's impact was as much symbolic as it was commercial. For the Duke
of Argyll, who visited Montreal in 1878, it represented imperial solidarity:
"the traveller in crossing the mighty stream feels, as he is borne high above
it through the vast cavern, that … its iron girders and massive frame …
stand, spanning the flowing sea, as firm and as strong as the sentiment of
loyalty for her whose name it bears." It was the *Times* of London, however,
that seemed most impressed by the bridge's impact on Canadian unity:
"The provinces of the North American Union are now so intimately
connected by iron lines that all that was wanting to bring the Union into
close communication with Canada was to span the St. Lawrence, and this
has now been done … by the very poetry of engineering."

BY THE TIME of Argyll's visit, however, the days of iron bridges already
were drawing to a close. English inventor Henry Bessemer had discovered

a process for making steel in 1856, and in the 1860s this new material, stronger and more durable than iron, was being used in bridges across the United States. When businessmen and railway barons set their sights on a permanent connection between Quebec City and the south shore of the St. Lawrence River, steel was the material of choice.

A bridge at Quebec had been considered at the same time as the Victoria Bridge was being designed—producing sketches for such a project was something of a hobby for engineers of the period—but not until the late 1880s did a bridge become an economic necessity. Montreal, with access to ice-free Atlantic ports over the Victoria Bridge, was stealing business from Quebec, and the only thing that could stop the drain was for the city to have its own link with the south shore. In 1887, the Board of Trade called a meeting of politicians and business leaders, all of whom spoke passionately of the bridge as a necessity, not only for the city's economy but for the good "of the whole Dominion, as it will be a complete and unbroken connection on Canadian territory." Part nation-building propaganda and part fiscal pragmatism (if the bridge could be sold as a national project, the federal government might help pay for it), the rhetoric had the desired effect: in June 1887, the Quebec Bridge Company (QBC) was chartered to erect a bridge across the St. Lawrence. Under the terms of the act, the company had three years to begin construction and six years to finish; if it failed to do so, the charter would become null and void. It was immediately clear that the QBC had little chance of meeting these deadlines. The project was anticipated to cost over $6 million (more than $110 million in current values), but the firm had limited financial resources. Even when various levels of government kicked in money to get the ball rolling—$1 million from Ottawa in 1889, $250,000 from the province of Quebec the following year, and $300,000 from the city of Quebec in 1891—the company remained desperately underfunded. So in 1891, in a cycle that would become tediously repetitive, the company's directors convinced Parliament to grant another three-to-six-year window to complete the project. Three more times they would return, and each time Parliament gave the requested extension. This should have set the alarm bells ringing, but if it did, no one was listening.

Perhaps that's because the company was doing what it could, within its limited financial capabilities, to keep up a show of activity. In 1897, it was busily considering sites along the St. Lawrence, and the directors eventually picked one near the mouth of the Chaudière River, 6 miles from Quebec City. But that was the easy part. In engineering terms, the bridge represented as much of a challenge as had the Victoria Bridge. Its centre span had to be long enough and high enough, at least 150 feet, that ocean-going ships could pass under it, and had to accommodate two railway lines, as well as streetcar tracks and two lanes of road, for a total width of at least 67 feet. The challenge was not insurmountable, so long as the company made the right decisions along the way.

Then, in 1899, the Quebec Bridge Company made its first bad decision: it hired American Theodore Cooper as consulting engineer for the project. Cooper had spent eleven years in the U.S. Navy before getting his first big engineering job, on the St. Louis Bridge. It was a great success, and Cooper moved on to build bridges in Providence, Pittsburgh, and New York, each one a triumph. But none of them was large, at least compared with what was envisioned for Quebec. Cooper was nearing the end of his career and desperately wanted to build a truly great bridge as a capstone to his professional life. The Quebec project must have been irresistible to him. There was just one problem: Cooper didn't want to have to come to Quebec. In fact, he didn't like going to job sites at all and his previous contracts had all limited his time at construction sites to no more than five days per month. As he got older, he grew less willing to travel, often claiming ill health as a reason for refusing to leave his New York office. In total he would visit the Quebec Bridge sites only three times, the last in May 1903, before the work had progressed very far. He was, as the *Engineering News* later put it, "an engineer who had never seen the structure for which he was actually carrying the entire engineering responsibility."

The QBC seemed undeterred by Cooper's odd contract clause, and in March 1899 its representatives met with him in New York to review the tenders submitted for the project. They apparently suggested (although no one would ever say how strongly) that, in making his decision, he should keep in mind the perilous financial state of his employer. When Cooper submitted his report on 23 June 1899, it was clear that he had taken the advice to heart: "I hereby conclude and report that the cantilever super- structure plan of the Phoenix Bridge Company (of Phoenixville, Pennsylvania) is the 'best and cheapest' plan." If there's one word that should never be attached to a complex engineering project, it's "cheapest." It was an unfortunate choice of words, and for the next eight years, every- one working on the project would have one eye on the bridge and the other on the bottom line.

The following summer, Cooper was officially appointed consulting engineer for the project, and within a matter of days, he made another fateful decision: the centre span would be lengthened from 1600 feet to 1800 feet. A longer central span would put the innermost piers in shal- lower, slower water where the ice was less dangerous; the cost of building those piers would be lower, and they could be built more quickly. The projected reduction in cost and time, combined with the fact that the change would give Quebec the longest cantilever bridge in the world, dazzled the directors of the QBC and they accepted Cooper's recommen- dation. Then, he suggested another major change: the structural members of the bridge should be redesigned to reduce the amount of steel needed, and therefore the cost of the project. The risk was that each piece of the bridge would now have to carry higher stresses, but Cooper believed the loads were still acceptable. In his original report, he had put "best" before "cheapest"; the order was rapidly reversing itself.

On 2 October 1900, Prime Minister Wilfrid Laurier and a host of dignitaries descended on the bridge site to lay the cornerstone of the first masonry pier. Four steamers were required to carry all the invited guests, and it may have seemed to spectators that every single person on those steamers was given a chance to speak. Almost all of them referred to the bridge as a national undertaking, but it was Simon Napoleon Parent, the mayor of Quebec City and the new premier of the province (and, not inci- dentally, the president of the Quebec Bridge Company), who described the significance of the bridge most explicitly: "We are at last realizing the cherished dream of every Quebecker for the last fifty years, and we long to hear the cheering sound of the hammer which is going to rivet the last link that was wanting to complete our national unity."

After the crowds had dispersed, though, not a hammer could be heard—not that day nor for months afterwards. For the next three years, the company teetered on the brink of financial ruin and did little to move the project forward. It should have been carrying out intensive testing on Cooper's redesigned structure to ensure that it could stand up to the demands that would be placed on it, but that cost money. Instead of recognizing that it was essentially working on an entirely new bridge, the company went on as if it were the same old bridge. Cooper's skill and experience were taken to be enough of a guarantee that the calculations were sound.

Finally, in 1903, after sixteen years of planning had yielded almost no results, the federal government stepped in. It was anxious to go ahead with the construction of another coast-to-coast railway to compete with the Canadian Pacific Railway, and needed the bridge at Quebec to realize that goal. The project was promptly declared to be "for the general advantage of Canada," which allowed Ottawa to guarantee a bond issue of $6.7 million to pay for the work. All at once the Quebec Bridge Company sprang into action. Now, they pleaded, there was no time to do the tests that should have been done on Cooper's structural changes. They were under the gun, so the engineers decided to accept the Phoenix Bridge Company's theoretical estimates of the weight of the redesigned bridge. The government made a half-hearted attempt to force the QBC to accept an independent bridge engineer to study the new plans, but backed off when Cooper protested this as an attack on his professional competence. There would be no independent oversight of the plans or of the construction as it proceeded.

The first hint that something was amiss came in February 1906, when Phoenix's inspector of materials reported that the bridgework weighed in at 38,800 tons, over 7000 tons heavier than anticipated. This would boost the already high stresses by a troubling 10 percent. Cooper was backed into a corner. He could either scrap everything and start again from scratch, which would be an admission that he had erred (and would also ruin the Quebec Bridge Company's plans to have the Prince of Wales officially open the bridge in 1908), or he could order work to proceed. He probably didn't deliberate for long: work would go ahead.

The following summer, Cooper received even more alarming news from Quebec. Workers reported that pieces of the south anchor arm, which connected the bridge structure to the stone pier, didn't match up when they tried to assemble it; they had to use two 75-ton jacks to force them into place, and even then the pieces didn't fit properly. On 6 August, Norman McClure, a bright young engineer hired by Cooper to be his eyes and ears at Quebec, reported that two pieces of the south cantilever arm were bent, a discovery that sparked a disagreement at Quebec. The local representative of the Phoenix Bridge Company said they had been bent when they left the shop (an admission suggesting that the company's quality control measures were not up to snuff), but McClure insisted the pieces had warped after being installed on the bridge, which suggested they were buckling under higher stresses than they could handle. Cooper's assistant took to measuring the affected pieces on a regular basis, and on 27 August was shocked to find that they had bent a full 2 inches in the previous week. The situation could hardly have been more serious, but no one at the job site knew what to do because not one of them was technically qualified to make any major decisions. The chief engineer of the QBC, Edward Hoare, was experienced in laying railway track but had never built anything larger than a 300-foot, single-track bridge. Phoenix's senior engineer at the site was Arthur Birks, a graduate of Princeton University, praised to the stars by all who worked with him, but only twenty-five years old. McClure, another Princeton alumnus, was even younger and less experienced. As a later report put it scathingly, "[T]he greatest bridge in the world was being built without there being a single man within reach who by experience, knowledge and ability was competent to deal with the crisis."

McClure immediately wrote to Cooper for advice, while Benjamin Yenser, Phoenix's general foreman at the site, declared the bridge unsafe, and suspended work. Rather than wait for a reply to his letter, McClure decided to go directly to New York, where he met Cooper on the morning of 29 August. Cooper immediately agreed that work should remain suspended until the situation could be studied carefully. McClure was dispatched to Phoenixville to consult with the engineers there, but in his haste he neglected to cable Quebec with Cooper's decision. He soon noticed his oversight, but wasn't unduly worried because he knew Yenser had stopped work. What neither he nor Cooper was aware of was that Yenser had ordered work to resume, for reasons that remain unclear; most likely he was pressured by officials from the Quebec Bridge Company, who were concerned about delays.

McClure got to Phoenixville around five o'clock that afternoon. He told the company of Cooper's decision that all work should be suspended, but company officials wanted to postpone any action until the next morning, when they were expecting a telegram from their engineer at Quebec. They expected it to confirm that the pieces in question had indeed been slightly bent when they left the factory and hadn't buckled under the high stress loads. McClure, very much the junior man in the room, could only defer. At 5:30 P.M., the meeting broke up.

While McClure was conferring with the managers in Phoenixville, the workers swarming over the Quebec Bridge were waiting for the whistle signalling the end of the workday. Instead, they heard what sounded like a cannon shot. A flawed piece of the south anchor arm failed and the bridge started to collapse, the superstructure on the piers falling, according to one witness, as if its supports were made of melting ice. In no more than fifteen seconds, 19,000 tons of steel crashed down, taking the lives of eighty-six workers. Some of them lay trapped and wounded in the wreckage of the bridge for hours because there was no equipment to free them. As their mates watched helplessly, the river slowly rose and drowned them.

The disaster was no respecter of position. Among the dead were two of the senior officials at the site, Birks and Yenser, and the youngest of workers, fourteen-year-old Stanley Wilson, who earned 10 cents an hour as a water boy. Thirty-three of the dead were natives from the Kahnewake Reserve, men who were starting to build a reputation as fearless ironworkers. Just a few days earlier, the Kahnewake lacrosse team had posed for a photo, the spidery form of the bridge looming ghost-like behind them. Over half of the team went down with the bridge.

The nation was horrified by the graphic accounts and photographs in the newspapers, and the federal government immediately appointed a Royal Commission to study the accident. Two of the commissioners were at the bridge site within two days of the disaster, and their inquiries also took them to Ottawa, New York (to meet with Theodore Cooper), and Phoenixville. Their exhaustive report, presented in February 1908, traced the collapse to the two pieces of the south anchor arm that Norman McClure had been watching for weeks, and put the blame squarely on the Phoenix Bridge Company's engineer for designing the faulty pieces, and on Theodore Cooper for approving them. The Quebec Bridge Company was also held partly responsible, for its "loose and inefficient supervision of all parts of the work." One of the commission's last conclusions was that a bridge of that design and size simply couldn't be erected given the state of engineering knowledge of the time.

The government was quick to restart the project and complete the much-needed link. In August 1908, the minister of Railways and Canals appointed a board of engineers to draw up specifications for a new bridge, and eventually the government selected a design submitted by the St. Lawrence Bridge Company. This time, the bridge segments would not be imported from the United States but would be built right at the site. No mills in Canada had the capacity to form rolled steel into bridge components of that size, so St. Lawrence had to build a factory on each side of the river, at a total cost of over $1 million. Even more time-consuming was the task of removing the wreckage of the old bridge and dismantling the piers, a job that took two years.

By September 1916 the superstructure on either side of the river had been completed; all that remained was to hoist the centre span into place. To do so, the pre-assembled span was put on two scows and floated down the river, which was clogged with rowboats, skiffs, and every manner of watercraft, all packed with people anxious to watch the final act in the bridge saga. People lined both shores—estimates put the crowd at fifty thousand—and among them were a host of dignitaries, including local, provincial, and federal politicians, representatives of the contractors, two hundred members of the Society of Canadian Engineers and their American guests, even a party of members of the Australia parliament on their way home after visiting their troops in France.

When the scows reached the bridge, they were anchored in place and the span was attached to the massive chains that would lift it. Then, the scows would be removed and the span slowly jacked upward, about 2 feet at a time, until it was level with the superstructure at either end and could be bolted into place. For the first few hours, everything went according to plan. The span was attached to the lifting chains, at which point the scows drifted away. So, too, did most of the spectators, who assumed that the rest of the operation would be a mere formality. And for a while, it did seem as if the big excitement had passed. The span was slowly elevated, and when it was about 30 feet off the water, the crews were given a break for a meal and a rest; within the hour, they were back at it. They had just completed another lift when disaster struck. A support piece at the southwest corner of the centre span failed, dropping that corner and then the southeast corner into the St. Lawrence; it was only a matter of time before the north end of the span plunged as well. For the second time in a decade, the great Quebec Bridge lay in ruins—this time killing thirteen workers.

It was wartime and there was considerable pressure on the supply of steel, but the government and the U.S. steel supplier immediately agreed to free up enough material to construct a new centre span (fortunately, the bridgework stretching out from either shore of the river was undamaged). On 17 September 1917, almost exactly a year after the most recent disaster, the process of lifting the centre span started again. This time, work proceeded without incident and the span was in place in four working days. When the last rivets were hammered home, a group of workers held an impromptu footrace to see who could be the first to run across the bridge. A month later, the first train, carrying some four hundred company officials, engineers, bridge workers, and government representatives, passed over the new structure, and on 3 December the bridge was turned over to the Department of Railways and Canals for testing. In August 1918, it was finally made available to regular rail traffic, and on 22 August 1919, the Prince of Wales unveiled four commemorative plaques to formally open the span.

Just two days later, Theodore Cooper died, lonely and disappointed, without ever having seen the bridge he had wanted so badly to be his.

THE UNION, Victoria, and Quebec bridges had been engineering challenges pure and simple. There had been no debate about the potential social consequences of linking Ottawa to Hull or Quebec to the south shore, and the phrase "environmental impact" had not yet been coined. All three were built in the days when the government neither sought nor desired the public's opinion on any infrastructure project. In contrast, the story of the Confederation Bridge linking Prince Edward Island and New Brunswick offers an interesting case study of how technical problems could be matched, and in some cases overshadowed, by other issues.

In August 1955, the largest crowd yet assembled in Nova Scotia converged on the Canso Strait to be part of the grand opening of the Canso Causeway, a 4300-foot strip of rock linking Cape Breton Island with the mainland. Cape Bretoners had been talking about some kind of link since the nineteenth century, but it took a decade of intense politicking to see the project through. It was well worth the wait, as far as lobbyist L.J. Doucet was concerned, for the causeway was "like a handshake across the water, a handshake whose clasp remained!" One local woman was a little more sanguine: "And, thank God," she said, "for having at last made Canada a part of Cape Breton!"

Even harder was the task of making Canada a part of Prince Edward Island. The process didn't take much longer, but there were significantly greater obstacles to be overcome: local opposition, environmental concerns, engineering challenges, and constitutional issues. But there was also, arguably, a greater need. Compared to Prince Edward Islanders, the residents of Cape Breton could hardly complain about the difficulties in reaching the mainland. The Canso Strait was only a few thousand feet wide; the Strait of Northumberland, at its narrowest point, was more than 9 miles across.

The first politician to grapple with the problem of communication was the island's governor, Walter Patterson, who hired a crew of men to carry the mail from Wood Island to Pictou, Nova Scotia, in February 1775. These winter mail runs continued sporadically over the next fifty years, but in 1829, the island government opted to stop using that 23-mile route and instead use the 9-mile crossing between Cape Traverse, PEI, and Cape Tormentine, Nova Scotia. The craft of choice was the classic ice-boat, 17 to 18 feet long with a bent cedar-plank hull covered in sheet tin. The men who worked the boats were the best and strongest paddlers around, experts in the kinds of ice that flowed through the strait and able to spot a patch of open water in the worst conditions. At the best of times, it was an exhausting trip; at other times, when a brilliant blue sky over Tormentine changed to towering grey clouds and gusting sleet before they were 3 miles into the strait, the crossing was a nightmare.

So dangerous was it that in 1885 the federal government decreed that boats had to carry survival supplies and fire-making equipment, be operated by a crew of six, and travel in convoys of three. The fare for men was $2, but they had to help haul the boat across the ice whenever necessary; a gentleman who didn't want to dirty his hands with manual labour could pay $5 to remain in the boat while others did the pulling. Women, the elderly, and invalids paid $4 but weren't expected to lend a hand with the hauling. These were not inconsiderable sums in those days—a century ago, $6 would buy food for a week, and $1.75 would pay the rent. Winter travel to and from the island, then, was only embarked on if absolutely necessary.

When PEI joined Confederation in 1873, it appeared that its isolation would end. Under the terms of union, the federal government agreed to provide efficient, year-round steam-ferry service to keep the island in "continuous communication" with the mainland. But the much-anticipated ice-ferries turned out to be a disappointment. In 1881, one of them was icebound for three weeks, and even the addition of three newer ferries, the *Minto,* the *Earl Grey,* and the *Stanley* (the same Grey and Stanley commemorated by Canada's premier sporting trophies), didn't help things much. In 1915, the federal government inaugurated a railway car-ferry service with the launching of the *Prince Edward Island.* It was so efficient that the old ice-ferries were soon taken out of service. The *PEI,* which was fitted with an automobile deck in 1938, crossed the strait faithfully until 1969. By that time, it had been joined by the *Abegweit*—which made 123,000 crossings before it was retired in 1982 to become the floating clubhouse of Chicago's Columbia Yacht Club—its successor the *Abegweit II,* and the new, larger, and more modern ferries that followed.

However good the ferry service was, though, it was still dependent on the weather; until an all-season link was constructed, the "continuous communication" promised in the terms of union didn't really exist. Not that there hadn't been plans. In 1885, PEI senator George Howlan thought about building a bridge, but believed it would obstruct ship traffic. His idea? A subway—5 miles of connected iron tubes, each 300 feet long, 15 feet in diameter, with a concrete base inside to support the railway roadbed, and with long, earth-filled wharves stretching out from each shore to meet the subway as it rose to the surface. The cost, according to his consulting engineer, would be about $2.1 million. That was good enough for Howlan; he established the Northumberland Straits Tunnel Railway Company, resigned from the Senate, and ran for a seat in the House of Commons, where he thought he stood a better chance of pushing his project. But, as historian Boyde Beck put it, "the project was popular, Howlan was not." He was trounced at the polls, taking with him any chance of seeing his subway become a reality.

Over the next few decades, the federal government occasionally revisited the notion of a fixed link, but was always scared away by the experts' reports. In 1955, when the Canso Causeway was opened for traffic, PEI premier A.W. Matheson petitioned Ottawa to build a Northumberland Causeway, but the numbers defeated him: the project would cost over $50 million and require at least 40 million tons of rock, four times more than the Canso Causeway. Not until 1962 did the federal government start to make noises that could be construed as positive interest. Prime Minister John Diefenbaker committed to paying $105 million for a fixed link between the island and the mainland, and consultants advised that a combination bridge–causeway–tunnel would be the best option. A causeway would stretch out from Bayfield, New Brunswick, for about 2 miles and would then become a bridge. As it neared PEI, it would become a causeway again, and then, close to the town of Borden, would become a tunnel to allow ship traffic to pass over it. Finally, a ramp would take the road back onto land again.

Diefenbaker fell from power in 1963, but in July 1965 the new prime minister, Lester Pearson, announced that Ottawa would go ahead with the project. On 5 November 1965, the sod was turned for the ramp approach road on the Prince Edward Island side. Another two years passed before bids came in for the New Brunswick portion of the causeway, and then they were far higher than anyone had anticipated. By 1968, the federal government had spent $15 million moving earth for the New Brunswick approach road and building the highway interchange on the PEI side, but then the project's yearly budget was cut to $5 million amid rumours that it would be shelved altogether. In March 1969, that's precisely what happened.

It was 1982 before the government took another look at the idea, but by then the estimated cost of a bridge had climbed to $640 million. Then, within a year, Public Works Canada (PWC) received three unsolicited proposals from private sector companies, one for a tunnel and two for bridges. Here was an idea that any fiscally conscious government could get behind: private sector loans would finance the construction, and the money that the federal government was already paying in ferry subsidies would be used to repay the loans. Perhaps Canada might become part of PEI after all.

In 1826, the Union Bridge had been proposed, approved, surveyed, and started in the space of three days; two years later, the work was done. The bridge linking PEI to the mainland would take a full fifteen years, from the time PWC reopened the file on the project to its grand opening, and would have to clear a succession of hurdles that would have mystified By and Mactaggart—feasibility studies, the examination of the unsolicited proposals, the call for Expressions of Interest, the Initial Environmental Evaluation. And then there was the plebiscite, called for 18 January 1988 after the provincial government decided that the matter was important enough to be put to the people. To help islanders come to grips with the issues involved, the University of PEI's Institute of Island Studies held public meetings in eleven communities. Two camps quickly emerged. The Islanders for a Better Tomorrow, representing mostly business, tourism, and labour groups, supported the plan, arguing that its economic benefits couldn't be ignored or understated. "If you vote no, you'll never know," they said. Opposing them were the Friends of the Island, dominated by academics, fishers, environmentalists, and social activists, who put the case against the link. They were determined to open people's eyes to what they believed were the potentially serious environmental and economic consequences of the fixed link—the slogan "If you don't know, vote no" captured their position.

The debate took on a curious character. As Island historian David Weale put it, "We are Islanders ... living in a place set apart by time and nature. And though it is denied by some, it is our Islandness which is at the centre of this debate." But the notion that an "island way of life" was at stake was itself contentious. Some people in the anti-bridge camp thought the very idea gave the pro-bridge group the upper hand; they could paint themselves as the proponents of progress, modernization, and the future, in contrast with the misguided defenders of "Islandness" who hopelessly clung to a stagnant past. The Friends fought hard against this characterization by publishing a collection of studies that avoided the rhetoric and instead made the anti-bridge case with hard science on the environmental impacts, economic studies and policy analyses, and exposés of the flaws in the process.

The debate was a bitter one—some friendships were severed forever as people took sides—but one person who refused to take a public stand was premier Joe Ghiz. At home, the subject was a constant source of spirited argument. Rose Ellen Ghiz opposed the bridge, while their son Robert supported it. The premier steadfastly refused to give his personal opinion. Only after his death was his deep secret revealed: he had voted against the fixed link. As things transpired, the premier was on the losing side. Voter turnout was only 65 percent, less than what the Island usually sees and surprising given the bitterness of the debate, and almost 60 percent of voters supported the fixed link.

Following that was another round of bureaucratic exercises. The twelve companies that had submitted Expressions of Interest were whittled down to seven, and then three by September 1988. The financial arrangements had to be worked out—Ottawa set an upper limit of $42 million (an amount equivalent to the yearly ferry subsidy) as the most it would pay on an annual basis—and it wasn't until 2 December 1992 that the federal government announced that it had selected the proposal from Strait Crossing Incorporated (SCI). But first, the project had to go through the courts, for on 6 December the Friends of the Island brought suit against the federal government for failing to follow certain procedures with respect to environmental assessments, and on the grounds that cancelling the ferry service was a violation of the 1873 terms of union. In March

1993, Madame Justice Barbara Reed agreed on both counts: the proper environmental studies had not been completed, and ending the ferry service would require a constitutional amendment in the House of Commons. PWC promptly went away and commissioned the court-ordered environmental assessment, but then the Friends were back in court to demand a full Environmental Assessment Panel. This time, the judge disagreed; he ruled that there had been enough studies and that there was nothing to stop bridge construction from proceeding as long as the constitutional amendment was passed before the last ferry sailed. That amendment was secured on 15 April 1994.

The way now clear, in October 1993 the federal government signed a contract with SCI that bound the company to certain deadlines. It had until 1 June 1997 to finish; if the bridge was not ready for traffic by that date, SCI would have to cover the $42-million cost of continuing the ferry service. SCI immediately got to work on the site preparation. The company had decided that most of the construction would be done on shore, but it had to find a suitable property on which to build and store everything. They fixed upon John Read's Amherst Point Farm, which his family had been working for three generations; once the sale of the land was finalized, it was transformed from a bucolic farm with trees, flowers, and cattle into an industrial yard. All of the bridge components would be manufactured at that site and then assembled in the water using a modified crane ship, the *Svanen,* which had been used to build a similar bridge in Denmark. Three times higher than PEI's tallest building, the Prince Edward Hotel, the *Svanen* soon became a tourist attraction in its own right.

Concrete, from which the new bridge would be built, had been used in Canada for bridges since the early twentieth century. One of the first spans was a reinforced-concrete-arch highway bridge built at Massey, Ontario, in 1906, but concrete bridges really came into their own in the interwar era, with structures such as the Ashburnham Bridge in Peterborough, Ontario (1920), and the Broadway Bridge in Saskatoon (1932). These boasted impressive spans to be sure, but nothing like the magnitude of the SCI project. The construction process itself, however, was not unlike that for the Victoria Bridge: piers would be built in the water, and then the pre-assembled sections of bridge would be mounted atop them. The first job was to prepare the sites for the piers. Work crews sank a series of cofferdams to the bottom of the strait, pumped them dry, and drilled holes over 16 feet deep into the bedrock; filled with reinforced steel and concrete, the holes would act as anchors for the pier bases that were cemented to the bedrock. On top of the bases were the pier shafts, with ice shields sloped at a 52-degree angle; just as with the piers of the Victoria Bridge, flowing ice would be forced up the sloped shields to break under its own weight. Once the pier shafts were completed, a main bridge segment was attached to each shaft, and then spans to join the main segments were dropped in. Some were fixed at both ends, while others slid on bearings at one end so that the bridge could expand and contract as a result of climatic conditions.

Once the actual construction began, it went smoothly. On 1 October 1995, the first main segment was put in place, and during the 1996 construction season, the work of setting the piers went on twenty-four hours a day, seven days a week. That fall, on 20 October, the ferry *Abegweit II* became the first ship to sail under the navigation span in the middle of the bridge. The last structural component was installed on 19 November 1996, and it looked like SCI would be able to meet its deadlines.

But what to call the bridge when it was finished? The Fixed Link was entirely too dull, and the federal government's name, the Northumberland Strait Crossing Project, didn't exactly roll off the tongue. Islanders seemed to prefer the Abegweit Crossing, which honoured the two ferries that had plied the route for fifty years and the ancient Mi'kmaq name for Prince Edward Island. Yet Abegweit crossing wasn't easily made bilingual, a priority for a federal government still reeling from the razor-thin result of the 1995 referendum on Quebec sovereignty. Instead, Ottawa chose a name that has been variously described as bilingually appropriate, nationally accepted, and politically correct: the Confederation Bridge.

Meanwhile, preparations were underway for the grand opening, to be known as BridgeFest '97. It began on 30 May 1997 with the Race of a Lifetime, which drew thousands of entrants to a footrace across the bridge. Later that day, fifty thousand of the less athletically inclined took part in the Walk of a Lifetime, the one and only chance to walk across the bridge; the lineups were so long that some people missed the walk altogether. Then, on 31 May came the official opening, assisted by six-year-old Benjamin and nine-year-old Sabrina Campbell, whose grandfather worked on the last ferry crossing the strait and whose great-grandfather had worked on the ice-boats. As a farewell, the three ferries then in service, the *Abegweit II,* the *Vacationland,* and the *Holiday Island,* positioned themselves abreast and blew their horns in a final salute. At five o'clock that afternoon, the bridge was officially opened to traffic; in the first three days, more than twenty thousand vehicles crossed its span.

The first consequence of the opening was to put six hundred ferry employees out of work, but after that, pundits predicted, the fixed link would add 150,000 tourists to the 740,000 who had visited the island in 1996 (in fact, the number of tourists entering the island grew by a staggering 60 percent in the bridge's first summer of operation). They said it would bring $24 million to the island's economy and create hundreds of new private sector jobs, and would save the PEI transport industry $10 million a year because truckers wouldn't have to waste time waiting for ferries. These numbers were certainly important to the politicians who had presided over the bridge's creation, but their rhetoric was also about nation-building. Diane Marleau, the public works minister, called the Confederation Bridge "a symbol of Canadian unity and an example of close cooperation between the Government of Canada, the provinces and the private sector," while New Brunswick's premier, Frank McKenna, praised "the progress we continue to make in uniting this great country of ours." Islanders, however, remained divided on what it meant to be physically attached to Canada. For some, it represented the end of PEI's unique status as Canada's island province. One native, as he flew over the bridge and into Charlottetown Airport, huffed, "[T]here's that great, jeesley slab of concrete ... an island's not a real island if you can drive to it."

ONE OF THE STUDIES published by the Friends of the Island was an analysis of what will happen if the Confederation Bridge reaches the end of its useful lifespan, as such structures often do. If we ignore the Canadian Forces helicopter that flew under one of the spans in August 1998, only to be caught on tape by a bridge surveillance camera, its short life has been uneventful. The Union Bridge in Ottawa lasted barely eight years, but the Montreal and Quebec bridges have fared better. The Victoria Bridge was altered in 1897 to deal with ventilation problems—the iron plate walls were removed and replaced with open truss sections—and if today few of the forty thousand Montreal drivers who use the bridge every day would refer to it as the Eighth Wonder of the World, it still stands as a tribute to Victorian engineering. The Quebec Bridge faced its own challenges when changes in Canada's railway network reduced its traffic to passenger trains of VIA Rail's Quebec–Montreal corridor and a few CN freight trains each day. Fortunately, its significance as the longest cantilever bridge in the world (at 3239 feet) was recognized when the railway and the federal and provincial governments came together in 1997 in a partnership to restore and preserve the landmark. The project is expected to continue until 2006.

So what's next? A British general in Canada once floated the idea of a causeway between Newfoundland and Labrador, in the belief that it would reduce winter ice in the St. Lawrence. The notion went nowhere in 1879, and was no more popular a century later when Newfoundland politician Steve Neary suggested a tunnel under the Strait of Belle Isle to link Newfoundland and Labrador. The idea of a bridge between Vancouver Island and the mainland was also raised in the 1870s, when a potential route for the CPR included a series of bridges across the Strait of Georgia near Campbell River. The suggestion still comes up occasionally, usually in the form of an island-hopping bridge between Tsawwassen and Vancouver Island, but opposition to any such project, even if we think only of people concerned with the potential environmental impacts, is likely to be fierce.

In a relative sense, the challenges facing John By and John Mactaggart at Wright's Town in 1827 were every bit as daunting as those facing SCI in the 1990s. In both cases, there were many people who said the bridges could never be built, but they were. And whatever economic benefits might have accrued, these projects and the others were undertaken on the assumption that anything that linked Canadians and helped them to know each other better could only be good for the nation. PEI's terms of union with Canada spoke of "continuous communication," which was the goal of all these bridges. In the ideal world that bridge-builders envisioned, familiarity would not breed contempt, but rather sympathy, understanding, and unity.

A UNITY BASED ON ROAD AND WHEEL

I n a country with so much water, it took a long time for people to see the point of building roads. For decades after the settlement of Quebec in 1608, they simply weren't necessary—why go to the effort to cut roads when the rivers and streams along which everyone lived were ready-made highways? But after the 1660s, as the colony's population grew and a second range of farming lots was opened behind those fronting on the rivers, farmers were obliged to build and maintain roads between the two ranges. They had to beat down the snowdrifts and the worst of the ruts and ridges in winter, and erect poles to mark the sides of the roads; the poles were so important in preventing travellers from straying off into the wilderness that to remove them could bring a punishment of flogging. These most basic of roads in New France were known as the *chemins de moulin,* but there were also the *chemins de communication* (18 feet wide) and the *chemins royaux* (24 feet wide); in today's transportation network, these would be analogous to local roads, secondary highways, and principal highways. By 1734, additions to this network allowed the traveller to travel from Montreal to Quebec City in four and a half days. There was even a highway superintendent, the *grand voyer,* who provided advice and assistance in road building. But his inspections were irregular at best, and farmers soon learned that they could neglect their section of road with impunity.

After 1760, the British tried to make road construction in Lower Canada more efficient, doing away with the forced-labour system and instead hiring contractors and paying them in land. They also employed idle soldiers to break roads but mostly relied on private companies to build toll roads, the first of which was opened in 1805. By charging travellers to use the roads, the toll companies had incentive to expand the road network; however, they had little interest in maintaining the roads once they had been cut. Dodging the toll collector, usually by sending someone ahead to open the toll gate quietly so that the horse and cart could dash through, became a popular pastime; people usually justified their actions on the grounds that the roads weren't well enough maintained to warrant the payment of a toll. Often, the government agreed—over the years, it had to take over many toll roads that had fallen into disrepair, fix them, and then sell them back to the toll companies.

Other colonies had followed similar paths. In 1761, the assembly of Nova Scotia demanded that every man perform four to six days of road work each year, as well as one day after any heavy snowfall. A 1793 act in Upper Canada compelled men to work on the roadways for two to twelve days annually, depending on the value of their property. In neither colony was the system efficient. In Nova Scotia, men frequently failed to show up to discharge their obligations, and when they did, their efforts could scarcely have been considered taxing. It was known as "doin' a little soddin'" because it usually consisted of a few hours spent shovelling chunks of earth or sod into holes in the road. This cavalier attitude, understandable though it was, infuriated colonial administrators, who believed that a good system of roads was essential. "This will be the most flourishing province in North America," declared Charles Lawrence, an early governor of Nova Scotia. "Nothing is wanting to forward it but money to make roads."

In the early nineteenth century, legislators started to admit the wisdom of this view. Beginning in 1815, the government of Lower Canada set aside specific funds for road construction, with each county and district receiving a set amount. Thanks to those efforts, and to the aggressive policies of a few far-sighted administrators such as Governor John Graves Simcoe, who was responsible for building two of Upper Canada's greatest roads, Yonge Street and Dundas Street, by 1827 it was possible to travel by road from Halifax in the east to Amherstburg, the westernmost settlement in Upper Canada. To describe what was being built as "roads," however, was to take a real liberty with the word. Most were so rough, rutted, and blocked by stumps, holes, swamps, and streams that they were suitable only for travel on foot and by horseback. In 1837, Anna Jameson travelled by farm cart to Chatham, in southwestern Ontario, an experience that left a deep impression on her:

> The road was scarcely passable ... those terrific corduroy paths (my bones still ache at the mere recollection!), and deep holes and pools of rotted vegetable matter mixed with water, black, bottomless sloughs of despond! The very horses paused on the brink of some of these mud-gulfs, and trembled ere they made the plunge downwards. I set my teeth, screwed myself to my seat, and commended myself to Heaven—but I was well-nigh dislocated! At length I abandoned my seat altogether, and made an attempt to recline at the bottom of the cart, disposing my cloaks, carpet-bags, and pillow so as to afford some support—but all in vain; myself and my well-contrived edifice of comfort were pitched hither and thither, and I expected at every moment to be thrown over headlong.

Even the sturdiest carts offered little resistance to these unforgiving conditions, as the English novelist Charles Dickens witnessed: "Here and there, and frequently too, we encountered a solitary broken down wagon, full of some new settler's goods. It was a pitiful sight to see one of those vehicles deep in the mire; the axletree broken; the wheel lying idly by its side; the man gone miles away to look for assistance; the woman seated among their wandering household goods with a baby at her breast, a picture of forlorn, dejected patience; the team of oxen crouching down mournfully in the mud." Up to 1841, Upper and Lower Canada spent some $2 million on road construction, but Jameson and Dickens might well have wondered what the money went into.

Gradually, construction techniques improved. The "corduroy paths" that threatened to shake loose Anna Jameson's molars—built by simply laying logs across the road—were gradually replaced by what were known as common roads. The logs were removed, the roadway groomed with a crown in the centre and ditches on either side, and the surface covered with gravel, making a road that would stand up well against all but the heaviest farm wagons. And by mid-century, the McAdam process, known as macadamization, was making its way into the Canadas. Introduced in England in 1815, the process involved laying a base of large rocks, and then layers of progressively smaller stones. The last step was to cover everything with a primitive kind of concrete made from a mixture of stone-dust and water. Macadamized roads represented the best available technology, but by Confederation, they still made up just a fraction of the roads in the country.

Much more common, because they were cheaper, were the plank roads for which Canada became known. The logs of the corduroy paths were replaced by split planks, up to 5 inches thick, of beech, maple, or elm, and the surface was covered with earth to protect the planks from the grinding of wagon wheels. They were much more carefully engineered than they sound—the planks were fitted together like the pieces of a jigsaw puzzle, rather than just being laid randomly—but they were cheap to build because the raw materials in the form of trees lined every road. They were also very smooth: "Fancy rolling along a floor of thick boards through field and forest for a hundred miles," wrote one traveller. "You glide along much the same as a child's go-cart goes over the carpet."

The nineteenth-century railway boom brought fears that road building would cease because of assumptions that railways would make roads obsolete, but those fears were unfounded. By the turn of the century, Ontario had some 8000 miles of railway and 60,000 miles of wagon roads, which were essential to the railways' survival. Roads were just as vital in the West. With a single rail line snaking across the prairie, there had to be some means of getting from the station to the homestead. Cart trails gradually started to meander across the plains, and with time and use they gradually turned into roads of a sort. Improvements were made as time and circumstances permitted—farmers might fill in a slough with logs or rocks, or dig a ditch alongside to provide some drainage—but little effort was expended to make them any fancier than necessary. But the time was fast approaching when all of these roads would have to be improved, and expanded too. The age of the automobile was around the corner.

IN 1864, the Stanstead *Journal* of Quebec reported, seemingly breathlessly, on a new attraction at a travelling circus, "the wondrous novelty of an ordinary road carriage driven over the common highways without the aid of horses or other draught animals." The contraption drew the attention of local inventor Henry Seth Taylor, who set about building a steam-powered car for himself. In 1867, he displayed the product of his labours at the Stanstead Fair; it was Canada's first automobile. Taylor lost interest in cars when he crashed his vehicle at the bottom of a steep hill—it hadn't occurred to him to install brakes. Fortunately others took up the mantle. In 1898, John Moodie imported the first gasoline-powered automobile, and Canada would never be the same.

Most people regarded the first cars with great suspicion. They were smelly and noisy, they frightened horses and people, and they seemed yet another example of an annoying eccentricity adopted by those who had more money than sense. But the automobile refused to go away, and when Henry Ford pioneered the assembly-line production technique in 1908 there was no going back. He could sell his Model T, stripped to its bare essentials, for only $290 (about $5000 in current values). At prices like that, he eventually sold millions.

In Canada, where mobility and geography had always been regarded as opposing forces, people went car crazy. What began as a fad soon became an inexpensive and simple solution to the problem of getting from place to place. In 1903, there were only 178 vehicles registered, but by 1914 that number had risen to 74,000. By 1918, despite the economic constraints of the First World War, there were almost 350,000 vehicles in the country, and within a few years, Canada was second only to the

United States in car ownership. It was only a matter of time before this rapid adoption of the automobile brought pressure on politicians to improve roads.

In the first place, it didn't take long for automobiles to start destroying roads. The macadamized surfaces, with layers of carefully compacted crushed stone, broke apart under the heavier, faster vehicles. The wooden blocks that some cities used to pave their streets were worn down and disintegrated just as quickly, while automobile wheels forced apart the planks on rural roads, making the surface undriveable. One intrepid adventurer who motored across the prairies in 1909 found the experience taxing to the point that he was reminded of the old tale of the mule driver who was so frustrated by a trip across the mountains that he finally drew his revolver and fired six shots into the air because he had run out of expletives to express his anger. Canadian roads were becoming something of a joke, as this contemporary rhyme suggests:

> *But from somewhere east of Suez*
> *Where the roads are at their worst,*
> *Down to rocky Alabama*
> *Of the motorists accursed,*
> *For bumps and thrills and all the ills*
> *That, travelling, one gets onto,*
> *The greatest jar you give your car*
> *Is Hamilton to Toronto.*

Politicians began to feel the heat from their constituents, who demanded better roads for their new vehicles, but they were also starting to realize that the automobile could bring in tourist dollars, a fact borne out by the government's own statistics. In 1908, two-thirds of the vehicles on Ontario's roads were registered to non-residents, mostly Americans. It's hardly surprising that Canada's first modern highway, completed in 1912, linked Montreal with New York State. Railway tourism had been the cash cow of the nineteenth century; motor tourism would be the cash cow of the twentieth.

The real impetus for road improvements, and eventually the construction of a trans-Canada highway, though, came from the small but rapidly growing car lobby. In 1894, not long after the province's first electric auto-mobile was built, a number of businessmen, municipal politicians, and travel writers founded the Ontario Good Roads Association, a lobby to convince the province to improve the lamentable state of its roads. The association succeeded in getting the government to appoint a provincial roads inspector, who confirmed everything the association claimed. The roads were worse than they had been ten years earlier; "the majority are little better than trails," and for five months each spring and fall, "by far the greatest part of the mileage of the province is mud, ruts, and pitch holes. There are at least two months when the roads are practically impassable." In response, the provincial government came up with the 1901 Highway Improvement Act, which made available grants totalling $500,000 a year to cover one-third of the cost of any road improvements. The plan sounded good, but counted on municipal governments being willing to spend $2 for every dollar the province kicked in, something that was by no means assured.

The Ontario Good Roads Association was just the first in a long line of groups that would pester politicians on behalf of automobile owners. Car clubs were founded in Hamilton and Toronto in 1903, and Winnipeg in 1904; the Ontario Motor League was established in 1907 and the Manitoba Motor League the following year; and the Canadian Automobile Federation came into being in 1913. But the group that was most concerned with a coast-to-coast road was the Canadian Highway Association (CHA), established at New Westminster, B.C., in November 1911. Its dominion charter stated explicitly its intention "to promote and encourage the establishment and construction of a continuous first-class trunk highway, to be known as the 'Canadian Highway,' from Alberni, British Columbia, to Halifax, Nova Scotia." If local groups would heed its call and lobby for road improvements in their own areas, the association believed, the coast-to-coast highway could be completed within three years.

This was not a new idea. In the 1860s Sir James Douglas, the governor of British Columbia, who had succeeded in having a 400-mile road built northwards from the town of Yale to the Cariboo goldfields, urged the British government to construct a wagon road linking British Columbia with the Canadas: "Trade would find an outlet," he argued. "Population and settlement would follow." In 1870, when British Columbia presented the terms under which it would consent to join Confederation, Douglas's scheme was resurrected, and the colony demanded that the Dominion government open a wagon road to Fort Garry (Winnipeg) within three years of signing any union agreement. But the prime minister, Sir John A. Macdonald, had his heart set on a railway, and the wagon road across the prairies quietly disappeared from the discussions that would see British Columbia join Canada in 1871.

The Canadian Highway Association, determined to breathe new life into the idea that had lain dormant for forty years and raise awareness of its cause, sponsored a series of publicity stunts. In May 1912 it organized a road trip to Alberni, B.C., and back. As many as fifty cars, from Victoria, Vancouver, New Westminster, Nanaimo, Seattle, and Tacoma, lined the streets ("accidents were conspicuous by their absence," reported a Vancouver newspaper) and on the afternoon of 4 May, their drivers and passengers made their way to the waterfront. There, in front of British Columbia's lieutenant-governor, representatives of the city councils of Victoria, Vancouver, Nanaimo, and Alberni, and probably every resident of the town of Alberni, CHA president W.J. Kerr had a solemn duty to perform. This wasn't just a joyride, he said; this was the beginning of one of Canada's greatest engineering projects. It was the start of "a highway that will eclipse anything that has ever yet been attempted in any part of the world," a single road that would link the Pacific to the Atlantic. To great applause, Kerr lifted a brightly coloured curtain to reveal a sign: MILE O — TRANS-CANADA HIGHWAY.

Even more famous was Thomas Wilby's now legendary drive across Canada in 1912. The British-born Wilby was a bit of a gadabout, a man who had worked variously as a tour guide, travel writer, and apartment building superintendent. His gift (aside from writing over-the-top prose) was in persuading others to fund his travels, and in 1911 he convinced an Ohio car company to take him and his wife on a three-month tour of the United States, which he would write up for newspapers and for the U.S. federal Office of Public Roads. A year later, he took the same idea to the Reo Motor Car Company of Canada, based in St. Catharines, Ontario, a subsidiary of an American manufacturer that had made a hobby of setting speed and distance records in the United States. With the sponsorship of Reo and the CHA, Wilby proposed to motor across Canada, from Halifax to Alberni, using only Canadian roads. To do the actual driving, Reo assigned American-born Jack Haney, the best troubleshooter at the St. Catharines factory and a man whose age (he was only twenty-three) belied his skill as a mechanic. If anyone could get Wilby and his Reo to Alberni, Haney could.

Wilby confined his efforts to providing colourful commentary for local newspapers and being wined and dined, while Haney spent long nights tinkering with the Reo to keep it in running condition. It didn't take long for Wilby to hone his rhetorical flourishes. When people in Halifax told him the trip couldn't be made, he dismissed their lack of vision and reminded them of the milepost that had been erected in Alberni as "the concrete expression of a great Canadian ideal. It is the first of a series of posts which will stretch for 4,000 miles across mountain and plain, prairie and forest, until … they have spanned a continent." At every stop, he preached the gospel of good roads ("good roads lead to social improve-ment" was one of his favourite phrases) and the need for a trans-Canada highway. "Do not highways mark the rate of human progress?" he mused on one occasion. "Have not nations risen from obscurity to greatness and world power along their trodden ways?"

And the dignitaries he met along the way echoed his sentiments. He collected messages from the mayors of cities they passed through, and they all expressed the same nation-building dream. Mayor F.P. Bligh of Halifax observed that a trans-Canada highway "would not only bring the differ-ent provinces into closer relation, but help to weld all parts of the Empire indissolubly together." Mayor G.A. McGaughey of North Bay, Ontario, called the highway "a matter of great national necessity. It will encourage our public and influential citizens to visit one another and thus become better acquainted with the necessities and possibilities of this great and flourishing country of ours." Mayor George Geary of Toronto promised that the people of his city "are much interested in anything that would tend to bring more closely together the East and the West, and more solidly to unite the different parts of the Dominion." And then there was the president of the Winnipeg Auto Club, who believed that only the car was capable of "bringing the provinces into the relations that they ought to have with each other. We do not know each other in Canada as well as we should, and the lack of highways is the cause of it. I can't think of a pleasanter way of bringing the provinces to know each other than by the use of highways."

Despite such cheery thoughts, the trip turned out to be fifty-two days of sheer torment, and for long stretches Wilby and Haney had to give up on the so-called roads and send the Reo ahead by train or ferry; thus the honour of being the first to drive across the country eluded them. By the end of it all, the two could barely disguise their loathing for each other (Reo eventually added a second mechanic to the team—officially, he was to help with vehicle maintenance, but historian John Nichol believes he was added to keep Haney and Wilby from strangling each other). But Wilby never let his personal feelings get in the way of a good speech, and when the pair finally reached Vancouver, he unleashed his oratorical skills. "Had I not seen them—Scotchmen, Irishmen, Welshmen, Old and New Englanders, United Empire Loyalist descendants, picturesque Habitants, the mixed races of the prairies and the mountains, thousands of incoming farmers from the great Republic to the south? Were they not isolated from each other as if Eastern and Western Canada were worlds remote and unrelated? What might not a connecting road accomplish for such diverse elements as these in common purpose, in common ideals? Does not Canada … need that continuous thoroughfare from border to border which has ever stood for unity and strength?" For Wilby, it was all about welding the regions into a nation: "Inch by inch the great white way of Anglo Saxon civilization will be wrested from mountain path and beetling crag, from sandy waste and alkali slough, from winding pass and dizzying height, stretching its way from the Silver East to the Golden West, along trails left by our pioneer fathers in their ceaseless march toward the setting sun, until the last link is forged in the 4,000-mile chain," he said. "Then and not until then will Canada be a true nation. The road will consolidate, will unite East and West, will wipe out all difference, racial and distinctions [sic]. The confederation of Canada will not become historically complete until we have a Canadian Transcontinental Highway to take up the work of nation-building at the point where the railroads left off. This transcontinental highway unlike the railroads, will be a people's highway, built for the people. Thus in a true sense it will be a national highway."

They were stirring words, but did they amount to anything? Ironically, the Canadian Highway Association that had sponsored the trip collapsed the same year, after only its second national convention. A medal that member A.E. Todd had donated, to be presented to the first person to drive across the country on Canadian roads, was given to the Victoria Automobile Club for safekeeping. It would remain in the club's hands for nearly forty years, until it was claimed in 1946 by Brigadier R.A. Macfarlane and Kenneth MacGillivray, who took nine days to drive their Chevrolet from Louisbourg on Cape Breton Island to Victoria, B.C. On the entire journey they suffered only four flat tires; Haney and Wilby had often fixed four flats in a single day.

The Canadian Highway Association disbanded, but other groups were quick to take its place. When the Canadian Automobile Federation (CAF) held its first meeting in Toronto in December 1913, the organization committed itself to promoting the idea of a trans-Canada highway. At its next meeting, in Montreal in May 1914, president Oliver Hezzelwood led a campaign to get all of Canada's automobile clubs to lobby their federal members of Parliament for support of a trans-Canada highway. Even with the intervention of the First World War, these efforts soon started to pay dividends. In October 1916, a delegation from the Canadian Automobile Association (as the CAF had become known) met with Robert Rogers, the federal public works minister, and secured his pledge to champion a trans-Canada highway scheme in Parliament and with the public. For the first time, a member of the federal cabinet had publicly endorsed their pet plan. In June 1920, at the seventh annual meeting of the CAA, Manitoba's lieutenant-governor, Sir James Aikens, spoke of "that highway from one end of Canada to the other along which the spirit of unity and progress should prevail. We ought to remove all the obstructions in the road, level up low places and take out all the stones of prejudice so that a national conscience might be created which would make it a habit to think over things not merely from the standpoint of the place in which we are located or the province in which we may be living." The words could have flowed directly from the pen of Thomas Wilby; the fact that they came from a highly placed public official gave them rather more weight.

The lobbyists had already started to win more than just friends in high places; in large part because of their efforts, provincial governments had finally started to see the necessity of funding road improvements. In 1908 the B.C. premier, Sir Robert McBride, had taken the public works portfolio away from the attorney-general and turned it into a separate ministry, with responsibility for roads. The first minister was Thomas Taylor, nicknamed "Good Roads" because of his sympathy for the ideas of the highway lobby. The Ontario government in 1913 appointed a commission that advised the creation of a separate agency to manage the province's roads (this came with the establishment of the Department of Public Highways in 1916) and recommended that the government pay 20 percent of the cost of building or improving county roads, and 40 percent of the cost of trunk roads. Across the country, provincial spending on highways gradually increased, and through the 1920s it was the single largest item on most provinces' budgets.

Still, a provincial highway wasn't a trans-Canada highway. If that was to become a reality, the federal government had to get involved, either in coordinating it or paying for it, or both. When Robert Borden's Conservatives were elected in 1911, they used the throne speech to promise legislation enabling the Dominion government to cooperate with the provinces in road building. But when the bill got to the Liberal-dominated Senate in 1912, representatives promptly shot it down. Roads, after all, were a provincial responsibility, at least according to the British North America Act. Federal involvement, they argued, would be unconstitutional.

In 1919, however, the Conservative-dominated Union government tried again, with the Canada Highways Act, a package of $20 million in federal money to help the provinces with highway construction. Influenced by the U.S. Federal Aid Highway Act of 1916, the legislation gave each province an $80,000 lump-sum grant, with extra money allotted on a per capita basis; the federal contribution to any single project could be no more than 40 percent. Funding under the act was conditional on each province providing a detailed, five-year highway plan, with emphasis on interprovincial highways. Ottawa would then determine how best to knit them into a series of long-distance highways, including one that would cross the continent.

The provinces eventually produced the requested maps, which showed a total of 24,709 miles of road (the only significant gaps were in northern Ontario and the Rockies), but few governments were won over by the plan. New Brunswick thought it was too cheap; once the costs of engineering studies, rights of way, and bridges were factored in, provincial highway officials figured the federal contribution would pay for a quarter of any project at best. Other provinces chafed at the nation-building aspect; they preferred to direct their road-building money to projects that their own citizens needed most, and often these projects didn't correspond to any transcontinental route. Furthermore, the program couldn't apply to northern Ontario above the Severn River, because highways there were the responsibility of the Ministry of Northern Development, which didn't qualify for funding; one of the biggest gaps in the proposed trans-Canada route, then, would not be closed.

Such concerns didn't cloud the vision of the first federal commissioner of highways, Archie W. Campbell, who also went by the nickname "Good Roads." In his first bulletin, published in 1922, he laid out his grand scheme. The distinction between local and national highways, he argued, was misleading, because a road network was like the human circulatory system—the major highways are arteries and the smaller roads are arterioles, but all are essential to the functioning of the national body. And the national body would be in much better health with a trans-Canada highway. But the medicinal value of the act was felt unevenly. It was great for some parts of the country, like southern Ontario, where there were plenty of matching funds to build roads, but did almost nothing in other places. Indeed, when Ford of Canada asked photographer Ed Flickenger to test the results of the act by following the new road system for some 4000 miles across Canada in 1925, he saw that the Canada Highway Act had not resulted in much improvement. Some stretches of road were asphalt or concrete and others were gravel, but the vast majority of roads were still dirt; at times, he could cover no more than 18 miles a day. And there were still big gaps—for 850 impassable miles in northern Ontario and the Rockies, Flickenger put flanged wheels on his car and drove along the railway tracks. The federal government had spent $20 million on improving highways, but thirteen years after Wilby and Haney's journey, Flickenger shaved only twelve days off their travel time.

Few Canadians, though, were trying to drive across the country; most simply wanted to get around their city or township. And it was those people who continued to push up the statistics on automobile use. In the short term, this brought a welcome windfall for the provinces. Alberta came up with the idea for a tax on gasoline in 1922 (the other provinces followed suit by 1928), and income from sales taxes, licence fees, and fines was considerable enough that automobiles soon became the single largest revenue source in many provincial budgets. But the days of worry-free automobile revenues could not last. Through the early 1920s, most provinces were taking in more from automobiles than they were spending on road improvements, but by the end of the decade, highway construction and maintenance costs began to exceed provincial revenues from automobiles. Particularly alarming was the explosion in the number of trucks on the road, which increased forty-fold between 1916 and 1937 and whose weight made them much harder on road surfaces than cars. The province of Alberta found that higher traffic volumes and more trucks meant that even dirt roads had to be better built; improved engineering meant higher costs, as much as 500 percent more than a decade earlier. In 1927, the provinces collected nearly $23 million in revenues, while the costs for road construction and maintenance were estimated at almost double that, $46 million. But the provinces were beginning to grow dimly aware of another number that made taking federal cash for highway construction seem not such a bad idea after all. That same year, the federal government collected import duties and excise taxes on cars and parts valued at over $21 million. The federal government was clearly making money from the car boom.

When the Depression started, federal–provincial cooperation suddenly looked even more appealing, especially when the new Conservative prime minister, R.B. Bennett, proposed building a trans-Canada highway as a make-work project. The federal government would contribute $20 million in total, or 50 percent of any highway construction project. Although it was most interested in closing the gaps in British Columbia and northern Ontario, Ottawa wouldn't dictate routes; it did, however, reserve the right to veto projects. As part of the plan, federal officials canvassed the provinces to find out which of their highways they wished to have designated as part of the Trans-Canada Highway. Even this proved to be surprisingly contentious. In Ontario, engineers bickered over a southern route that followed the shore of Lake Superior from Sault Ste Marie, and a more northerly route going west from Hearst. All of this took time, and the delays eventually sapped Bennett's enthusiasm for the project. When the Liberals returned to power in 1935, they had even less interest than the Conservatives in going ahead with Bennett's program.

Like the 1919 Canada Highways Act, Bennett's scheme produced mixed results. From 1920 to 1940, the federal government put about $44 million into highway construction, but over half of that total went to Ontario, which could afford to put up the matching funds that Ottawa demanded (in addition to Ottawa's contribution, the Ontario government spent about $140 million on highways during the 1930s). No other province got more than $3.5 million and, because of its reluctance on principle to accept federal money, Quebec drew only $3,756.28 from Bennett's program. What was called the Trans-Canada Highway now stretched for 4244 miles across the country, but only about half of it was paved, and there were still major gaps in the Rockies and northern Ontario.

IRONICALLY, the Second World War proved to be a boon for highway building. In the first place, the federal government faced a desperate foreign exchange crisis. Canadian dollars were flooding south to pay for war materials, and few U.S. dollars were coming back in return. Highways were still seen as a way to lure American tourists and their dollars; a rush of holiday-makers from south of the border might not prove to be decisive in reversing the exchange crisis, but every little bit helped. Perhaps more important, the federal government embraced highway construction as a worthwhile public works project. In 1940, an official of the CAA asked a conference in Ottawa "if a first-class coast to coast Highway is to be rated as a national necessity, should not Canada as a whole be prepared to meet a large part of the bill?" and successive federal committees agreed that a trans-Canada highway was indeed a work of national importance and deserved to be given priority once the war had been won. The constitutional issue remained a thorny one—roads were still a provincial responsibility—but the Liberal government took the plunge in August 1945 with its Green Book Proposals, which reshaped federalism and ushered in a new era of federal activism. One of the areas that Ottawa singled out for special mention was transportation initiatives of a national character, such as the Trans-Canada Highway. The federal government had finally accepted, at least on paper, that it had an interest and a responsibility in funding such projects.

Fortunately, provincial highway construction had continued during the war, finally closing the two gaps in the national route. In June 1940, British Columbia opened the Big Bend Highway (and it certainly was a big bend—some dubbed it the world's longest detour, for it consisted of more than 185 miles of driving that brought you back to just 50 miles from where you started) between Golden and Revelstoke, meaning that it was now possible to drive from Alberta to Vancouver without having to go through the United States. Later that year, the road between Nipigon and Geraldton in northern Ontario was completed, and in October 1942 the Hearst–Geraldton section was finished. For the first time, the motorist could drive from Halifax to Vancouver on an all-Canadian route.

Still, much of the route was dirt, not the kind of modern paved highway that automobile lobbyists wanted. What they desired was something like Ontario's Queen Elizabeth Way (QEW) between Toronto and Fort Erie, opened in August 1940 as Canada's first modern superhighway. With four lanes of smooth, fast pavement, modern cloverleafs and access ramps, and striking architectural touches such as the sculpted Henley Bridge west of St. Catharines and the lion monument marking the highway's northern end in Toronto, the QEW became the ideal for highway lobbyists. It was an ideal that would only partially be realized, and even then it would take decades.

The fact was that the federal government remained ambivalent. Despite all the arguments in favour of a trans-Canada highway, Prime Minister Mackenzie King had shifted little from his belief of the early 1920s that roads were a provincial, not a federal responsibility. He knew that public works projects would be needed to cope with the expected post-war economic downturn. He knew that better roads would improve traffic safety (between 1946 and 1950, more than twice as many Canadians were killed and injured in road accidents than were killed and wounded in the Second World War). He knew that automobile use was exploding (between 1945 and 1950, it nearly doubled, and the number of trucks on the road increased by an even greater proportion). He knew that Canada, where 75 percent of all roads were still dirt, compared badly with the United States, where only 44 percent of roads were dirt. But he still didn't want to tread on the provinces' toes, especially for undertakings that, because they claimed the lion's share of automobile revenues, would benefit mostly provincial governments.

King, however, was about to be nudged into retirement, to spend his last months engaged in a campaign to have a bridge in Ottawa named after him. In August 1948, at the federal Liberal convention one cabinet minister, C.D. Howe, called the Trans-Canada Highway a "rainy day" project, but this wasn't good enough for the provincial delegations. Leading Liberals from British Columbia, Nova Scotia, and Saskatchewan ganged up on him, introducing a resolution that the government should take immediate steps to complete the Trans-Canada Highway. Its passage forced the federal cabinet's hand.

In December 1948, the government convened a federal–provincial highway conference and immediately put its offer on the table: Ottawa would fund half the cost of the Trans-Canada Highway, with the provinces determining the routes and accepting responsibility for securing rights-of-way. The reaction from the provinces was mixed, and the new prime minister, Louis St. Laurent, who had been far from thrilled when the party convention passed its resolution, grew concerned. He didn't like any program which, because of its funding structure, would benefit the "have" provinces more than the "have-nots." He also didn't want to give Quebec premier Maurice Duplessis, who had made his career defending provincial rights, any more cause to complain about federal centralizing. In the end, the prime minister decided that cabinet wouldn't proceed with the plan unless it could get every province onside.

During the 1949 federal election campaign, all parties came out in favour of the Trans-Canada Highway, and when the Liberals won, they had no choice but to include its construction in their first throne speech. Nova Scotian Robert Winters, the new minister of Reconstruction and Supply, contacted provincial premiers with a proposal containing a new stipulation, that the highway should follow the "shortest practicable east–west route." Some provinces remained cool to the idea, but because of a looming downturn in the economy and the higher unemployment rates that seemed inevitable, cabinet elected to introduce the Trans-Canada Highway Act into the House of Commons on 25 October 1949. Ottawa would reimburse provinces up to half the cost of highways built between April 1928 and December 1949 that could be incorporated into the Trans-Canada Highway, and would also pay 50 percent of the cost of new construction (the full cost where the route passed through a national park), excluding the expense of securing rights-of-way. The federal government would also impose common standards for aspects such as rights-of-way, curvature, gradient, sight distance, pavement, shoulders, and bridges. By the time the program would be completed in March 1956, Ottawa planned to spend $150 million.

Immediately, provincial governments began to raise objections. Once again, New Brunswick said that the federal contribution was too low and that, after factoring in the cost of surveys and rights-of-way, most provinces would end up paying two-thirds, not half, of any project. British Columbia went even further, saying that Ottawa should pay for everything because it was a national project. New Brunswick and Nova Scotia objected to having to upgrade roads to the standard of the Trans-Canada Highway when their roads already met provincial standards. This "common standard," a principle that the short-lived Canadian Highway Association had adopted at its founding convention in 1911, was itself a concern. For rights-of-way, the Trans-Canada Highway standard was to be 100 feet. This presented no problems in western Canada, where some highways had a 200-foot right-of-way, but in New Brunswick the provincial standard was 56 feet, and in Newfoundland, roads needed only a 24-foot right-of-way. And then there was the route. Ottawa interpreted its "shortest practicable east–west route" to be as the crow flies, as long as it was physically possible, but this often didn't accord with provincial priorities. The proposed route through Nova Scotia would miss Halifax, while the route through New Brunswick would bypass St. John. Ontario opposed the northern route because it left out the majority of the province's population centres. Quebec's Union Nationale government, under Maurice Duplessis, was still severely allergic to accepting federal funding and didn't like anything about the plan.

When the premiers met on 24 April 1950, none of these concerns had yet been dealt with. However, the spectre of unemployment had frightened St. Laurent into dropping his demand for provincial unanimity, so those provinces whose objections could be overcome signed on to the deal. When the meeting concluded, only Nova Scotia and Quebec were excluded. In 1952, Nova Scotia finally opted in, when the federal government agreed to pick up the tab for the Canso Causeway linking the mainland and Cape Breton Island. The government of Quebec, which refused to accept federal conditions as the price for receiving federal money, didn't come on board until after the Union Nationale administration was ousted by Jean Lesage's Liberals in the 1960 provincial election.

By then, the rhetoric of nation-building had started to fly again. The trade journal *Roads and Bridges* praised the federal government "for recognizing its obligations in connection with the development of a coast-to-coast highway that will be the pride of all Canadians and a unifying bond among the provinces." The National Film Board also gave the project a bit of publicity with its 1953 documentary *Canada's New Main Street,* the title suggesting the kind of small-town, traditional relations that would be created across Canada with the highway's completion. In the House of Commons, Robert Winters recalled the great national dream of an earlier era, saying that the Trans-Canada Highway "would help to weld the country more closely together and … to contribute to national growth and development just as the railways did in the nineteenth century."

For all the rhetoric, progress was painfully slow. In the first place, probably because of Ottawa's initial ambivalence toward the project, the federal government hadn't done enough preparatory work in the months leading up to the signing of the agreement in April 1950. Many engineering problems that should have been worked out before construction began had to be dealt with on the fly, which meant delays as engineers brainstormed to solve problems. And then there were some route changes suggested at the last minute. British Columbia, after much consideration, decided against using the Big Bend route, opting to push its portion of the highway through the Rogers Pass. The official reason was that the new route was shorter; unofficially, the reason was that the new route went through two national parks, meaning the federal government would have to pick up the entire bill for those sections. Then, when the Korean War broke out in June 1950, materials like steel and cement were diverted away from highway building and into defence. The shortage of steel became so acute that Ottawa had no choice but to put up more money for temporary wooden bridges along the route and also agreed to pay a bigger chunk of the cost of permanent steel and concrete replacements when those materials became available. Furthermore, provinces were building other highways at the same time, some of which they deemed to be more important than the Trans-Canada Highway. On a single Labour Day weekend, the Queen Elizabeth Way in southern Ontario carried more cars than were projected to travel the Trans-Canada Highway in an entire year. With statistics like that, it was difficult for provincial officials to make the national highway a top priority.

These factors, however, were nothing like the engineering problems involved in construction. The Rogers Pass section was built on an abandoned railway roadbed, which should have reduced the construction costs, but it still ended up being one of the most expensive sections of the highway, with much of the money going to snow protection devices. The average annual snowfall in the area was 338.5 inches and avalanches were common, so the engineers had to come up with ways to minimize the risks and make the highway safe for winter travel. Eventually, they came up with a variety of weapons: conical earth dams to block the path of snow, ice, rock, and earth, or at least change the course of avalanches; bench defence systems designed to catch and hold snow-slides; permanent emplacements for mortars to fire bombs into mountainsides where avalanche conditions were deemed to be dangerous; and, as a last resort, snow sheds, 9000 yards of them, which covered the highway completely, sending avalanches over the top of the road and down the other side.

The other particularly challenging area was between Marathon and Agawa Bay in northern Ontario, a 165-mile section that included 98 miles of bush that had never been traversed by any kind of road. Workers, supplies, and equipment (including more than three million pounds of explosives) had to be brought in by barge, and collectively they cleared 3,000 acres, moved 3.1 million cubic yards of rock and 9.8 million cubic yards of earth, and built twenty-five major bridges. Muskeg, that soggy, spongy carpet of moss and decomposed plant matter that covers large parts of northern Canada, was a real problem—as one engineer recalled, "one evening we finished a two mile stretch of paving over a muskeg and by morning the entire road had sunk out of sight." The worst patch was a 5-mile piece of highway north of Agawa, which involved blasting cuts through solid rock that were up to 600 feet long and 75 feet deep. That one section of highway cost $1.695 million to build, or $339,000 a mile. All told, the workers spent four years putting the highway through from Marathon to Agawa Bay.

Sections like that brought the government face to face with two problems: money and time. An audit prepared in late 1955 revealed that two-thirds of the allotted money had been spent, but only one-third of the highway had been completed. At the same time, an official on the project told the federal government that no province would finish its portion by the time the agreement ended on 31 March 1956. Newfoundland hadn't paved a single mile by the end of 1956—there, too, engineers had to dump thousands of tons of rock into the seemingly bottomless muskeg, just so they could get a surface on which to build the roadbed. The Trans-Canada Highway, said the official, would not likely be finished until 1970.

The problem was even more acute because an election was looming and, having invested significant political capital in a trans-Canada highway, the government faced the embarrassing prospect of admitting to the electorate that it had failed. The Liberals reacted in the time-honoured political tradition—by compromising and by throwing more money at the project. The compromise came with the construction standard: the controversial "common standard" was replaced with a much weaker "good standard," allowing certain provinces to announce the completion of portions, even if these roads didn't meet the earlier standards. Financially, to jump-start construction on the problem sections, the government agreed to increase its contribution to 90 percent of 10 percent of any provincial section, as well as 50 percent of the remaining 90 percent. The nine provinces signed on to this new agreement, and work proceeded.

The honour of being the first province to complete its section went to Saskatchewan, which in 1957 finished paving all 406 miles of its portion, just hours before a blizzard blew in that would have stopped work for the season. Construction in other provinces would continue for more than a decade, and by the time the funding window provided for under the Trans-Canada Highway Act closed in 1970, Ottawa had contributed $825 million of the nearly $2-billion total cost. By then, the Trans-Canada was the longest national highway in the world, running, at that latitude, a fifth of the circumference of the globe.

Eager politicians wouldn't wait until 1970 to celebrate the achievement. As soon as the Rogers Pass section was completed, John Diefenbaker's government took advantage of the milestone to declare the Trans-Canada Highway finished. (Oddly enough, no one seemed to question Dief's claim, even though the government used different benchmarks in different provinces; in some, completed meant just that, but in others it meant only paved, but without guardrails or culverts, or even graded but not paved.) The official opening was held near Revelstoke on 3 September 1962, largely because of the site's historical associations; it was, after all, only a few miles from where the last spike was driven to complete the Canadian Pacific Railway. Like the highway itself, the ceremony took too long to finish and was plagued by problems. The band of the Princess Patricia's Canadian Light Infantry had been invited to play "O Canada," but their instruments didn't arrive until the end of the ceremony. The speech-making dragged on for an hour over schedule, although it was not without its highlights—such as when the minister representing Saskatchewan said how pleased he was to be in Quebec. But it was Diefenbaker, who had played almost no role in having the highway built but at least had the good sense to keep his remarks short, who best summed up the meaning of the project: "This event has generated a renewed sense of national unity. It has brought about a sense of oneness from the Atlantic to the Pacific Ocean, comparable to that which moved Canadians when the first Canadian transcontinental railway was completed.... It is a day when another landmark is met and passed in the building of a strong Canadianism."

When Edwin Guillet wrote a history of Canadian roads as a Centennial project in 1967, he observed that the full impact of the Trans-Canada Highway had not yet been felt: "Canada could start her second century with a new tie, a ribbon this time of concrete and asphalt, a unity based on road and wheel." Today, most of us take the Trans-Canada for granted. We think little of the impact that it might have on national unity, and can easily dismiss Guillet's ideas as the over-optimistic musings of the Centennial year. We complain about ruts and potholes, construction delays, the amount of truck traffic, and overly aggressive drivers. It would never occur to us to refer to the highway, as Thomas Wilby did, as a "continuous thoroughfare from border to border which has ever stood for unity and strength."

So it makes sense to leave the last words to someone who passionately wanted Canada to build a national highway but would not see it completed in his lifetime. In his first official publication, released in 1922, Archie "Good Roads" Campbell laid out his philosophy of road building, something he shared with thousands of his contemporaries. For Campbell, "the march of civilization has been rapid when and where facilities for transportation have advanced." In his view, this kind of progress meant building a strong Canadian nation: "Upon the ability of Canadians to work together in the ends of common concern, and to consider the questions affecting the commonwealth from the point of view of the national, rather than sectional interest, will legislative union endure and national progress depend." But such a state of affairs wasn't possible if the nation was burdened with a poor transportation infrastructure. Bad roads intensify racial differences, he wrote. Bad roads lower the value of each citizen to the country as a whole. Good roads, on the other hand, "promote a better, broad-based citizenship ... [and] have a tendency to break down sectional prejudices, and to create mutual understanding and appreciation between families, clans, classes, and races." For Campbell, the ideals of Confederation would be realized only when Canadians had the kind of easy access to one another that a national highway provided: "Were it possible for the westerner to travel entirely over Canadian highways, using their own transport equipment, the journey would doubtless be made oftener, with advantage to all concerned. Better understanding of the points of view of both east and west must arise from the intimate associations formed by leisurely and interprovincial travel."

Like Guillet, Campbell might be dismissed as an idealistic dreamer; hard experience tells us that the Trans-Canada hasn't made the Albertan love the Ontarian, or the Quebecker love the British Columbian. Before casting aside Campbell's vision, though, we might well ask ourselves what the Canadian nation would be like today if the coast-to-coast road that he and others worked so hard to build had never been achieved. If we think about transportation in those terms, it's hard to dispute that the Trans-Canada Highway was, and remains, just what Campbell called it: "indispensable to the general welfare of the community, the province, the Dominion."

A VAST AERIAL HIGHWAY

The age of flight came to Canada on a frosty day in February 1909, when J.A.D. McCurdy wrestled the *Silver Dart* off the frozen surface of Great Bras d'Or Lake on Cape Breton Island. But in those days, airplanes didn't seem to be good for much. When they flew, the experience was sublime, but all too often these early experiments with flight ended in a cloud of dust and a heap of shattered wood, wire, and canvas. Doug McCurdy tried to convince Canada's generals of the airplane's potential as a weapon of war, but a crash at the end of his 1909 demonstration at the Petawawa military base brought a collective harrumph from the assembled generals; they retreated into the comforting certainty that airplanes would never have any real use in war, or in anything else for that matter. Anyone who suggested that airplanes would one day carry passengers from coast to coast was dismissed as a lunatic. Even Alexander Graham Bell, whose work made the *Silver Dart* flight possible, was, in the eyes of some of his colleagues, ruining his reputation by his obsession with airplanes.

It was another decade before these notions were seriously challenged. During the First World War, the airplane demonstrated beyond all doubt that it could perform a dozen tasks, from aerial reconnaissance to carrying bombs, safely and effectively. The hothouse of war also fostered dramatic technological improvements that transformed the airplane from a fragile crate lumbering through the sky at 50 miles per hour into an agile and manoeuvrable craft capable of travelling at three times that speed. Just as important, when the war ended in November 1918, hundreds of demobilized pilots and mechanics returned to Canada, all in search of outlets for their new talents. Skilled and experienced fliers and technicians, they were determined to build on the lessons of war to make the airplane an everyday part of Canadian life. This small group of enthusiasts, and a handful of others who believed in their ideas, became the apostles of flight, trying to convert nonbelievers to the gospel of wings. Their doctrine was known as air-mindedness, a wonderfully evocative term that encompassed a faith in the airplane and its potential as a positive force in the world. The twentieth century would be the age of aviation, they argued; the way to the future lay in the skies. Any country that didn't embrace the new technology would be left behind.

Of course, the veterans of the Great War were not the first to foresee this brave new world. In 1883, Ralph Centennius (the pen name of an obscure futurist in Peterborough, Ontario) had looked forward to the day when travel by air would draw the country together, replacing fractiousness with "a powerful unanimity that renders possible great social movements." But in the days of Centennius, "flying" meant drifting through the clouds in a gas-filled balloon, a mode of transport that was hardly going to revolutionize anything. For the new generation of air-minded Canadians, on the other hand, the technology to achieve their dreams was close at hand, if only governments had the wisdom to harness it. The airplane was the railway engine of the twentieth century, the machine that would draw the provinces together and complete the work of Confederation. When the Air Board, newly established to guide Canada into the aviation age, promised in 1920 that the nation's scattered air routes and landing fields would soon be knit into "one vast highway across the Dominion," the air lobby was filled with optimism.

Nothing of the sort emerged in Canada, however, much to the dismay of the air-minded. Plenty of private airfields and a few commercial routes served parts of the country in the 1920s, but most were unconnected. Instead of one vast aerial highway, Canada had a patchwork of dead-end streets. Most air-minded Canadians blamed this state of affairs on the federal government, which had shown little interest in supporting the infant aviation sector. It did sanction a few experimental flights, but the frugal civil servants in Ottawa had a ready response to every suggestion. Funding for municipal airports? Any city that really wants one should pay for itself. Regularly scheduled airmail services? Only the mining companies seem interested, so they can foot the bill. Passenger services? Canadians don't seem especially keen to travel by air. Aerial surveys of forest resources? Why should taxpayers fund something that will benefit only the lumber barons? To every request for financial support for aviation the response was the same: no money was available.

The federal government had an answer for everything, except, that is, aggressive U.S. airlines. Through the 1920s, those companies expanded dramatically south of the border; soon there were four complete transcontinental services, most of them with a foothold in Canada. Even more notorious was PanAm, which had no U.S. domestic routes but was eagerly gobbling up routes around the globe. Inevitably, it cast eyes northward and, after years of lobbying, secured the Canadian government's permission to fly a mail route between Boston, St. John, and Halifax; a few months later, PanAm extended the service to Newfoundland, as a prelude to opening trans-Atlantic services. Ottawa recognized the thin edge of a wedge: freight and passengers that had once used Canadian railways were now using U.S. airlines, and one internal memo warned of the "threatened invasion of the principal centres of industry and commerce in Canada to make their traffic tributary to American transcontinental lines." To resist that invasion, the federal government had always steadfastly denied permission for U.S. companies to operate passenger services in Canada, but that couldn't go on indefinitely. If Ottawa were going to keep turning down U.S. carriers, it would have to offer a Canadian alternative.

But unlike the United States, Canada didn't have a national airline—it was one of the few western nations without one—and lacked even the infrastructure to support one. Airmail services had been operating in the United States since 1918, and by the late 1920s there were airports and navigational facilities in virtually every major city. In Canada, things were very different. Huge areas of the country were completely unserviced, and many cities didn't even have suitable emergency landing facilities, let alone proper airports. As the air lobby realized, that had to change. If there was to be a national airline and airmail service, there had to be places for the aircraft to land.

And so was born the idea of the trans-Canada airway, a line of airfields that would stretch across the country, linking the regions together in a communion of the skies. Passenger travel and communications would be revolutionized. When the airway was finished, a letter mailed in Montreal or Toronto in the late afternoon would reach Vancouver the following morning, while one posted in Vancouver would get to Britain a scant five days later. But the airway would also lay the groundwork for Canada's emergence as an aviation superpower. U.S. mail would begin flowing north to use the quicker Canadian air lanes to Europe, and air travellers from the United States would soon follow. Before long, predicted a government official, "Canada would control this important Great Circle international route between the old world and the new."

The scheme was hatched in 1927 when, after years of prodding, the federal government finally agreed to put up $75,000 for the transportation of airmail across the country. Some of this money would go in subsidies to airlines, but much of it was intended to build up the infrastructure of the airway—the airports, emergency fields, navigational aids, and meteorological services that were essential to scheduled mail or passenger services in those days. Early projections suggested that the airway could cost as much as $6 million, and the government of Mackenzie King swallowed hard and threw its support behind the plan. The nervous and obsessive King never liked flying (he was known to draw up a new will before a flight), but he could see the value in a national air service. He also accepted the military's argument that in the event of a war in the Pacific, the airway could play a valuable role in the movement between the coasts of aircraft, troops, and supplies.

The first rough surveys began in 1928, to determine the facilities required along the route. The trans-Canada airway was envisioned as a kind of railway line, a chain of airfields and radio beacons, between which scheduled flights would travel. The cornerstones would be nineteen principal airports, mostly in urban centres; each would have two or more paved runways at least 3000 feet in length (longer as elevation increased), as well as full field and runway lighting, a one-million candlepower rotating light beacon, navigational aids (the airway took advantage of the new science of radio-direction finding [RDF] apparatus, which used Morse code signals to guide pilots to airports), and meteorological services. Connecting these principal airports were twenty-four intermediate fields equipped with RDF ranges, and forty-two emergency fields that had minimal services and were suitable only for forced landings. Because the transcontinental service required night flying, builders installed beacons, in the form of acetylene lanterns on steel towers, at frequent intervals to guide the way and to mark obstructions such as antennas and factory chimneys.

The first surveys also revealed the sorry state of landing facilities across the country. Vancouver's airport was substandard, something that became an embarrassment in 1928 when the great transatlantic flying hero Charles Lindbergh refused to visit because he said the city didn't have an airfield fit to land on. In Montreal, the airport at St-Hubert was being configured to handle not passenger aircraft, but the massive British airship R-100, which was expected to visit in 1930. Some major cities, including Halifax and Toronto, didn't even have municipal airports and were in the midst of bitter public debates over the location of future facilities. The situation was much brighter in western Canada, where most landing fields were fairly well equipped. Some needed only to be lengthened or resurfaced (in 1932, Regina would become the first airport between Montreal and Vancouver with asphalt runways), while others merely required additional lighting. Even most of the intermediate fields on the prairies needed only minor upgrading.

Because of that head start, the prairie section of the airway was completed first, and the postmaster general in Ottawa began taking bids for the prairie airmail, which would be the first scheduled service to use the airway. On 25 June 1929 the government announced that the successful bidder was Winnipeg-based Western Canada Airways (WCA), founded in 1926 to serve the mining districts of northern Ontario and Manitoba. Under its charismatic and ambitious president, James Richardson, WCA had grown from a two-plane operation into a major player in the air-freight business. Within a few years of its founding, WCA was the biggest airline in the country, flying more miles and operating more aircraft than the Canadian government. No other carrier had as much experience or equipment for carrying the nation's mail.

The first flight, a Winnipeg-to-Regina return trip to deal with the Christmas mail rush, took place on 10 December 1929, but the regularly scheduled service didn't begin until March 1930, and even then got off to a rocky start. WCA pilots often complained that the airway's field lights and rotating beacons were useless in bad weather, forcing them to navigate by city street lights, and that the government's much-vaunted RDF ranges were unreliable. Richardson himself made few friends in the Post Office by insisting that the mail flights would also carry passengers; bound by the terms of the contract, postal officials grudgingly agreed, but never stopped believing that pilots would be reluctant to take risks if there were passengers aboard. Not that tagging along on these flights was particularly pleasant. WCA used eight-passenger Fokker F14s or four-passenger Boeing 40Bs that flew at under 140 miles per hour, and the conditions were spartan to say the least. Sound-proofing, cabin heating, upholstered seats—these were luxuries of the future. In those days, flying was uncomfortable: noisy, bumpy, and cold. Furthermore, postal regula-tions demanded that the mail be carried in a locked compartment to prevent tampering; until the planes were retrofitted with secure storage holds, the mail bags were simply locked in the toilet. Not surprisingly, a flight became all the more unbearable when, to preserve the sanctity of His Majesty's Mail, the toilet was locked. Don McLaren, a wartime flying ace who became one of WCA's leading pilots, later recalled that passengers often fortified themselves with a drink before flying and wondered "whether they flew because they had been drinking or drank because they wanted to fly."

Still, the prairie airmail was a great success. In its first season, it achieved a 92.8-percent completion rate on 4864 scheduled trips; for a brand-new service, this compared favourably with the U.S. rate of 93.9 percent on a service that had been running for more than a decade. Perhaps more important, the prairie airmail was a moral success. For many Canadians, it was a sign of progress, and for Westerners, a symbol of the commitment to integrate the West into the national fabric. They were proud of their airmail, and of their homegrown Western Canada Airways. They could see no good reason why the airline and the trans-Canada airway on which it depended should not expand as planned. Then trouble appeared on the horizon. The first obstacle came in a form that was all too familiar to Canadians, the Constitution. At a 1927 Dominion–provincial conference, the government of Quebec challenged the right of Ottawa to legislate in matters regarding aviation; flying, after all, was a means of transportation, and the British North America Act (BNA Act) gave responsibility for such matters to the provinces. In October 1930, the Supreme Court of Canada agreed: federal control of aviation was not absolute, as Ottawa had blithely assumed, and because transportation was a provincial responsibility, the two levels of government must share in the regulation of air transport. Although the case did not specifically consider the matter of interprovincial flights, the decision nonetheless put a scare into supporters of the trans-Canada airway. If the chief justices were ever asked to consider that question, their pet project might well be declared unconstitutional. Federal officials probably cared less about aviation than they did about a precedent that extended provincial powers, and decided to seek the opinion of the Judicial Committee of the Privy Council (JCPC) in Britain, Canada's final court of appeal until 1949. To the great relief of airline executives, federal politicians, and air-minded journalists, the committee overturned the Supreme Court decision. "The whole field of legislation in regard to aerial navigation belongs to the Dominion," concluded the JCPC in October 1931. The airway could go ahead.

By then, however, a bigger problem had already emerged. The economic chill signalled by Black Monday in 1929, when panic hit Wall Street and the financial districts across North America immediately felt the shock waves, had, with frightening speed, morphed into a full-blown depression. The stock-market crash in the United States, a steep drop in agricultural prices, and a series of natural disasters of almost biblical proportions conspired to drive Canada into the deepest depression it had ever seen. Across the country, farming districts emptied, factories closed their doors, and the jobless took to the streets, the highways, and the railways in search of work. Within a few years, as much as a third of the workforce was unemployed.

The villain of the piece, in the minds of many Canadians, was their new prime minister, R.B. Bennett. In July 1930, he had swept Mackenzie King from office on a promise to rebuild the economy by blasting a way into foreign markets. But his blustery pledge couldn't stop the locusts that plagued the West, or keep the windstorms from blowing away the very soil upon which prairie farmers depended, or force foreign brokers to pay more for Canadian wheat. Despite his best efforts, the crisis deepened, and nothing he did seemed to make any difference. Over time, his name became attached to the Depression's most visible symbols. A car pulled by horses because its owner couldn't afford gas was called a Bennett buggy, a newspaper covering a drifter on a city street was a Bennett blanket, an abandoned farm was a Bennett barnyard.

Despite the characterization of him as a heartless capitalist, Bennett felt the economic disaster profoundly. In public, he was the picture of strength and confidence—"the manners of a Chicago policeman, and the temperament of a Hollywood actor," observed one of his political opponents—but in private, he could seem very different. He was deeply troubled by the economic depression gripping Canada, and Bennett, a shrewd businessman with a knack for turning a profit, was at a loss as to what to do. He looked for answers in the Bible, but would frequently turn to the letters that poured in from jobless young men, desperate parents, and children who little understood what was happening around them. All they wanted was to work, to hang on to a farm that meant the world to them, or to buy a decent suit of clothes; all they wanted was a little human dignity. And Bennett, whose government was being vilified in the newspapers for its inability to deal with the catastrophe, did what he could out of his own personal fortune; cheques, food hampers, clothing, and christening gifts issued forth from the prime minister's office. One account estimates that he gave away as much as $250,000 a year, until his advisers convinced him to stop reading his mail lest he bankrupt himself.

Provincial governments, too, teetered on the brink of ruin, and even the federal government searched desperately for places to cut spending. Under the circumstances, it was inevitable that the prairie airmail would be sacrificed. After all, as Bennett told the House of Commons, "there was very little gratification in seeing an aeroplane passing day by day, when the unfortunate owner of the soil could hardly see the aeroplane because his crop had gone up in dust." Overall spending on aviation, including the Royal Canadian Air Force (RCAF), was slashed by 70 percent, the budget of the airmail service by more than 80 percent. Despite the protests of WCA, western politicians, and a handful of noisy newspaper editors, the airmail routes were slowly whittled away. When they were mothballed, many aviation boosters feared that the need for a trans-Canada airway went with them.

IF THE DEPRESSION was the death of the airmail system, it was also the salvation of the airway. One of the most tragic consequences of the economic disaster was the idling of hundreds of thousands of workers. According to the BNA Act, they were the responsibility of municipal governments, a practice that had never been a problem when times were good. But in the deepening economic crisis, the municipal level was increasingly unable to provide relief for its own people, let alone itinerants from elsewhere. How could they be helped? Even if governments could afford it, handouts were a problem—the practice of direct relief, what in Britain was known as "the dole," was proof of that. Going cap in hand to the government for assistance was demeaning; charity destroyed a worker's self-esteem. Instead, concluded the government in Ottawa, relief would be given in the form of a wage that would be earned for labour on public works projects. That way, everyone benefited. The nation got much-needed building projects and the unemployed escaped the stigma of charity, getting the help they needed in a scheme that was carefully contrived, in the words of one observer, "to safeguard Canadian manhood and self-respect."

Initially, the works projects were funded by the three levels of government, but this practice proved to be ruinously expensive. The Relief Act of 1930 paid out some $69 million, which worked out to $9.22 per man per day, a figure that was deemed extravagant for unskilled labour. Quite apart from the cost, however, was the whole question of whether the jobs were worth doing. Most of them involved moving huge quantities of dirt from place to place and relied on large gangs of labourers to accomplish tasks that could be done much more quickly and cheaply with machines that were readily available. Some projects came in at twice the normal cost, and it was not unknown for municipal engineers to devote hundreds of man-hours to filling in a hollow or levelling off a knoll, work that would never have been done under other circumstances.

The 1930 Relief Act's inefficiency was a primary motive for change, but the potential for unrest was also a powerful factor. Canada's top soldier, a thin and grizzled First World War veteran named Andy McNaughton, toured the country in the summer of 1932 and observed first-hand the deteriorating situation for unemployed males. The danger, in his mind, was twofold. Although small and ill-equipped, Canada's army was capable of suppressing any unrest that might bubble over. But no one, least of all McNaughton, was anxious to send young Canadian soldiers into battle against young Canadian men looking for work. Furthermore, these were the very men who would be called upon to serve in the armed forces in a future war. McNaughton saw them slowly losing their hope for the future, and their faith in the country. Such men were not good raw material for an army.

Bennett was no more optimistic. Alarming reports were coming in of single, unemployed men riding the railways in search of work. Though this was still a disorganized exodus, there was the real possibility that it could become more serious. Should these men decide to get together, they could become a threat to public order. Revolution was in the air, and Bennett didn't intend to be the prime minister who turned Canada over to the Bolsheviks.

McNaughton had an idea. After returning from his cross-country tour, he presented Bennett with a plan for a system of public works projects, paid for by the federal government and administered by the Department of National Defence. Get the men out of the cities and off the railways, and put them in remote camps where they could work for the benefit of the nation—improving roads and erecting buildings in national parks, working on reforestation projects, expanding military bases, repairing historic sites, and, not incidentally, helping Canada take its place in the air age. Ottawa would pay them the most modest of wages, just enough to remove the sting of charity. The prime minister liked what he read and told McNaughton to present the scheme to cabinet. Once the provinces had been brought onside, the way was cleared for Order-in-Council PC2248, which on 8 October 1932 provided for the maintenance of two thousand single homeless men needing relief. At first, they would be put to work on just three projects: repairs to the citadels of Halifax and Quebec City, and the construction of the trans-Canada airway. Successive orders would extend the plan so that, all told, some 170,000 men would spend time in the work camps, labouring on dozens of projects.

While the manpower problem was being dealt with, federal officials had returned to planning the airway. It was immediately clear that the need was greater in some areas than others. Except for a few emergency fields, the western section was largely finished, and the part of the route going east from Ottawa was also well in hand. The priority area was also the most challenging: the section through northern Ontario, between Ottawa and Winnipeg, which was essentially a black hole for transcontinental flying. For hundreds of miles between the nation's capital and the Manitoba border, there were plenty of lakes and rivers that could accommodate float planes or flying boats, but few facilities that could handle a modern passenger aircraft. Until that gap was filled, there could be no safe flying across Canada.

The government decided that it made sense for the airway to follow the rail lines. Although construction on the airfields would be done by manual labour, the project still required supplies and building materials that could only be brought into the bush by rail. So, the surveyors decided that from Montreal to Ottawa to North Bay, the airway would follow the Canadian National Railway, then strike north along the Temiskaming and Northern Ontario Railway to Cochrane, where it would turn west and follow the route of the National Transcontinental to Winnipeg. They chose this route over the other railways because it had fewer elevation changes, a more stable climate, more flat ground than the Shield country to the south, and better access to Ontario's remote mining communities.

Across the prairies, the airway followed the route of the Canadian Pacific Railway, and for the mountain section, the surveyors decided to use the Crow's Nest Pass through the Rockies. This meant that Alberta's major cities would be bypassed (Lethbridge was on the route, but Calgary and Edmonton had to be content with a feeder line to the airway), something that was regrettable but unavoidable. The northern passes, the Yellowhead and the Kicking Horse, would take the airway too far away from the more densely settled southern part of the region, and from the string of airfields in southern British Columbia—at Fernie, Cranbrook, Trail, Grand Forks, and Chilliwack—that were ready to be incorporated into the network. The objections of Calgary and Edmonton were waved aside, and eventually the airway pushed through Lethbridge to its western hub, Vancouver.

With the route laid out, the government dispatched from Ottawa in June 1932, two RCAF officers, a South African émigré named J.H. Tudhope, and Robert Dodds—who had worked for a Montreal airline before joining the air force—to select the airfield locations. In a Fairchild 51 float plane, they flew westward along the rail line looking for possible sites; when they saw an area that looked promising, they put down on the nearest lake and explored on foot, all the while battling mosquitoes and blackflies, and occasionally stopping to help fight forest fires. Their exploration work was a bigger challenge than they had been expecting. Once, engine trouble forced Tudhope and Dodds to put down in northern Ontario and paddle the machine 5 miles down the White River, which twisted and turned through spruce swamps and lakes, to a mill that had facilities for replacing the motor. First, however, they had to get to the telegraph office in the town of White River, another 10 miles away, to send for a new engine from Ottawa. So Dodds cocooned himself in mosquito netting to keep from being eaten alive and trudged through the forest to the railway line in hope of flagging down a passing freight train. It was late at night, and the sight of Dodds emerging from the trees swaddled in netting and waving his arms wildly was enough to frighten the first train engineer who came along into pouring on the coals and speeding right by. Dodds eventually got a ride from a passing track inspector and sent his message. While waiting for a lift back to the mill (it would be 36 hours before the engine arrived, and another 8 to install it) he overheard a train engineer regaling his pals with a story of having seen, the night before, a ghost on the line.

By the spring of 1933, Tudhope and Dodds had selected all of the sites between Ottawa and Emsdale, Ontario, as well as most of the sites west to Winnipeg. Now it was up to McNaughton's army of unemployed to do the hard work. Through the spring and early summer of 1933, work camps sprang up across the country. In all, there were forty-eight camps along the trans-Canada airway; most were in northern Ontario and British Columbia, with the rest scattered through Alberta, Manitoba, Quebec, and New Brunswick. The average camp was intended to hold 109 workers, but in reality they varied greatly in size. One of the biggest was at Hope, B.C., with 126 men, while at Upper Brockway, New Brunswick, only half a dozen men laboured on the airfield. By January 1934, the workforce at camps along the airway numbered more than 1900.

At each site, the first order of business was to clear enough ground to erect the barracks and other buildings, which railcars dropped off as prefabricated sections. Once the men had somewhere to live, the real work began. All of the brush on the site had to be cleared, and then the stumps and roots were removed in a process known as grubbing. The site then had to be graded, usually with hand tools, surfaced, and planted with grass seed. Some sites, of course, were more challenging than others. At Grant, Ontario, the field was to be situated on an abandoned railway yard, which meant that the men had to slog away at removing embedded railway ties and concrete foundations. Seventy acres of burned-over and boulder-strewn forest awaited the work crews assigned to build the emergency landing strip at Yakh, B.C. From the opening of the Yakh camp in February 1933 to the completion of the project three seasons later, men cleared almost the entire acreage, removing 162,000 cubic feet of boulders and excavating more than 297,000 cubic feet of earth and loose rock, to create a landing strip 200 feet wide by 2750 feet long.

In the first year of work, McNaughton's department learned some valuable lessons, in part by maintaining and analyzing meticulous records of the man-days spent on each part of the project (the final report for Yakh, for example, stated that 2744 man-days had been spent erecting the workers' huts, as opposed to 44,646 man-days to build the airfield). The clearing and grubbing was best done by hand, by gangs of men working with axes, saws, and shovels, but the grading was a tedious and time-consuming job that often produced a surface that was not really flat. The government eventually decided that heavy equipment should be brought in, to speed things along and produce a better landing surface. Still, there was much waste and mismanagement. Work gangs spent eight months hacking away at the bush outside of Kenora before the engineers decided that the site wasn't suitable for a landing strip. The men packed everything up and moved a couple of miles away, where they started the whole process again. Two years later there was still no airport, and the engineers were once more beginning to wonder if they had picked the right site. Down went the saws and axes, and there was much collective scratching of heads. Finally, officials concluded that there was no point in moving again and that work should proceed. Kenora Airport finally opened in early 1939, more than five years after work had begun at the original site.

None of these problems, of course, found their way into the many public pronouncements on the work scheme. In a March 1934 radio address, Douglas Sutherland, minister of National Defence, painted a rosy picture of the project. The men were doing "useful work on undertakings to the general advantage of Canada," he announced, and what's more, they were being well taken care of in the process. Yes, the men lived on standard army rations (variety in food was permitted only if it didn't increase the cost), but "great care is taken to ensure that only capable cooks are retained." The department provided food, accommodation, clothing, and tools free of charge, and the quality of medical care meant that the death rate in the camps was only 3 per 1,000, roughly a third of the rate in the general population. Furthermore, he emphasized, "no military discipline or drill is permitted, and no powers of compulsion or punishment have been taken by the Department of National Defence."

Magazine articles published around the same time fleshed out the picture that Sutherland sketched. One photograph featured white-hatted chefs standing indulgently in a spotless dining hall, while another showed the men passing their idle time in canvas-covered huts outfitted with bunk beds and linen tablecloths. There were recreation huts, with comforts provided by the Imperial Order of Daughters of the Empire or the National Council of Women, barbers and tailors on-site, Frontier College personnel to provide educational courses, and religious services where possible. No one should be concerned about the men being militarized by the Department of National Defence, assured the magazine; the scheme was "a practical illustration of the possibility of turning swords into ploughshares."

The reality of life in the camps was often rather different. So much depended on the supervisor—good headman, good camp, recalled one worker. If the supervisor was efficient, well organized, and sympathetic, the camp might well resemble what the press described. If not, it could be little better than a prison, with brutal discipline, dreadful living conditions, inedible food, and alternating periods of punishing labour and mind-numbing boredom. An inspection of one camp in British Columbia in 1936 revealed a long list of problems. The workers' huts were infested with mice and bugs, while rats roamed the kitchen, dining hall, and food storerooms. Dishes were not always washed, and occasionally not even rinsed. The mattresses were stuffed with old newspapers, some dating back to the early 1930s, and the camp's grounds resembled a kind of urban wasteland, strewn with garbage, bottles, tins, paper, and at least two dead cats. But when pressed on conditions in the camps, the government hastened to point out that nothing compelled the men to stay. Nothing, that is, except the hundreds of miles of wilderness that separated the typical camp from civilization.

Soon the critics were lining up to denounce the scheme. Trade unions protested when the men did anything but the most menial, unskilled jobs. Any skilled work should be done by their members, the union insisted, not by casual workers who would inevitably dilute the labour pool. For his part, McNaughton thought this was merely a blind; the reds were behind the unions, and their real agenda was to close the camps so that the disgruntled workers could flood back into the cities and start a revolution. In the House of Commons, the Liberal and Cooperative Commonwealth Federation (CCF) opposition both attacked the Conservative government's scheme as a boondoggle, the order-in-council method allowing the government to spend money without parliamentary checks. The president

of the Ontario CCF charged that the work-camp system could be manip-
ulated to ensure that the men were unable to exercise their right to vote.
Prompted by a willing press, public opinion, never very sympathetic to
anything military, soon began to turn against the camps. The workers
came to be known as Royal Twenty Centers, a nickname that came from
the daily allowance they were paid, and some critics dismissed the whole
project as simply a thinly veiled attempt to militarize the young men of
Canada. And then there were the agitators who stirred up discontent in
the camps. Many of them were probably just disgruntled, but the government thought it knew better. According to its sources, the Communist
Party of Canada had been looking for an opportunity to take the next step
on the road to its "ultimate seizure of power," and the work camps were
the perfect incubator. The Department of National Defence claimed to
have conclusive proof that the rumblings in the camps could be traced
directly back to the subversive activity of Canada's Bolshevik fifth-column.

Communist-inspired or not, trouble was certainly brewing in the
camps. The worst outbreaks were in the road-building camps of British
Columbia, but the sites along the airway were not immune. The government's response wasn't always heavy-handed. When the men in Rock
Creek, B.C., refused to work because their unheated tents offered no
protection against the October cold, the authorities brought in iron stoves
and the men willingly went back to work. But more often than not,
National Defence took no chances with workers who were branded as
troublemakers. At Hope, B.C., sixty-six men downed tools to protest bad
food and a filthy dining tent, demanding that the cook be sacked, but
instead, twenty-one of the protesters were sent packing. The same thing
happened at South River, Ontario, where twenty-two men were behind a
disturbance to protest the culinary transgressions of an inexperienced
cook. The authorities agreed to have him replaced, but also decided to
discharge all of the protesters for good measure. Sioux Lookout, Nakina,
Kowkash, Pagwa, Kitchener—all along the airway, camps were struck by
work stoppages, and in each case the so-called agitators were swiftly
removed.

Disturbances like this only gave more ammunition to people who
wanted to see the camps closed. June 1935 brought a new prime minister.

Although Mackenzie King, by his own admission, was not much interested in the camps ("Returned to H of C [House of Commons] at 8 but discussions was on relief camps and desultory, so I returned to L.H. [Laurier House]," he recorded in his diary in March 1935), he had nevertheless campaigned on a promise to close them. But a committee that he himself appointed surprised everyone, especially King, by concluding that the camps should remain open, at least until the economy improved to the point where it could absorb the unemployed workers. Most camps were well run and showed no traces of militarism, the committee found, and the grievances publicized by the press and opposition politicians were largely baseless. On the contrary, most of the problems could be traced to a small group of young men who were "viciously rebellious against and defiant to authority." King then faced the political truism that it's easier to criticize than to govern; having campaigned on a pledge to cancel the scheme, his own committee now recommended that it continue until the economy began to create some jobs.

As an expedient, the King government had already taken responsibility for administering the camps away from the Department of National Defence and given it to the Department of Labour, to counter the impression that they were "places for the internment of alien enemies and seditious-minded youths who must be kept under the watchful eye of the military branch." There was also a salary increase—the Royal Twenty Centers would now be the Royal Fifty Centers—but nevertheless, the end was in sight. It was dawning on the government that the camps were beginning to do just what they were supposed to prevent: they were fostering a feeling of hopelessness among the men who passed through them. In March 1936, the government decided that the economic indicators were sufficiently promising that they could reduce the camp populations immediately, with the last camp closing by 1 July. By then, McNaughton's army had completed eleven airfields and made substantial progress on thirty-seven others.

Meanwhile, the federal budget was finally starting to creep upward again, so the government's Civil Aviation Branch was able to continue work on most of the remaining airfields by letting contracts, now with the full use of mechanical equipment. The funding was boosted again in

1937, allowing work to continue at an even faster tempo. By year's end, there were 101 airfields between Halifax and Vancouver either completed or nearing completion, not including 5 fields in Maine that were linked to the airway by a bilateral agreement with Washington. Progress continued through 1938, until there were fully equipped airports and aerodromes about every 100 miles between Montreal and Vancouver, and intermediate aerodromes every 35 miles between the airfields; the feeder lines linking the airway to Edmonton, Saskatoon, and Toronto were similarly equipped. In February 1938, Trans-Canada Air Lines (TCA), which had been chartered as a Crown corporation the previous year to be the country's national airline, began its training flights on the route. Mail and express flights followed soon after, and on 25 March 1939 the government mounted a special Vancouver-to-Ottawa flight to show off the airway to a handful of dignitaries.

In the early evening, they boarded the TCA aircraft and set off. Three hours of flying took them to their first stop at Lethbridge, and fifteen minutes later they were airborne again for the six-hour flight to Winnipeg. Stops at Kapuskasing and North Bay followed before the aircraft reached Ottawa at 11:30 A.M. after thirteen hours in the air. On board for that trip was Vancouver banker E.E.W. Rhodes, representing a B.C. veterans' organization. In recalling the flight, he could hardly contain his enthusiasm: "In the moonlight the shining silver wings gave off a radiance that was almost golden and seemed to express the glory of the thing which had come to pass." The whole experience, he declared, was "very grand, very thrilling," and he predicted that TCA and the trans-Canada airway were "destined to bring such comfort and happiness to Canada, to bind the Provinces closer together, and to make its citizens so much more easily know each section intimately."

On April Fool's Day 1939 the first regularly scheduled passenger flight left Montreal for the West to open Canada's transcontinental air service. Like Rhodes, most people in those days saw flying as a grand and romantic adventure. Not that it was much more comfortable than it had been a decade before—it was still bumpy; noisy; the passengers had to make frequent use of the oxygen masks; and the less said about the toilet facilities the better—but the level of service had improved immeasurably with the advent of the stewardess, an American innovation that TCA brought to Canada in 1938. These "angels of the air" became like the porters on the best trains or luxury liners, who knew the passengers by name and were never without a friendly, calming smile. They served meals, refilled coffee cups, stowed luggage, plumped pillows, tucked blankets, and generally made flying a much more enjoyable experience, all on a salary that was anything but generous. Thanks in part to their presence, flying in Canada became an event that demanded a jacket and tie, one's best pearl necklace, and perhaps even white gloves. After all, this was the first generation that could cross Canada by air in a matter of hours, an experience of which their ancestors who chugged across the country for a week on a railway carriage could scarcely have conceived.

The great irony was that by the time passenger services were inaugurated along the trans-Canada airway, it was already becoming obsolete because of improvements in aviation technology. In 1927, when the government first drew up plans for the airway, Western Canada Airways flew slow and lumbering biplanes with limited range and ceiling, aircraft that frequently needed the emergency fields provided by the trans-Canada airway. Twelve years later, when the sleek, polished Lockheed took off from Montreal to open the service, airliners were being built on a weight-reducing monocoque design, were streamlined to improve speed and fuel efficiency, and had more powerful engines and variable-pitch propellers that boosted speeds to over 240 miles per hour. That all added up to greater range and reliability, and less need for the airway's intermediate and emergency fields. After all that planning and construction, many of those fields never had a single visit from a transcontinental flight.

A number of them remain in use today, some with upgraded facilities, some in a form little different from that which was wrought from the wilderness in the 1930s. Others have not fared so well. The strip in Yahk, B.C., which workers had created from a boulder-covered field, was officially closed in November 1988; the most recent plans envision the field being used as a landfill site. The emergency strip at Salmo, B.C., eventually found itself in the middle of a golf course. In 1960, a newspaper in nearby Nelson reported a club rule that all golfers had to clear the course when they heard an airplane approaching.

Still, the trans-Canada airway was a remarkable achievement for its time. As Depression-era relief projects went, Canada's was widely regarded as one of the best. It certainly was one of the cheapest. The Relief Act of 1930 cost the government over $9 per man-day and produced results of dubious value. McNaughton's scheme, in contrast, averaged about $1.30 per man-day, and bestowed on the country the beginnings of an infrastructure of inestimable value. The British government tried a similar scheme, but Britain's labour minister eventually admitted that it didn't come close to the efficiency of McNaughton's. The U.S. government also thought enough of McNaughton's work camps to pattern its own Civilian Conservation Corps (CCC) after the Canadian example; that the CCC was so popular in the United States can be explained by the fact that the administration of Franklin Delano Roosevelt promoted it, not as a way to control dissent by isolating potentially rowdy young men, but as a way to inject money into the economy.

What's more, even if most of the emergency fields were never used, the trans-Canada airway did precisely what it was supposed to do—launched Canada into the air age. The first months of TCA's transcontinental service attracted few paying passengers—the tickets were far too expensive for anyone but well-heeled businesspeople or vacationers—but that changed with the coming of war in September 1939. Speedy and reliable transportation between major cities became a priority for politicians, civil servants, businesspeople, military personnel—anyone who was serving the war effort—so TCA began to expand, adding flights, acquiring larger aircraft, and developing new routes. To the Montreal–Vancouver service was added service to Moncton in 1940, Halifax in 1941, Sydney and St. John's in 1942, and Victoria in 1943. That same year, the Canadian Government Trans-Atlantic Service began flying regularly to the United Kingdom, using converted four-engine bombers. All of this growth would have been much more difficult if the trans-Canada airway had not already created the infrastructure. The principal airports were ready to handle TCA's expansion and could also accommodate the growth of Richardson's Western Canada Airways, which went through a number of incarnations before being reborn in 1943 as Canadian Pacific Airlines. By war's end, Canada had a fully functioning national passenger and airmail system, and a trans-Atlantic service anchored on the airway's eastern hub. A trans-Pacific service, based on the airway's western terminus, was soon to come.

More than sixty years after its completion, the trans-Canada airway is still the framework of our air transport system, its principal airports still the nation's largest and most important facilities. Little remains of some of the emergency fields that were carved from the bush at now-forgotten places in northern Ontario and central British Columbia, but the airway of which they were a part has left an important legacy for Canadians. To paraphrase the words of a contemporary, Canada, by virtue of its geography, was at the crossroads of the world in the air age. The trans-Canada airway was intended to take advantage of that lucky circumstance and to ensure the nation was not left behind by progress.

"LET US THINK THAT WE BUILD FOREVER"

IN EVERY WAY WORTHY
OF THE PROVINCE

On 23 March 1938, any number of couples would have strolled through Regina's Wascana Park and stopped to marvel at the magnificent provincial legislative building, then a quarter of a century old and comfortably settled into a place of honour in the Saskatchewan capital. With a glorious dome rising over 180 feet it was still the tallest building in the city, as well as the longest at over 530 feet, and the stately portico and colonnaded pavilions at each end gave the edifice a dignity and a grandeur that made the people of the city justifiably proud.

A thousand miles to the east, the registrar of the Homewood Sanitarium near Guelph, the first private psychiatric institution in Ontario, was recording the death of a seventy-year-old patient. The elderly gentleman, after becoming agitated during an argument with an attendant over a library book, had fallen and broken his hip. His death, according to the coroner, was caused by a blood clot. So ended the life of T. Walter Scott, the first premier of Saskatchewan and the man who, more than anyone else, had been responsible for the architectural gem of Regina, arguably the greatest of Canada's provincial legislatures.

That Scott would one day rise to such heights would probably have surprised people who knew him as a child. Born near London, Ontario, in the year of Confederation, he was an indifferent student who frequently missed school because of chronic asthma, and he gave up on education as soon as he finished the eighth grade. But in his mind, the darkest cloud hanging over him was his illegitimacy. (It was such a burden that, for the rest of his life, he maintained the fiction that his father had died before he was born.) Knowing that he would never inherit his stepfather's farm and perhaps tiring of the sideways glances that an illegitimate child could expect in puritanical, small-town Ontario, he decided to try his fortunes in the West. Although he wasn't yet eighteen, he packed his few belongings and set out for Portage-la-Prairie, Manitoba. A year later, he had settled in Regina.

The story of Scott's transformation from illegitimate farm boy to provincial premier is the stuff of legend—from a floor-sweeper in a small Manitoba newspaper office to the owner of the Regina *Leader* and the Moose Jaw *Times,* from a journalist with liberal inclinations to the Liberal member of Parliament for the federal riding of Assiniboia West and finally the premier of Saskatchewan in September 1905. His life to that point was a great Prairie success story.

And there was more to come, for the West was booming. Manitoba (which had become a province in 1870), Saskatchewan, and Alberta (the latter two created in 1905) saw their populations and economies explode in the decades before the First World War. Between 1881 and 1911, the region's population grew from under 120,000 to over 1.3 million, and the cities of the new West burgeoned even more dramatically, some by as much as 10,000 percent. All three provinces were in expansionary moods, and few people exemplified the prevailing optimism as fully as did Walter Scott. Fortunately for the history of Canadian architecture, two others who did were Scott's fellow Prairie premiers.

Alexander Cameron Rutherford was ten years older that Scott and had headed west from Kemptville, near Ottawa, a decade after Scott had established himself in Saskatchewan. Already a successful lawyer when he reached Edmonton, Rutherford's rise was less surprising but much faster—from his election as a member of the territorial legislature in 1902 to premier of Alberta in September 1905. The eldest of the three was Rodmond Roblin, born in Prince Edward County, in eastern Ontario, in 1853. Insatiably ambitious, he had been hatching a grand scheme to make a fortune in cheese when one day his horse bolted and put him in hospital with severe injuries. As he recuperated, he started to read about the West and became convinced that it was the only place big enough for a man of his ambition. In 1877, he and his family climbed off a riverboat in Fort Garry, all set to make a mark on the province. Three years later, Roblin entered local politics, moving to the provincial legislature in 1888. By the time Scott and Rutherford took over Saskatchewan and Alberta, Roblin had been premier of Manitoba for five years.

The three men, whatever their political differences, shared a common belief: if their province was to have any pretension to greatness, it needed grand public buildings to express that greatness. A modern, prosperous province demanded a fitting seat of government, a building that would awe everyone with its solidity and grandeur. All three men fell under the sway of this tantalizing dream, committing millions in public funds to building campaigns that were the most ambitious yet embarked upon in the West. Ultimately, as with so many government mega-projects, those campaigns left a trail of frustrated architects, disgraced politicians, and ruined contractors. But they also produced some of the most impressive public buildings in Canada. Scott was aware of this potential as the plan for a legislative building in the Saskatchewan capital took shape in his mind. He may well have recalled what Sir John A. Macdonald had once said of Regina—"it would be improved by a little more wood, and a little more water, and here and there a hill"—and saw the legislative complex as a way to transform the city and express the province's potential.

Parliament buildings had certainly had that effect elsewhere in Canada. Scott had never travelled east of Quebec, but he proceeded to make it his business to study from afar the legislative buildings of the Maritime provinces for inspiration. The oldest was Halifax's Province House, completed in 1819, a triumph of Georgian architecture that novelist Thomas Raddall would later call "a little grey gem in the heart of Mammon." Charles Dickens too declared himself most impressed by the building. He couldn't help remarking on the faithfulness with which England's legislative traditions were replicated on a much smaller scale in Nova Scotia; looking at Province House and its doings was, he thought, like "looking at Westminster through the wrong end of a telescope." Charlottetown had its own Province House, although it was known as the Colonial Building when the legislature first met there in 1847. It too had the stately columns that characterized the Georgian style of architecture, although it was smaller and a little more restrained. It may have been inspired by the public buildings of the designer's native Yorkshire, but Islanders were more interested in the fact that they had a building to rival Halifax's. That it was constructed from Nova Scotia sandstone was better left unsaid. New Brunswick's legislature dated from 1882, by which time fashions had changed, and the government's chosen architect had opted for the Second Empire style, a French-inspired form characterized by rich ornamentation and a complex design. Corner towers and a cupola that positively glowed in the sun made for a lively and exuberant building that one editor observed was "in every way worthy of the province."

The Saskatchewan premier looked closely at the construction of Canada's newer legislatures as he contemplated what might be built in Regina. In Quebec, the government had voted to spend $200,000 to erect a legislative complex that drew inspiration from the Louvre in Paris; the plans were largely the work of someone with little architectural training, Eugène-Étienne Taché, the deputy minister in the Department of Lands and Forests and the man who coined the provincial motto *"Je me souviens."* The construction would be done in stages: the office wings of the new complex first, then a small connecting section, and finally the legislative assembly block itself, an opulent building with a grand central tower and two false turrets, or pepper boxes, at either end. This would address the greatest needs first, and also spread out the cost a little.

And cost quickly became an issue. When the first estimates came in, they had ballooned to $500,000, more than double the original vote. The government felt it had no choice but to accept the lowest bid, but before long it became painfully clear that the lowest bid was not necessarily the best. The new building had more stone sculpture than any other in the city and the contractor, facing ruinous labour costs, began to slash the wages of its stone-cutters. At first, they earned $1.50 a day, but in 1877 when the contractor started paying them on a piecework basis, daily wages fell to about 80 cents. It was only a matter of time before the workers were in open revolt. On 3 June 1878, they could stand the wage cuts no longer, and downed tools. The contractor responded by bringing in strikebreakers from Montreal and Trois-Rivières, which in turn spawned rioting, and the government summoned the army. By the time order was restored, dozens of workers were injured and two were dead.

Despite these problems, the government offices were completed by 1880. But that section alone had cost nearly $400,000, and the government began searching for economies on the second phase, the small section to link the office wing to the legislative building. Once again, they took the lowest tender, but this time Pierre Gauvreau, the chief engineer in the Department of Public Works, found another way to cut costs and avoid labour trouble: he borrowed convicts from the city jail, paying them 40 cents a day as manual labourers. But the eagle-eyed Gauvreau fell ill in late 1882, shortly after tenders were called for the legislative building, leaving no one able or willing to exercise the same control over costs. An odour of corruption began to rise over the building site. Three local contractors claimed that the specifications for this phase changed so frequently that they couldn't submit bids; they believed it was a shallow ploy by the Conservative premier, J.A. Mousseau, to ensure that the contract went to a Montreal builder named Alphonse Charlebois. A commission of inquiry cleared Mousseau, but the controversy was the last straw in his short and ill-starred premiership, and he was forced from office. What was worse, costs continued to climb alarmingly. The original tender for the legislative building section had been for $185,000, but design changes and cost overruns quickly pushed it to over $1 million. Even then, the construction ran behind schedule, and only a few months of working around the clock enabled the contractor to finish the job in June 1885, two months after the original deadline.

The building had one more victim to claim. Liberal member Honoré Mercier had led the charge against Mousseau with his accusations that

Charlebois had bought the contract, but in the wake of the official opening, Premier Mercier himself became the target. The Conservatives were quick to use their former leader's downfall as a weapon, charging that Mercier had accepted a bribe to meddle in the work of the commission. The charge was never proven, but it was enough for the province's lieutenant-governor to call for Mercier's resignation. Erecting a legislature, it seemed, was bad for one's political career.

In Ontario, the province of Scott's birth, the construction of the new legislature had been just as controversial. On 27 April 1880, the government announced a design competition for a new building costing up to $500,000 (later raised to $700,000). The jurors, Alexander Mackenzie, the federal public works commissioner, and architects W.G. Storm of Toronto and Richard Waite of Buffalo, New York, eventually selected three finalists, but were less than enthusiastic about them. "In architectural character these designs are inferior to some of the others," they concluded; not one was worthy of the site and all of them showed "a grievous lack of that distinctive character in design." The architects themselves were not to blame, they pointed out; the fault lay with the government for being so miserly in the money voted for the building. The public works minister, Christopher Fraser of Brockville, decided to ask the top two bidders to resubmit their designs, with the construction costs spelled out.

When the revised proposals reached the government, Fraser was dismayed that both forecast costs in excess of $750,000. With no alternative but to commit the extra money, the government then had to plot its next course of action. Unable to choose between the two, it decided that one of the expert judges should be called upon to pronounce—but which one? Mackenzie was not an architect, so he was not an option, and because Storm lived in Toronto and had worked with both of the leading bidders, it was thought that he could not be impartial. That left Richard Waite. But if Fraser thought that Waite was now ready to offer a warm endorsement of one of the schemes, he was sorely disappointed. Waite stuck to his guns: neither design was suitable. After two failed competitions, Fraser must have felt like washing his hands of the entire affair, but instead he advised the government simply to appoint an architect to the project. It should be someone with experience in designing and constructing large buildings and preferably some familiarity with the situation in Toronto. Perhaps someone like … Richard Waite!

To the casual observer, and certainly to the two firms whose designs had been rejected (Gordon and Helliwell, and Darling and Curry), this looked like a boondoggle of the first order. Waite, they charged, had sabotaged the entire process, ensuring that the two local firms were shut out so he could step in and pick up the lucrative contract. Despite official denials— Waite was out of the country when the decision was made, the government said, and there had been no clue that he had been interested in winning the contract for himself—the controversy hung over the project like a cloud.

Still, Waite's design was not unpopular. The new legislature was the first major Canadian building done in a style that was sweeping the United States, Richardson Romanesque, and had all of its characteristic features: a profusion of heavy, rounded arches; warm, dark stonework; a squat appearance that suggested solidity; and curious elements of asymmetry. The *Globe* came out strongly in favour of it and dismissed claims that the money could be better spent elsewhere. On the contrary, said the newspaper, Ontarians should be willing to pay for a building that expressed the strength and stability of the province.

If Waite thought that a big government contract would make him a wealthy man, he was mistaken. He earned less than half of what he was due based on the cost of the project, and eventually gave up trying to squeeze his rightful fees out of the province. And the legislature wasn't an easy assignment. The first two builders who were offered the construction contract declined; it eventually went to the third choice, a Toronto builder named Lionel Yorke. Then, Fraser developed a deep distrust of the architect, and relations between the two deteriorated as project costs climbed. When it became clear that extra excavation and concrete work was needed to give the building solid footings, Fraser reluctantly agreed but suspected that the province was being hoodwinked by Waite, or Yorke, or both. "The exact amount of extra work done should be ascertained and fixed from time to time as completed, and not left to be disputed afterwards," he wrote testily. Not even the fact that the ten million bricks needed for the inner structure were made by cheap convict labour from Toronto's

Central Prison made a dent in the ballooning bills. With the overruns, discontent at the process of awarding the contract flared. In 1892, a poster circulated around the city showing Darling and Curry's design, with the full cost of $612,000 noted in large print, and Waite's design, which carried the ominous caption "Nobody yet knows what complete Building will cost, but practical men estimate it at not less that $2,000,000."

The grudge would die hard—into the 1960s, local newspapers would remind readers of the controversies that had swirled around the project— but all was temporarily forgotten when Torontonians flocked to Queen's Park for the official opening of the building on 4 April 1893. The weather was uncooperative, a sudden gale smashing a large window and shredding the brand-new Red Ensign hoisted above the building, but the star of the show was the grand old man of Ontario politics, the seventy-three-year-old premier, Sir Oliver Mowat. A living link with the province's past, he recalled the days of his youth, when Muddy York was little more than a village, a tiny outpost of civilization between the lake and the wilderness. But as he matured, so too did his province: "Its progress in population, in wealth, in education, in intelligence, in political freedom, and in most other things which serve to make a country attractive and great, has in fact been enormous." Such progress often made him feel his age (he noted that he had outlived most of his political friends and foes), but Mowat was still full of optimism for the province. His enthusiasm was symbolized by the new building, which he credited to the public works minister, Christopher Fraser (there was not a word about the long-suffering Richard Waite): "This building, erected under his care and supervision ... will, as long as the building stands, be a monument of his administrative ability, his energy and his economy."

Things had been no better in British Columbia, where Premier Theodore Davie had struggled mightily to convince legislators to vote $600,000 for a new legislature in Victoria. A competition was announced, and in due course judges A.G. Taylor of Montreal and W.S. Curry of Toronto (one of the much-aggrieved losers in Ontario's design competition) closeted themselves in the Rocabella Guest House to go through the sixty-seven entries. They short-listed five, including one that was signed "A B.C. Architect." The eastern Canadian judges may not have noticed this blatant attempt to use local sentiment to sway them (in fact, their report listed the creator as A.B.C. Architect), but they had to admit the design was impressive. In the end, that one got the nod.

That Francis Mawson Rattenbury would try to curry favour with so transparent a ploy was entirely in character. At the time the twenty-five-year-old Yorkshireman received the congratulatory telegram from the B.C. government, he was an architect of undoubted promise but limited accomplishment. Indeed, he had never built anything even close to the size of the legislative buildings when he entered the competition in 1893, just a year after arriving in British Columbia. But Rattenbury could never be accused of lacking self-confidence, and his skills as an architect were matched by even greater talent as a self-promoter. Embellishment was his watchword, whether in architectural detail or his own biography. Shortly after the award was announced, the Vancouver *Daily World,* perhaps with Rattenbury's connivance, exaggerated the architect's accomplishments to the point of untruth, suggesting he had been involved in the design of the Bradford Town Hall, an architectural triumph in northern England. Considering Rattenbury was six when it opened, that was hardly likely— he was certainly a young prodigy, but not that young.

If his resumé was dubious, his design certainly wasn't. It combined a variety of architectural styles, from the Gothic to the Italianate to the Romanesque, with the entire facade dominated by an immense central dome and more than a dozen smaller domes on the wings. The handling of the various elements was so confident that the judges might have assumed they were viewing plans drawn up by a senior architect with decades of experience. If they did, Rattenbury would have felt it was only right. He installed himself in the best hotel in the city (a need for economy later asserted itself, and he moved to a more modest guest house), and got to work.

The headstrong and imperious Rattenbury soon found the construction site full of obstacles to his creative vision. The first was builder Frederick Adams, who had matched the lowest bid, submitted by a Washington firm, so that the work could go to a local company. Adams, an experienced contractor from Ontario, was hoping to translate this project into a successful business on the West Coast, but he got more than he bargained for in Rattenbury. After shipping to Victoria a load of stone from the very quarry that Rattenbury himself had inspected, Adams was shocked to be told that the stone was inferior in quality. The real problem was that Rattenbury had mistakenly chosen a stone that was too dark for the effect he wished to achieve—rather than admit his error, he pinned the blame on the hapless Adams. And, because Adams had unwisely agreed to do the work at a fixed cost, he was soon staring at financial ruin and had to surrender the contract, just a few months after he had started work. He vowed to pester the architect and the provincial government until he was vindicated, but a fatal boating accident in 1895 removed that thorn from Rattenbury's side.

Soon, however, another adversary appeared in the person of George Martin, the newly appointed commissioner of Lands and Works. A reluctant public servant—he always regretted that he hadn't followed in the family footsteps and joined the navy—Martin was alarmed by the cost overruns that seemed to grow every week and made it his business to wrestle control of the project away from Rattenbury. The two butted heads over every imaginable detail, from the paving of sidewalks to the space designated for individual departments, but Martin was invariably bested by the smoother and more urbane Rattenbury, who regarded any suggestion, whatever its merit, as an attack on his professional judgment. After one clash, the government asked if Rattenbury would like to resign from the project; a few months later, the architect inquired if the government would prefer that he step aside. But almost every time, Rattenbury got his way. The project soured Martin's last drops of enthusiasm for public service and he retired prematurely, shortly after the legislature was officially opened.

The great day was 10 February 1898, just in time for the new sitting of the assembly. Schools had been closed for the day, and the best and brightest in Victoria society turned out for the festivities. There were dignitaries, military bands, curious citizens, politicians, civil servants—everyone who was involved in the project was there, except the architect himself. Rattenbury was already thousands of miles away, back in London trying to drum up investors for a hare-brained scheme to build and operate riverboats (the company eventually launched three boats, quaintly named *Flora, Nora,* and *Ora*) to serve the Klondike goldfields.

Few people, however, remarked on Rattenbury's absence. The press was generous in its praise, the Victoria *Times* observing that "The beauty of the structure calls forth the admiration of everyone who has seen it, while the perfection of the work and the thoroughness in which details have been carried out is a surprise to visitors. In general design and in choice of the stone for the buildings the good taste and judgement displayed has been decidedly happy, the result being a harmonious picture delightful to the eye." King George V would later call it one of the two finest architectural achievements in Canada. Only with use did the shortcomings of Rattenbury's *magnum opus* become clear: the terrible acoustics in the assembly chamber (rumour has it that they were improved by hanging salmon nets from the ceiling), the fact that the press gallery had no desks, and the absence of washrooms in the lieutenant-governor's suite. The architect would probably have dismissed such matters as inconsequential to his grand vision, and perhaps he would have been right.

AS HE LOOKED around at the other provinces, Walter Scott saw plenty of examples of how not to build a legislature. But he also had greater incentive to do things right, thanks to the competitive spirit among the three Prairie provinces. Each felt it had something to prove, to the nation and to each other, and was determined to use public architecture to accomplish it. And Scott had great dreams for Saskatchewan and its capital. He directed his deputy premier, James Calder, to hunt out potential sites, and Calder eventually came up with seven possibilities, some closer to downtown, others on the outskirts. Much to the dismay of municipal politicians, Calder's interest soon focused on a property south of the Wascana Creek and, in those days, outside city limits. The land featured good frontage on the waterway, was large enough to be turned into a major urban park, and could accommodate a building that would dominate the city's skyline. Brushing aside council's complaints that it was too far from downtown, the provincial government bought the property for $96,250 and got down to work.

At first, Scott was tempted to use the privileges of power to appoint an architect with a good Liberal pedigree, or at the very least one of his own acquaintance, like Rattenbury or the great American architect Cass

Gilbert, whose state legislature in St. Paul, Minnesota, deeply impressed Scott. But prudence won out. Scott knew that he was erecting not just a public building but a symbol of the province and that everything about the process had to be above reproach. So, he appointed a panel of expert judges, headed by Percy Nobbs of Montreal, one of Canada's most influential architects, which decided to invite seven respected firms to submit designs, among them the Maxwell brothers of Montreal, Francis Rattenbury, Darling and Pearson of Toronto (Darling was another veteran of the Ontario legislature design competition), and Cass Gilbert.

The government's guidelines were straightforward. The cost should be somewhere between $750,000 and $1 million, and the building should be made of the latest fireproof materials. As to exterior finish, brick with sandstone trim was preferred, but the primary consideration was that it be able to stand the extremes of prairie weather. The legislature should be designed so that wings could be added in the future, to accommodate the growth of the government, and, as a further indication of the prevailing optimism, the legislative chamber should be designed to seat 125 members (this at a time when there were only 25 members in the assembly). The government had little to say about the desired style, except that it should have a tower or dome to dominate the table-flat landscape. Percy Nobbs added his own afterthought to the guidelines: Saskatchewan being within the British Empire, the design should express that connection. On 21 December 1907, the results were announced: the winner was the Montreal firm of Edward and W.S. Maxwell.

The Maxwells' description of the design revealed just how seriously they had taken Nobbs's final condition: "In designing the exterior of the building a free adaptation of English Renaissance work has been employed, as being best suited to the requirements, and offering a logical, sensible and architecturally interesting solution of the problem that marks it unmistakably as representative of the British sovereignty under which the Province is governed." In awarding the construction contract, Scott again faced pressure to use the power of patronage. The lowest bid came from a local contractor, but the premier believed that only a large, well-established, and financially stable firm could handle a project of this size. So, the government chose a Montreal contractor recommended by the

Maxwell brothers, risking the wrath of the local building community for the sake of posterity. In every other respect, though, Scott did all he could to ensure that this was a local project. The labourers would all come from Regina, and to avoid charges of preferential hiring, each man had to present letters of reference and proof of competence to show that he didn't get the job through political connections. All materials would be Canadian, or at least British—the builders would resort to U.S. suppliers only if nothing else was available.

Work began on 31 August 1908, with Scott being a hands-on manager, involving himself in most of the decisions regarding the project. Firmly in his mind was the notion that the building would be erected only once, and so it had to be done right. This explains the ninety-one separate modifications made over the course of the construction, changes that early on boosted the cost estimate to $1.75 million. Some of these changes were relatively minor—such as adding a light atop the dome that would be illuminated every night that the legislature was sitting—but others involved significant reorientations in the original design. Perhaps the biggest was that the exterior, instead of being clad in red brick, should be done in Manitoba Tyndall limestone. Everyone agreed that it improved the appearance of the building, but it added an extra $50,000 in total for the stone, the new quarry that had to be opened, and a new rail line to transport it to Regina. For Scott, though, the extra expense was worth it. As he told the crowds who mobbed the work site to see the governor general, Earl Grey, lay the cornerstone on 4 October 1909, "[I]t will be in appearance, stability, and durability such a building as will appropriately represent the character and ambitions of the people of the province."

Not that the project didn't have its hiccups. There were a few work stoppages by bricklayers, carpenters, and electricians, but none of them lasted more than a few weeks. Then, as if to confirm that Scott's project was somehow blessed, it escaped virtually unscathed when a cyclone swept through Regina on 30 June 1912, killing twenty-eight and injuring hundreds more. The building suffered little damage—only the wing in which the Department of Education had been working was grazed, the most serious consequence being that the year's provincial exams, which were waiting to be graded, were blown out of the windows and scattered across the countryside. That year, students in the province received a pass or fail based on their teachers' recollections of their academic progress.

The new legislative chamber was ready for the opening of the 1912 session in January, but the formal dedication had to wait until 12 October 1912, when the new governor general, the Duke of Connaught, and his wife and daughter came to Regina to do the honours. The royal representatives drove through city streets adorned with processional arches and lined with cheering crowds, to a building illuminated by huge searchlights for the occasion. The event boasted everything—fireworks, a riot of flowers, local worthies in their best formal evening dress, an honour guard from the North-West Mounted Police. The only thing missing was the man who had done more than anyone else to see the project through to completion, Walter Scott. The bouts of depression that he had long battled secretly were starting to take over his life, and within a few years his illness would drive him from politics. Tragically, on what should have been his night above anyone else's, he was too ill to attend the ceremonies and asked Calder to represent him. Scott did, however, leave behind the text of the speech he would have made, and it captured the great optimism that battled against his deepening mental illness: "What a field for speculation is opened by this occasion—what unlimited room for imagination in the thought of history which will be made in this building, the history which will centre here and which in both the figurative and literal sense, this building will share in and preserve."

Every province is proud of its legislature, but it's hard to deny that Saskatchewan's achievement was a little greater than the others'. When completed, it was the largest reinforced concrete building in the Canadian West, and it had all been done at a cost of $1.8 million, the last payment being made to the contractor on 12 March 1914. There were a few glitches—"We will make no comment on the wonderful clocks which ornament certain portions of the Department but which were evidently never intended to give any reliable information regarding time," wrote one deputy minister after the building opened—but the verdict has been overwhelmingly positive. Nowhere else in Canada is a legislature surrounded by so much parkland, something that made a deep impression on journalist Bruce Hutchison: "No other provincial government building approaches this in beauty. No setting is equal to it.... Nowhere has man struggled with less promising materials and achieved so much."

In a perfect world, Hutchison's words would apply to any legislature, but the experience of Alexander Cameron Rutherford in Alberta was decidedly less happy. The legislative assembly of the new province first met in the grand setting of Edmonton's Thistle Rink, with later sessions convening in the MacKay Avenue School. Neither was satisfactory. "It is most important," said the public works minister, W.H. Cushing, "that the government at the earliest possible moment take up the matter of providing legislative buildings in this province." Everything depended on which city would be named the capital. Almost every community in the province went to great lengths to sell its own virtues: Edmonton ("the nearest suitable point to the ultimate centre of population in the Province"); Calgary (the choice of R.B. Bennett); Banff ("already known to travellers all over the world as one of the great sights of the continent"); Red Deer ("nature has provided a site there for a beautiful city on a splendid river"); Vegreville, population seventy-eight ("she has made such gigantic and tremendous strides during the last decade and a half who may not venture to prognosticate what good things are in store for her?"); even the tiny village of Blackfalds ("so suitable, so beautiful, so adaptable and so recommending"). In the end, Edmonton carried the day, winning by a vote of sixteen to eight in the new provincial assembly.

By the fall of 1906, the government had chosen a property on a hill overlooking the North Saskatchewan River. Its physical prominence was a factor, but so too was the site's historical significance, located as it was near the site of Fort Edmonton, the fur trade post run by the Hudson's Bay Company and the earliest ancestor of the city of Edmonton. "We are ... aiming only to establish for our people the most important and imposing structure in the province upon a site in our judgement well suited for the purpose," said one government official, "and in doing so following in the footsteps of the officers of the historic trading company who established themselves upon the same ground two generations before." The province duly bought 21 acres at $4,000 an acre and set in motion the process of building a legislature. The Edmonton *Journal* predicted confidently that it would be "the handsomest parliament building in the Dominion."

The next order of business was to find an architect. This would be the biggest public works project of the pre-war era, with a budget of nearly $2.5 million, and everything had to be just right. The province's established architects, of which there were more than a few, were rubbing their hands with glee at the prospect, not just of a lucrative contract but of the chance to design such an important structure. But then the government announced its choice: Allan Merrick Jeffers, United States born and trained, and living and working south of the border. The architectural community was thunderstruck—the government's choice was not just an outsider, but also someone who had never even been to the province, and an easterner to boot, from Rhode Island! It didn't help that he arrived in Edmonton in April 1907 carrying two thick books filled with drawings, not of an English public building, but of the recently completed Minnesota state capitol.

Though the appointment was badly handled, there was some logic behind it. The government had first approached Francis Rattenbury, who offered to provide a design but wasn't interested in supervising the entire project. Edward Hopkins, an architect in the Public Works department, then presented a set of plans to Alberta's assembly. Some members thought they looked familiar, and so they should have, because they were actually plans of Rattenbury's legislative building in Victoria. Whether Hopkins presented them in error or because he hadn't come up with anything else is unclear, but his gaffe didn't sit well with the government. Hopkins was sent away to produce another set, but Cushing didn't think much of those either. Perhaps it was then that the government decided to bring in someone with more experience. Or, perhaps it was after Cushing and Rutherford visited the state capitols in Minnesota and Wisconsin, which they much admired. Rutherford, after all, had a deep personal interest in the project, and may have been influenced by the fact that Jeffers shared his admiration for the U.S. government buildings.

Jeffers was appointed provincial architect in the summer of 1907, with his first design, presented in September 1907, showing the influence of the Rhode Island state capitol, as well as the capitols in Minnesota and

Wisconsin. The style was known as Beaux-Arts, but Jeffers's design represented a restrained version. The main stairs were less monumental than on many such buildings, and it was conspicuously lacking in the ornate sculptural detail of which Beaux-Arts architects were so fond. But if the government liked the design, its consultants didn't. Percy Nobbs thought it was "thoroughly non-British in feeling," which for him was the strongest possible criticism, and he also had a more practical, not to mention prescient, comment: Beaux-Arts was expensive, and tended to give less usable space than other popular styles of the period.

So construction hadn't even started yet and the local architectural community and one of the country's leading architects were already expressing doubts. Site-clearing had begun, however, which demanded the removal of Hardisty House, a once-grand structure that had served as the home of Edmonton's chief factor since 1874 and had later done duty variously as a golf clubhouse and a smallpox hospital. Workers began excavating the basement in August 1907 and pouring the concrete foundations in October—by which time Jeffers had only just presented his preliminary plans (the diagrams for the first storey were still being finalized), and the design hadn't yet been shown to the public. It wouldn't be the last time that, by all appearances, Jeffers had to work hard to keep ahead of the builders. The foundation was finished early the next year, just as the architect was finishing the drawings for the roof framing and the south elevation. Then, someone noticed that an important issue had been neglected—the securing of a building permit. Though only a formality, it betrayed a lack of experience that would plague the project. With the necessary permit duly obtained in February 1908, the work proceeded. In 1909, while Jeffers was still working on drawings for the dome, the steel skeleton went up and crew laid the first courses of the external masonry. There was a break in the construction on 1 October 1909 so that Governor General Earl Grey could officiate at the ceremonial laying of the cornerstone (he then left immediately to do similar duty in Regina), but other than that, the work gangs kept up a torrid pace. So too did Jeffers.

In November 1911, the assembly met for the first time in the newly completed chamber, and the Edmonton *Journal* pronounced favourably on the project: "There is no difference of opinion as to the wisdom of the expenditure which has provided the government of the province with quarters in keeping with the pretensions of Alberta." Within a few months, however, problems became evident. The plaster in the legislative chamber and the library began to show cracks; more seriously, some of the interior arches had to be rebuilt because the stonemasons couldn't get the keystones to fit. A later historian put this down to miscalculations in the design drawings, perhaps because Jeffers was designing as the building was going up around him. The problems may also have had something to do with his resignation from the project in January 1912, to become Edmonton's new City Architect. The site was turned over to British-born architect Richard Blakey, who finished the remaining features such as the rotunda and the main staircase leading to the legislative chamber.

The last stone was laid in the building's dome on 6 May 1912, though the steel work atop the dome had not been completed by 12 September of that year, when the Duke of Connaught came to Edmonton to perform the official opening. And once again at such an opening ceremony, a key figure was missing. Rutherford, who had been a constant visitor to the construction site and had done so much to bring the building to fruition, had been chased out of office in 1910 by a scandal, not of his own making, involving the shady financing of the Alberta and Great Waterways Railway. He never got to sit in the chamber he had worked so hard to create.

And alas, Percy Nobbs had been right; the building simply didn't have enough usable space, and by the time construction was finished it was already too small. The government had always intended to centralize operations in the new legislature so that the nearby Terrace Building could be emptied of civil servants. But even after all the offices in the new structure were occupied, the Terrace Building was still full of bureaucrats. It's tempting to put such faults down to the government's lack of experience with major building projects, but one wonders if the Alberta government felt the pressure of competing with Saskatchewan and rushed the process to beat its neighbour. Alberta did indeed win the race by a month, but only at the cost of erecting a building that has never drawn the praise of Saskatchewan's. Some have criticized Jeffers's choice of greyish yellow sandstone for the upper storeys, one architectural historian suggesting that "the sallow, murky colour gives a dingy appearance to the stone even in the bright Alberta sunlight." Nor did the building have the grandeur that it might have. The fact that the legislature was too small was part of the problem—the interior "spaces are compressed, even oppressive," thought architectural historian Diana Bodnar, and the design itself was not sufficiently expansive for the purpose or the setting. It "lacks an overall effective monumental quality," wrote Bodnar. "It is and has always been dominated by its environment." As we shall see, later architects would consider this a virtue.

Throughout these years, Manitoba's premier, Rodmond Roblin, was fully aware of the buildings that were going up in Regina and Edmonton, and he had no intention of being upstaged. Saskatchewan and Alberta had both laid the cornerstones of their new legislatures in October 1909 and had held their official openings less than a month apart in 1912. These facts would irritate Roblin like a bad blister. Canada's fifth province would not, could not be outdone by the country's eighth and ninth provinces; Roblin was determined to see to that. The Manitoba *Free Press* might have been speaking for him when it wrote that "no loyal citizen of Manitoba will be satisfied with any building not commensurate with the province's importance and dignity." Roblin's government had created the office of the Provincial Architect in 1904 and intended to redevelop Winnipeg's downtown. A new legislature would be a major part of that plan.

Roblin had his eye on a downtown property where the current legislature sat, but part of the property was owned by the federal government, which wanted $1 million for the land and the dumpy barracks and drill shed that stood on it. Luckily, the federal election of 1911 brought to power Robert Borden's Conservatives, with the help of Roblin's notoriously corrupt political machine. Federal gratitude began to flow toward Manitoba—the province's northern boundary was extended, the premier became *Sir* Rodmond Roblin, and the price for the parcel of land in downtown Winnipeg miraculously dropped. Roblin had himself a site.

The government decided to open the design competition only to Canadian or British firms, and when the competition closed on 31 March 1912, four of the top five entrants were Canadian architects. Roblin's opponents assumed that the Conservative government, notoriously corrupt even by contemporary standards, would find a way to reward a loyal Conservative firm, but the judges chose the lone non-Canadian finalist, Frank Simon of Liverpool, whose best-known work to date was the splendid Liverpool Cotton Exchange. The legislators wanted a building with four important facades, so Simon designed an H-shaped structure, with a 250-foot central dome. Fluted columns flanked each of the four entrances and lined the tower that supported the dome. For Simon, the grandeur of the building was significant: "Here you have no mountains to which you can lift up your hearts. And so you have all the more need of great architecture to lift them up." Despite this idealism, Simon almost immediately found himself at loggerheads with the province. He argued that he should serve as supervising architect so that he could control what went on at the job site, but the government instead appointed the Provincial Architect to the position. This gave Roblin's government exclusive control over the construction and all the patronage opportunities that a major public building project offered. The seeds of disaster had been sown.

The province's economy took a nose-dive in 1913, but the government remained committed to the project and awarded the contract to Thomas Kelly and Sons, a Winnipeg firm. Kelly had lost out on the contract for the Regina legislature because of accusations that he had acted improperly by submitting two bids; he was accused of trying the same tactic in Winnipeg, but this didn't bother the Roblin government. Kelly got the contract, and work began in August 1913. In short order, however, problems began to emerge. The government had originally budgeted $2 million, but by February 1914 the building was projected to cost nearly double that, in part because of additions to the plan but also because of questionable practices on Kelly's part. Subsequent investigations revealed that the government had been billed almost twice the going rate for the structural steel, with almost all of the money being paid up front, before construction even started.

Roblin may have heaved a sigh of relief when the First World War began—the day after Canada entered the war, he announced that work on the building would be suspended so that funds could be diverted to the war effort. If he thought the ploy would buy him some time to sort out the mess, Roblin was wrong. The public outcry, from the people of Winnipeg as well as from the organized labour movement (which was counting on the project to provide jobs over the winter), was so strong that Roblin was forced to convene a special session of the provincial legislature to float a $2-million loan that would allow construction to continue. On 22 September 1914, the workers were back at the building site.

In solving one problem, however, the government created another. To get approval for the loan, Roblin had to agree to allow the legislature's public accounts committee to investigate the project, and there was always the chance that it would turn up dirty secrets. So the government took the precaution of destroying all the paperwork related to the steel purchase, shuttling any potentially embarrassing witnesses out of town, and searching for a scapegoat on which to blame the mess. They looked first toward Simon, but the architect was having none of it—far from taking the blame, he said bluntly that he was prepared to walk away from the entire project. Then, the government found the ideal patsy, a former civil servant noted in the records as Syncox. He was a minor player, but at his door was laid the responsibility for failing to keep an eye on the builders. In the end, Roblin needn't have worried. The public accounts committee was dominated by his own caucus members, and their report exonerated both the government and the contractor.

Lurking in the shadows, however, was a minority report, and its findings so outraged public opinion and the press that the lieutenant-governor forced on Roblin a royal commission. Construction slowed and eventually stopped altogether as the commission began hearings in April 1915. The process was a disaster for the government. Key witnesses failed to testify, and Kelly was uncooperative, refusing to produce most of the documents that the commissioners wished to examine. It didn't really matter, though—independent experts hired to examine the work came back with enough evidence of shoddy workmanship that Kelly was removed from the project. Roblin, facing not just the legislature debacle but public anger over disastrous forays into grain elevator ownership and public telephones, had had enough. He informed the lieutenant-governor that his administration was resigning.

Worse was to come. In the wake of the commission report, the new government launched a suit against Thomas Kelly, who stood trial in Winnipeg on five charges relating to corruption. Against an onslaught of evidence from the Crown, Kelly mounted almost nothing in the way of a defence, saying only that it was unfair to judge him on a half-finished building. The court was unimpressed, and sentenced him to two years in Stony Mountain Penitentiary. He was also ordered to repay over $1.2 million to the government; twenty years later, only about $30,000 had been recovered. At the same time, Roblin and three of his former cabinet ministers were arrested and charged with conspiracy to defraud the government. Little came of the proceedings—one died before trial, and the Crown eventually dropped the charges against Roblin and the other two—but the entire episode revealed the cesspool into which Manitoba politics had sunk. Roblin's Conservative Party, which had elevated machine politics and influence-peddling to a high art, had been consumed by its own machine.

That left Frank Simon to pick up the pieces. Now acting as Supervising Architect, he tried to strike a balance between erecting an impressive structure and doing what he could to save the province money it didn't in fact have. After Simon redrew his plans with an eye to financial constraint, the new Liberal government of Premier T.C. Norris found an affordable contractor, the James McDiarmid Company, and awarded the job on 16 April 1917. Yet there remained one tiny problem: the government had no money to restart construction, even on this scaled-back contract. Norris was forced to go to Ottawa for permission to issue provincial bonds in the amount of $1 million. Finally work could continue, but this would eventually cost the Norris government dearly—its majority was lost in the next provincial election, in part because of accusations that Norris had let project costs spiral out of control.

At least the end was in sight, barring any unforeseen difficulties, the public works minister reporting in early 1919 that the exterior walls were completed, most of the interior stonework was done, and the plastering, heating, ventilating, plumbing, and electrical work were progressing nicely. The Winnipeg General Strike, which shut down the city in the summer of 1919, held construction up for six weeks, but finally in

November, the bronze figure (now known as the Golden Boy, although he wasn't painted gold until the 1940s) that Simon had designed for the top of the dome was raised into place. Intended to represent the province's potential, he faces north, where Manitoba's future riches lay, and holds in one hand a sheaf of wheat, representing agricultural prosperity, and in the other a torch to light the path to the future for the youth of Manitoba. Cast in France, it had spent eighteen months travelling back and forth across the Atlantic in the hold of a troopship—demands on shipping were so great that there was no time to off-load it.

When the legislature was officially opened on 20 July 1920, Manitobans must have heaved a collective sigh of relief that their eight-year odyssey was finally over. Roblin had wanted to build a legislature that would outdo those in Regina and Edmonton, and in one sense he had. Each of those buildings had cost around $2 million, but when the final accounts were presented to Manitoba's legislators in July 1920, they learned that their building had cost nearly $9.4 million. It would be thirty-four years before the debt accumulated during the project was retired, during which time the people of Manitoba paid out another $13.7 million in interest charges. But despite the scandals, broken careers, and wasted public money, Manitobans were justifiably proud of their new legislature. Fifteen years after the opening, the Winnipeg *Free Press* declared proudly that "it is only the plain truth to say that we have an incomparably finer building here than the one at Regina or the one at Edmonton." The old spirit of competition died hard.

BY THE TIME the *Free Press* issued its verdict on the three Prairie legislatures, the premiers behind them had slipped from prominence. Rutherford attempted unsuccessfully to return to politics and in 1935 was re-elected to his third term as the chancellor of the University of Alberta. He was halfway through a fourth when he died in 1941. Roblin re-entered the business world, something that brought him more success and wealth than politics ever had. He was enjoying a comfortable retirement when he died in Arkansas in 1937. Walter Scott finally left politics in 1916, a combination of asthma and his worsening mental state making it impossible for him to continue in public life. For nearly twenty years, he moved frequently, seeking a peace that always eluded him, and in 1935, he was injured in a car accident on a country road not far from his birthplace. Early the following year, after an altercation with a hotel manager, he was committed to the Homewood Sanitarium, where he would live out his days, alone and largely ignored by the province he had helped to build.

And so none of these men lived to see the construction of Canada's last legislatures. In 1960, Newfoundland opened the Confederation Building, a modernized version of the structures in Regina and Edmonton but with a soaring, twelve-storey tower topped by a hipped roof and a beacon. It was the last legislature built to the old ideals, which emphasized the principle of monumentality, using size and style to create a presence. These edifices were like elaborate billboards—they advertised, to all who passed, the prosperity and stability of the province.

In the territories, the emphasis instead was on harmonizing with the surroundings. Whitehorse's legislature, opened in 1976, is a low building that blends in with adjacent structures, symbolizing the integration of the people and their government. In Yellowknife, architects Ferguson Simek Clark and Pin Matthews adopted the philosophy that the building should complement rather than dominate the environment. Working with the power and beauty of the natural landscape, they attempted to veil the legislature, completed in 1993, as much as possible in its surroundings. It is situated on the edge of a lake between three rock promontories; the combination of the rock and the surrounding vegetation, which is dense in the summer months, means that the building appears to have grown out of its environment. At certain times of the year, the only visible feature is the dome that rises above the treetops. Outside, the walls and roof are covered in panels of zinc, a northern mineral chosen for its subtle weathering qualities. The extensive use of glass on the exterior walls alters the look of the building as the seasons change. In the summer, the windows become mirrors, reflecting the surrounding environment; in the winter, the interior light shining out through the windows makes the building seem transparent.

Canada's newest legislature too is anchored in its environment. The building in Iqaluit, completed in 1999, was constructed of steel imported from the south, but in all other respects it belongs to the North. The grey-blue steel exterior is divided into blocks by metal strips, giving it a marked resemblance to an igloo. For Tagak Curley, the president of the builder, Nunavut Construction Corporation, the legislature was more than simply another government edifice: "[T]his building is for you as you take the dream and vision into the next millennium with pride in who you are, where you live and what you will accomplish." It was a timeless sentiment, and one that Walter Scott certainly would have appreciated.

As Scott knew, erecting a legislature was about expressing through architecture grand thoughts about the society's past, present, and future. But grand buildings, especially those built in the days before fire codes and accessibility issues, require grand maintenance. Time too takes a toll, necessitating periodic renovations that range from minor refits to major structural repairs. In Regina, crews had to sink nearly 1800 new pilings under the legislative building as changes in soil and moisture conditions weakened the original pilings, causing cracks in the plaster and stonework. The four-year restoration project cost $20 million, or ten times more than the original building. In 1993, crews began work on a renewal of the Ontario legislature that involved refurbishing the exterior sandstone walls and the slate and copper roofs, installing sprinkler systems, and providing additional stairs to meet safety requirements. The chamber itself was also renovated, a process that revealed, under nine layers of over-painting, a series of allegorical figures by Toronto artist Gustav Hahn: on the south wall, above the Speaker's chair, MODERATION and JUSTICE; and on the north wall, above the members' desks, POWER and WISDOM. Most Canadians today would accept the first as a suitable allegory—but the second?

In Victoria, the issue was not what should be revealed but what should be covered up. In 1935, George Southwell had painted a series of murals in the B.C. legislature that used historical events to symbolize values: COURAGE (the meeting of Captains Vancouver and Quadra at Nootka Sound in 1792); ENTERPRISE (future governor James Douglas's landing at Victoria in 1843); LABOUR (the building of Fort Victoria); and JUSTICE (Sir Matthew Begbie, British Columbia's first judge, holding court in Cariboo in the 1860s). Sixty years later the murals were drawing criticism from Aboriginal groups because one depicts bare-breasted native women hauling timber, and another shows a native standing submissively before the judge. A government-appointed advisory panel concluded that the murals were offensive to our modern social ethos, and that they should be chiselled from place and put somewhere more appropriate (at a cost of $280,000), so long as experts could guarantee that they wouldn't be damaged. Some Victorians were outraged, among them journalist Terry O'Neill, who likened the outcome of the proposal to the Taliban's destruction of the 2000-year-old Bamiyan Buddhas in Afghanistan in 2001. O'Neill thought the plan lunacy, and probably would have said that Frank Simon had it dead wrong in predicting that a fine legislative building "would, in the course of time, make people around it more perceptive, more intelligent, better balanced and altogether more civilized human beings."

Frank Simon was writing in a different era, when Canadians still retained a modicum of respect for what occurred within the walls of their legislatures. He did, however, put his finger on the intent that motivated each of these building campaigns in the first place. Some were grand and imposing, dominating the landscape in the same way that they were intended to dominate the people who saw them. Others were more in harmony with their surroundings, reflecting the notion that a legislature should be part of its community rather than loom over it. All were linked by the idea that they should serve the public good by improving their societies. The provincial and territorial legislatures were not part of a single building campaign, but they did share this singularity of purpose, something that was articulated by Walter Scott, whose speech at the cornerstone-laying for the Saskatchewan legislature could apply to any of these seats of government. Of all of the public officials involved in these building campaigns, Scott showed the greatest vision and the greatest determination to see things done right. His conception of the role of government as expressed by a legislature should be as valid today as it was in 1909: "How many thousands of feet may climb these stairs in this entrance in the years to come, —carrying a burden of responsibility as legislators, one long continuous line of them, year after year. Generation after generation, century after century, —the trusted, invaluable administrative officials and experts and staffs, contemporaneous lines of them, generation succeeding generation."

IN CHARACTER WITH
A NORTHERN COUNTRY

O ur national style of architecture had modest beginnings, but its roots were tied to one of the great stories in the nation's history. As the Canadian Pacific Railway (CPR) pushed through the Rocky Mountains in the 1880s, the line's directors realized they had struck gold—tourist gold. The natural beauties of the Rockies were unmatched in North America, and surpassed anything in Europe. For Europeans, who had become obsessed with the sublime views of mountain peaks and glacial streams but were finding Switzerland increasingly crowded with holidaymakers, the territory along the CPR line could become a mecca. "Since we can't export the scenery," declared William van Horne, the American railway-man who became the CPR's general manager in 1882, "we shall have to import the tourists."

It wasn't enough simply to stuff travellers on carriages and trundle them through the mountains. The railway claimed to have the most opulent sleeper and dining cars available, with polished mahogany and satinwood, rich upholstery, and gleaming brass lamps and fittings, but there were times when the trains had to stop, either to take on water or fuel, or to switch engines. There were also passengers who couldn't afford the luxurious meals served in the dining car, and in any case, those cars were too heavy to haul up and down steep mountain grades. So, the railway decided to build small dining stations at points along the line where the natural beauty was particularly stunning. Travellers could disembark, get a decent meal, and stretch their legs before continuing their journey.

These stations soon became so popular that they were destinations in their own right, and the railway realized that it could capitalize by adding basic accommodation. The CPR built a series of lodges—Mount Stephen House in Kicking Horse Canyon (1886), Glacier House near Rogers Pass (1887), and Fraser Canyon House (1887)—to cater to the growing number of travellers who wanted to spend a few days hiking in the Rockies. Simple structures that resembled the mountain chalets of Switzerland, the lodges were by no means fancy, but they were an immediate hit with tourists. The railway made plans to expand them and also started to think in bigger terms.

In 1885, a CPR survey party discovered hot springs on the eastern slopes of the Rocky Mountains, near present-day Banff. Immediately, the line's directors saw the potential of a luxury resort patterned after European hotels that offered healing waters as part of the traveller's experience. They commissioned a series of plans from U.S. architect Bruce Price, then working on the railway's new Windsor Station in Montreal. Price (whose daughter, the etiquette authority Emily Post, eclipsed him in fame) produced an eclectic design that seemed to draw inspiration from a number of sources. Observers compared it to a Rhineland castle, a Tudor hall, or a Swiss chalet, while others insisted it was modelled after the châteaux of France's Loire Valley. More likely, it was intended to be Scottish baronial in style, in deference to the fact that Sir George Stephen, the president of the CPR, was born in Banff, Scotland. If it was a mix of architectural forms, it also had a number of distinctive features: steeply pitched roofs with a profusion of dormer windows peeking out, an asymmetrical and uneven roofline, smooth wall surfaces, and towers and turrets sprinkled around the building apparently at random. In time, these features would come to be known as the château style, an architecture that was promoted as being particularly suitable to a northern country, its elements in harmony with our environment and expressive of our character. Over time, the impression grew in the popular consciousness that this form of architecture was somehow naturally Canadian.

The Banff Springs Hotel opened for business in the summer of 1888 and was a success almost from the beginning. The only incident during construction had come when van Horne noticed that the builder had reversed the plans, so that the best views of the mountains were from the kitchen rather than the luxurious public rooms. He quickly fixed the problem by ordering the addition of a guest pavilion and terrace. Guests paid $3.50 per day for a room, including all meals (this at a time when the average railway worker earned $1.50 a day), and within a few years of the hotel's opening, a Baedeker travel guide rated Banff Springs one of the five best hotels in Canada. By the early years of the twentieth century, the Banff Springs was turning away as many guests as it was able to accommodate. Seeing that it had a winner on its hands, the railway immediately started to look for similar sites. The CPR built a lodge at Lake Louise in 1890 and small hotels at Sicamous and Revelstoke, British Columbia, but patterned them after the dining stations. Not that the CPR had cast aside Price's château vision—the railway was simply looking for another suitable site on which to realize that vision. As it happened, that setting was thousands of miles to the east, in Quebec City.

The heights of Quebec had long been regarded as the most desirable piece of real estate in the city, if not the country. Samuel de Champlain, often called the founder of New France, had built his first *habitation* there in 1620, and ever since its replacement, the Château St-Louis, had burned down in 1834, architects and entrepreneurs had cast hungry eyes on the piece of property that dominated everything around it—the Plains of Abraham, Lower Town, the walled city, and the river approaches. In 1875, an Irish architect published drawings of a fancy hotel that might be built there, and in 1890 two others, including Eugène-Étienne Taché, who had designed the Quebec provincial legislature, submitted plans for hotels to adorn the heights. With each new set of plans, Quebeckers hoped that they might soon get a splendid hotel to draw the wealthy tourists of the world to their doorstep; each time, money woes got in the way and entrepreneurs quietly backed away from their grand schemes.

Finally, realizing that inaction was costing them valuable tourist revenues, a group of Quebec businessmen lobbied city council and in January 1892 convinced them to offer a ten-year tax exemption to any group willing to erect a $150,000, 150-room hotel in Quebec's Upper Town. The phrase "tax exemption" was music to the ears of any prospective hotelier, and less than six months later, the Château Frontenac Company was incorporated with the express purpose of building such a hotel. Its principals—William van Horne, Sir Thomas Shaughnessy, Sir Donald Smith, and Sir Sandford Fleming—were all in the top echelons of the CPR, although they hastened to point out to the public that the new company was entirely separate from the railway. After years of having their hopes raised by underfunded and over-optimistic investors, the people of Quebec finally had a suitor with some financial muscle.

Van Horne was keen to take advantage of the hordes of tourists expected to pass through Quebec on the way to the 1893 Chicago World's Fair and had already inspected some possible sites. He was immediately drawn to the heights, which he thought offered possibilities for a remarkable building. He secured a lease from the city for $1250 a year (the company bought the property outright later, in 1941, for $25,000) and placed a call to his architect of choice, Bruce Price. Van Horne impressed upon him the importance of the project: this was to be a landmark hotel, a structure for the ages. It had to make a statement, and it had to be unique. Price took this as an indication that money was no object (although that's not really what van Horne meant—he had amassed such a fortune because, in his eyes, money was *always* an object) and immediately began to study the site's possibilities. He dug up the drawings for the hotels that had been proposed in 1875 and 1890 and also pored over the plans of the old Château St-Louis. He even went to France, to visit Frontenac's home at Saint-Germain-en-Laye and to study the châteaux of the Loire Valley. A detail that rarely made it into contemporary accounts was that Price also looked carefully at a structure built by U.S. architect H.H. Richardson (who had popularized the Romanesque style used in the Ontario legislature): the Buffalo State Asylum for the Insane.

All of these buildings were echoed in Price's design, but other factors influenced him as well. He was aware of van Horne's reluctance to disturb the old city unnecessarily, so the hotel had to harmonize with the medieval atmosphere of old Quebec. This made sense to the architect, who believed that the steep roofs and large wall surfaces that characterized the old city were most suitable for a northern climate. Price also knew that van Horne was a man who liked big things, whether they be fat Cuban cigars, immense meals, or a commercial and transportation network that spanned the globe. For the hotel, the railwayman wanted something monumental, something whose impact would "depend on broad effects, rather than on ornamentation and detail." The structure had to dominate the skyline, whether one approached it from the city or from the river (on one occasion, Price and van Horne went out on the river in a small boat, to ensure that the hotel looked sufficiently impressive to travellers arriving by ship). But for Price, the site itself was the final determinant. He was a great believer in "naturalness," the notion that any given spot demanded a certain style of architecture; the design grew organically from the site, rather than the architect choosing a style and plunking it down without regard for the site's characteristics. For Price, the heights of Quebec could only be topped by a structure with high, steep roofs, round towers, dormer windows, and large, smooth wall faces. In short, only the château style of architecture would do.

Work began in May 1892, but not even an accelerated construction schedule could keep the Château Frontenac from missing the crowds on their way to the Chicago World's Fair. When it did open on 18 December 1893, however, the evening had it all—van Horne beaming like a proud parent; Shaughnessy happily showing parties of guests around the hotel and regaling them with his waggish impersonation of Edward, Prince of Wales; Price graciously accepting the congratulations of the guests; a midnight buffet of lobster salad, Gaspé salmon, cold roast beef, and pheasant; and even a specially composed piece of music, the "Château Frontenac Quadrille" (which had to be retrieved from a coal bin after someone accidentally threw it out). Dawn was approaching before the last of the guests trickled home from the new castle on the heights.

Like the Banff Springs Hotel, the Château Frontenac was an instant success. Tourists lined up to book rooms at $3 a day or suites at $6 a day (including all meals and afternoon tea), and the hotel's public rooms—the gold and blue grand ballroom, resembling the Hall of Mirrors at Versailles; the Rotunda, whose richly carved beams and stone mosaic floor made it impossible to call it a mere lobby; the Salon de Verchères, where huge potted plants jostled with Grecian-style pillars—became gathering places for the city's elite. All of the 170 guest rooms had open fireplaces, but only the wealthiest could afford one of the three luxury suites: the Habitant, finished in a traditional French-Canadian theme; the Chinese; and the Dutch. The press couldn't say enough about the new hotel, and novelist Max Pemberton called it "a great hostelry like no other one can name—majestic in the fashion of a medieval fortress, yet as up-to-date as any hotel in America and more comfortable than most … See Naples and then die! Rather, see Quebec and find a new inspiration to live." A year after it opened, the Château Frontenac joined the Banff Springs on Baedeker's top-five list. Perhaps the best indication of its success, however, was that within five years of its opening, the CPR took over sole ownership of the hotel. The railway had watched the Frontenac recoup its costs in the first year, almost unheard of for a new luxury hotel at the time, and in the summer months it was boosting railway earnings by as much as $750 a day. Not bad for a building that sponsors had believed would never make money by itself.

Four years after its grand opening, the Frontenac was already too small, and Bruce Price was preparing plans for extensions. The Citadel Wing and Pavilion were completed in 1899, and, with the addition of the Mont Carmel Wing (designed by another U.S. architect, Walter Painter, because Price had died in 1903) eleven years later, the Château became the largest hotel in Canada. Within a decade, still more space was needed, and so in 1919, the CPR turned to the Maxwell brothers, who were still basking in the triumph of the Saskatchewan legislature. They proposed two new wings and a seventeen-storey central tower that would add 658 rooms. These latest additions were completed in 1924. In January 1926, one of them, the Riverside Wing, was devastated by fire, but, determined that its crown jewel not be out of commission for long, the railway mobilized an army of labourers, who replaced the wing in just 127 working days. The Château Frontenac was fully reopened in the summer of 1926, looking much as it does today.

Back in 1894, though, van Horne was too busy enjoying the success of his new hotel to foresee these additions. He rightly predicted that the Frontenac would be "the most talked about hotel on this continent" and envisioned a chain of similar properties in cities across Canada, each of which would bring to the CPR the kind of praise that the Frontenac was garnering. And out in British Columbia, the people of Victoria wondered how they might get in on the action. Though it enjoyed status as the provincial capital, Victoria was being eclipsed in size and commercial importance by Vancouver, and many feared that the city would become a kind of backwater, off the tourist track. To avoid that fate, declared one alderman, they need look no further than Quebec: "Ten years ago that city was practically dead, but today it is one of the finest and most prosperous cities in the Dominion. The whole character of the city has been changed by the influence of the CPR hotel there." Victorians now had a plan of action to use tourism as their new economic engine: they would make their city "the leading health and pleasure resort of the Pacific Northwest."

When the CPR bought the Canadian Pacific Navigation Company and its fourteen steamships in 1901, a flicker of hope caught hold: perhaps the railway might develop a presence in Victoria and make their dreams of tourist dollars a reality. So when new CPR president Sir Thomas Shaughnessy visited in June 1902, city officials wined and dined him, taking him on a tour of potential hotel sites. When Shaughnessy returned to Victoria a year later, the Victoria delegation was shocked to hear him state categorically that the railway had no intention of building a big tourist hotel there. But immediately it became clear that this was just a bargaining ploy. If we did build a hotel, continued Shaughnessy, what could we expect from the city in return? If the railway built a $300,000 hotel, would the city be willing to provide free land, free water for twenty years, and exemption from taxes for the same period?

As to the location, Shaughnessy had his sights set on a spot at the end of James Bay, in Victoria's inner harbour. At the moment, it was a tidal mud flat, a nauseating mixture of industrial waste, garbage, rotting fish, decaying seaweed, and sewage, but the city planned to turn it into a prime piece of real estate. In 1901, citizens had voted in favour of building a causeway across the end of the bay, isolating the tidal flats so they could be filled in. Situated as it was right next to the provincial legislature, the site was an admirable one for a grand hotel, Shaughnessy believed. City officials could barely contain their glee, although they drove what they thought was a hard bargain with Shaughnessy: free land, but only fifteen years' worth of free water and tax exemptions. The shrewd railway baron, however, squeezed even more valuable concessions out of the city, which ended up agreeing to fill the site so that it was suitable for building and constructing good roads and sidewalks around the new hotel. All things considered, the railway probably got the better of the negotiations. Then again, it usually did.

The people of Victoria loved the deal, voting in favour by a margin of better than twenty to one. For the hotel's design, the railway turned to Francis Rattenbury. By 1901, he was free of his failed Yukon riverboat venture, which had stalled when the Klondike gold rush tapered off. As a consolation, he would have the honour of designing the finest hotel west of the Rockies. To prepare for the job Rattenbury went to Quebec to visit the Château Frontenac, which greatly impressed him as "a magnificent feudal castle built on the edge of the heights." In May 1903, the Victoria *Colonist* published a sketch of what the inner harbour would look like once the hotel was completed. While it showed off Rattenbury's legislature and the other public buildings being erected in the area, the centrepiece was the grand hotel, inspired by Price's additions to the Frontenac and by the Scottish baronial elements of the Banff Springs Hotel. Later writers would call it the first example of the mature château style, Rattenbury carefully choosing elements that symbolized the hotel's medieval character, its heritage in the cultures of English and French Canada, and its location in the British Columbia capital. In short, it was every bit as much a triumph as Rattenbury's legislative building.

So it was with some perturbation that Rattenbury received his plans back from the railway with suggestions for rather extensive changes to address problems—the baggage elevators were poorly located, the guest bathrooms were too large, the hallways were too wide. For the moment, the architect acquiesced politely to most of the demands, probably realizing that the CPR wouldn't be as easy to push around as the hapless civil servants he had bullied on the legislature's building site. But that exchange probably planted in his mind the first doubts about the project. They grew as construction was delayed. Although the first contract had been let in March 1905, work didn't start until August, when the foundations were prepared. To ensure that the hotel wouldn't sink into the reclaimed mud flats, nearly three thousand pilings, each of them 50 feet of good Douglas fir, had to be driven deep into the ground, the ends encased in concrete piers, and the entire site filled with 19 feet of crushed rock, sand, and cement.

Rattenbury was concerned that delays were killing public interest in the project. To relight the fires, he convinced the *Colonist* to run a name-the-hotel contest. Calling for something "dignified and attractive … [with] some historical associations," he proposed a few ideas of his own, but admitted all were lacking for one reason or another: the Camosun was too obscure, the Royal Oak too hackneyed, the Douglas Arms more suited "for places of lesser consequence," and the San Juan de Fuca "rather too much of a mouthful, besides having other euphonic objections." In the end, the railway made the decision and couldn't have picked a hotel name more suited to the city and its imperial connections: the Empress.

Over a year later, the hotel still was not finished, and Rattenbury told the *Colonist* that he blamed the city for being too slow to finish filling the tidal flats. Then in December, a shock: Rattenbury resigned suddenly as director. There were probably many reasons behind his abrupt departure, but most of them related to control of the project, which was slipping away from him. While building the provincial legislature, Rattenbury had become used to running the worksite as his own private fiefdom. With the Empress, he had started out in the same manner, making unauthorized changes to the design and ignoring requests from the railway's directors in Montreal. But the CPR was not interested in a prima donna architect who wouldn't listen to head office. The railway had appointed Walter Painter as chief architect, and he had a few suggestions about the Empress as it rose from the mud flats. So too did the construction supervisor whom the railway dispatched to run the site.

And then there was input from Kate Reed. The daughter of a Supreme Court justice, Kate was married to Hayter Reed, the former manager of the Château Frontenac. He was a great success at the job, being promoted to director of hotels in 1905, but his wife was even more successful. With a large clientele of wealthy Canadians whom she advised on their art collections, she was one of the great style authorities of Edwardian Canada. She had been responsible for the interior redecorating of the Château Frontenac while her husband was the manager, and her work was so highly praised that when Hayter was promoted, Kate was as well— when he travelled the country to work with architects on hotel construction, she provided advice on matters of design.

After the intrusions of Painter, the site supervisor, and Hayter Reed, having to listen to Kate Reed's design ideas must have been the last straw for Rattenbury. He walked away from the project and, just as he had done with the legislature, didn't even bother to return for the official opening on 20 January 1908. The occasion was a great one, and writers competed for purple prose to sum it up adequately. The *Colonist* drew the obvious comparison with the Frontenac and said the Empress would "make the Western gateway of the great transcontinental system a fitting companion to the historic pile on the heights of Quebec." But none did better than the province's unofficial poet-laureate, the big-game hunter and writer Clive Phillipps-Wolley: "This is a wedding feast. Victoria has been waiting long for her Prince Charming. She has been sleeping for half a century. The Canadian Pacific Railway has finally roused her. Victoria waited for the kiss of love and now comes into her own."

With the completion of the Empress, the CPR had succeeded in creating a brand. Through its exhaustive promotional efforts, which brought a huge growth in passenger traffic (from 4.3 million in 1901 to 15.5 million in 1913) and which always featured its hotel properties prominently, it had established the château style of architecture as its own. The steep, hipped roofs, the pointed dormer windows, the rounded towers and turrets, and the massive flat wall surfaces were certainly not unique to CPR hotels, but they had become inextricably linked with the railway. The fact that the same features distinguished CPR stations across the country cemented the connection. And because the railway was selling

Canada as much as it was selling itself, the château style was becoming identified as symbolic of Canada.

Just as its brand was becoming fixed in the public mind, however, the CPR started to move away from it. Having constructed what were arguably the most recognizable hotels in Canada, the Banff Springs, the Château Frontenac, and the Empress, the railway turned its back on the very style that had become such a significant part of its image. A few of the later CPR hotels—the Royal York in Toronto (1929) and the new Hotel Vancouver (1939)—had château elements, and when the Banff Springs Hotel was rebuilt between 1910 and 1928, Walter Painter returned to the French château and Scottish baronial models, and to the architectural features that Bruce Price had brought to the Château Frontenac. But the CPR's other properties, such as the Royal Alexandra in Winnipeg, the Palliser in Calgary, and the Saskatchewan Hotel in Regina, were inspired not by the château style but by classical or renaissance models, which the railway had decided were more suitable for modern, urban hotels. It would be left to others to carry Canada's national style to its fullest extent.

ONE OTHER REASON for Rattenbury's hasty departure from the Empress Hotel project may also have been behind the CPR's abandonment of the château style. Rattenbury had been in discussions with the Grand Trunk Railway about its program of hotel building. In Shaughnessy's eyes, that might have been enough to damn the architect. Rattenbury was, after all, consorting with the enemy.

The Grand Trunk had been incorporated in 1852, and by the end of the century stretched from Chicago through Toronto and Montreal to Portland, Maine. Keen to compete against the CPR in western Canada, it eventually struck a deal with the federal government: Ottawa would build a line from Winnipeg to Moncton (for which the great Quebec Bridge was required) and lease it to the Grand Trunk, while the railway would build and operate a line from Winnipeg to British Columbia. In 1903, the Grand Trunk Pacific was incorporated but, as the line began moving west, its general manager, the U.S.–born railwayman Charles Melville Hays, grew ever more jealous as the CPR hotels were showered with praise. He watched as the Banff Springs Hotel turned away hundreds of well-heeled customers every year and wondered if his line could enjoy the same success. Hays had been hired to get the railway out of debt but soon fell to dreaming of a chain of opulent hotels. He identified two sites—the Miette Hot Springs, in Jasper National Park, and the foot of Mount Robson, the highest point in the Canadian Rockies—for resorts that would match anything the Canadian Pacific had. Rattenbury, his connection with the CPR now severed, promptly prepared designs, using all the towers, turrets, and steep roofs that had come to define the château style. But the Grand Trunk needed something to rival the hotels that anchored the CPR's eastern and western terminuses in Quebec and Victoria—it needed its own Château Frontenac or Empress. And that star was to be located in the Grand Trunk's western hub, Prince Rupert.

At the time, the town was little more than a collection of warehouses, fishing sheds, and bunkhouses near the mouth of the Skeena River in northern British Columbia, but Hays envisioned it as a new San Francisco: "To this new port will come the ships of the Seven Seas. Ships of the East, laden with silk and rice will soon be riding at anchor in this splendid harbor, to sail away laden with lumber; … Ships from the shore of far-off continents, trading through the new and picturesque port of Prince Rupert." The project allowed Rattenbury to give full rein to his creative impulses, and he didn't disappoint. He created a combination steamship dock, railway station, and hotel, all designed in the château style to the highest standards of comfort and luxury. The $2-million, 450-room hotel was to be twice as tall as the Empress, its high-pitched roofs, turrets, and towers becoming the jewel of a beautifully landscaped downtown.

And Canada's new national railway had no intention of stopping with the Prince Rupert complex and a couple of mountain lodges. The Grand Trunk set its sights on the nation's capital, and in 1907 incorporated the Ottawa Terminals Railway Company to build a railway station and hotel complex in the city. Hays picked a site right downtown, secured the support of Prime Minister Wilfrid Laurier (for whom the new hotel would be named), and went to Ottawa city council with an offer to build a $250,000 station and $2.5-million hotel. The railway immediately appointed Cass Gilbert to the project; his design (an adaptation of the Château de Longeais, near Tours on the river Loire, southwest of Paris) was approved by the governor general and cabinet, and in October 1907 a sod-turning ceremony got things underway.

Then the trouble began. Hays asked Gilbert if he could shave a million dollars from the budget, which meant chopping entire floors and leaving a design that was, practically as well as architecturally, a shadow of its former self. At least that's what city councillors thought when they got a look at the revised plans in February 1908. They started asking questions about the changes, which breached Hays's original agreement with the city. A railway official responded that Gilbert had "exceeded his instructions" with the original design, but Gilbert, who was in Ottawa at the time and knew that the railway's explanation was patently false, refused to be the scapegoat. He promptly resigned from the project to protest the Grand Trunk's lack of professionalism. Hays quickly called in the Montreal firm of Ross and MacFarlane, which presented revised plans in May 1908. Unfortunately, they looked so similar to Gilbert's design that his assistant in Ottawa claimed Gilbert's work had been stolen by Ross and MacFarlane. A leading trade journal, the *Architectural Record,* had to agree, noting that the changes made by the new architects were confined to removing some decorative elements and reshuffling the interior space; none of these changes, according to the *Record,* were for the better. Still, the Château Laurier was back on track, and in February 1910, work at the site began again.

Meanwhile, the railway had other hotels on its drawing board. In Winnipeg, Ross and MacFarlane were commissioned to design the Selkirk, later renamed the Fort Garry Hotel. Like the Laurier, it was strongly château in style, with the same large, flat wall surfaces and high-pitched roofs; far away from the commercial districts, it would tower over the homes of the city's wealthy as the tallest building in Winnipeg. The Manitoba *Free Press* predicted that "the Citizens of Winnipeg can look upon this stately building with admiration akin to that of the Greek, who … viewed with pride the Parthenon." In 1910, the Grand Trunk got a ninety-nine-year lease on a property near the proposed site of its new station in Regina and commissioned Ross and MacFarlane to design the Château Qu'Appelle—everything was planned to the last detail, right down to the six-stool barbershop and the basement oyster pantry. The same year, the railway bought Douglas Gardens in Victoria. The Gardens had been one of the sites considered by Thomas Shaughnessy for the Empress, and the Grand Trunk saw a nice irony in erecting a Rattenbury-designed château-style hotel right next door to the competition.

Then, disaster struck the railway in an unlikely place: the middle of the Atlantic Ocean. Hays had been in England with his family, and they had decided to travel home in the style to which they were accustomed. In 1912, could one travel any better than on the newly launched *Titanic?* But just four days out of Southampton, the *Titanic* struck an iceberg and sank. Mrs. Hays and their two daughters were saved, but Hays and his private secretary died. With them went the hopes of the Grand Trunk hotel chain.

The railway's new president, E.J. Chamberlain, wasn't very interested in running hotels and immediately started re-evaluating the company's plans. The Château Laurier was already completed and opened its doors in June 1912 with no official ceremony; a gala had been planned for April, and one of the reasons that Hays had chosen to travel on the *Titanic* was to get to Canada in time for the opening, but upon his death, the gala was quietly called off. The Fort Garry too was well advanced and proceeded to hold its opening ball in December 1913. The railway also decided to go ahead with the Ross and MacFarlane–designed Hotel Macdonald, Edmonton's "Château on the River," which had been in the planning stages when Hays died. Construction began in 1913 at a commanding site overlooking the North Saskatchewan River, and the hotel opened in July 1915, destined to tower over the city for decades. The other projects, however, were quickly shelved. The Château Qu'Appelle got no farther than five storeys of steel framing; ironically, materials from the building site were later used for the CPR's Hotel Saskatchewan, and the fill from the Canadian Pacific hotel's foundation found a home in the Qu'Appelle's basement. At about the same time, the Grand Trunk suspended work on its rival to the Empress in Victoria.

The fact was that, quite apart from the construction costs, running a hotel of this standard was expensive. The calibre of guests that the railway wanted to attract demanded a certain level of service, which meant employing a veritable army of staff. The pay ledgers from the Fort Garry's first month in operations have been preserved and reveal an enormous variety of employees and a great range in their monthly pay, from the chambermaids ($15), waiters ($25), and cleaners ($30) to the manicurist ($60), bartender ($100), and laundry superintendent ($100). The importance of fine dining is clear—the oyster man took home $55 a month, the vegetable cook $60, the roast cook $90, and the head chef $225—as is the value placed on entertainment, for the violinists, cellists, clarinetists, and pianists each earned $30 a week. It was the same at all the great hotels, and operating profits were hard to come by. In its first fourteen years, the Château Laurier turned a total profit of just $42,000, or a paltry $3000 a year. The CPR had the financial resources to weather bad years; the Grand Trunk, with its mountain of debt growing by the day, did not.

Nevertheless, Rattenbury still held out hopes for his mountain lodges and his complex in Prince Rupert, and was buoyed when the Grand Trunk's first train pulled into Prince Rupert on 8 April 1914; the railway predicted confidently that its line would be swamped by tourists and settlers as soon as regular service started in September 1914. But the First World War started instead, and the hoped-for travellers never materialized. Already snowed under by the costs for the mountain section of its line, the Grand Trunk pulled the plug on the Prince Rupert complex when it was nothing more than foundation trenches and some piles of building materials. Rattenbury's plans for the San Francisco of the north, as well as for the Château Mount Robson and the Château Miette Hot Springs, were quietly filed away. Decades later, the Prince Rupert plans were discovered in the attic of a school that Rattenbury had designed as his private residence.

For Rattenbury, this was a cruel blow. He had invested much of his earnings from the provincial legislature and the Empress in land along the Grand Trunk line, confident that when it became as desirable as the land along the CPR, he would make a fortune selling farm lots; instead, he lost almost everything. From that point on, Rattenbury did little else in the way of architecture and moved back to England to live out his days battling depression and alcoholism in genteel poverty. The final act in the life of this gifted yet flawed architect came when he was murdered as a result of a tawdry love triangle involving his second wife and their teenaged gardener.

In time, the federal government pulled the Grand Trunk's chestnuts out of the fire, folding the railway into the new Canadian National Railways (CNR) in 1923, but there was one more great château hotel to build. After the CPR completed the Hotel Saskatchewan in Regina, the Saskatoon Board of Trade began to lobby for a project of equal magnitude in its city. On 31 December 1928, CNR president Sir Henry Thornton finally made the much-anticipated announcement in his New Year's greeting to Mayor G.W. Norman: "[A] hotel consistent in size and character with an enterprising and progressive city" would be built in Saskatchewan's second city. The railway announced that the structure would be called the Bessborough Hotel, in honour of Canada's new governor general.

Excavation at what had once been a city garbage dump began in February 1930. Almost all of the building materials were Canadian, including Manitoba Tyndall limestone, brick from Claybank, Saskatchewan, and tile from Estevan, and the construction quality was second to none, a fact that some historians have put down to the determination of local workers to keep their jobs as long as possible by working meticulously. They finished the project in late 1932, but the hotel had by then amassed such debts that the railway couldn't afford to open it; over the next three years it was used only three times, once for a Shriners' Ball and twice for visits by the hotel's namesake. Finally, in December 1935, the Bessborough accepted its first registered guest, Horace N. Stovin (a lounge in the hotel is now named in his honour) and celebrated the occasion with a dinner for a thousand of Saskatoon's best and brightest. According to the *Star-Phoenix,* it was well worth the wait: "The Bessborough stands as a monument to the resourcefulness of man, who takes from the natural resources of fields and mines and forests, the stones, clay, marble, iron, and various woods, and fashions them into castles of beauty."

With the Bessborough, the CNR continued the work that its rival had started in making the château style an identifiable brand—most of Canada's major cities now had hotels and railway stations that were linked by common architectural features. The style had also established a foothold in domestic architecture, thanks to Bruce Price and the Maxwells, who went on to design a handful of château-style city houses and country estates for Montreal's rich and famous. Some were for directors of the CPR, who wanted the corporate brand echoed in their homes; others were commissioned by wealthy Montrealers interested in emulating the national style. There was even an apartment block, the Château Apartments on Montreal's ritzy Square Mile, inspired by the domestic architecture surrounding it, and in time château elements would find their way into more modest house designs across Canada. Later scholars would debate endlessly the precise lineage of any given building, but to the casual observer, they were clearly part of the same family, a family that was distinctly Canadian. Yet there remained one more step in the elevation of the château to a national style. This final step would not involve a railway.

IN 1924, National Parks Commissioner J.B. Harkin was mulling over the plans for a replacement to the CPR's Château Lake Louise, which had recently burned down. His final verdict was to reject them for one simple reason—they were not in the château style. Harkin's decision was important because by then, the château style had gone beyond railway architecture; its popularity and recognition factor had caused the federal government to adopt it as a preferred style. And because Lake Louise was in a national park, Harkin believed that any building constructed there should conform to the national style.

In 1913, the government of Prime Minister Robert Borden had established an advisory panel, the Federal Plan Commission, to come up with a comprehensive plan for the government precincts in downtown Ottawa and to consider the style of architecture most suitable for federal buildings. The commission's 1915 report on land use around Parliament Hill had some pointed things to say about architectural styles. Changing the style of government buildings, it stated, would be a mistake: "One cannot look without reluctance upon any project to change the general architectural character of the present group of buildings ... because of the general harmony of the group, and the happy expression which has been given to them, seemingly in character with a northern country." Because the existing buildings were so successful, "the architectural design of the proposed new building[s] should be in harmony and not in contrast. They should be planned to have an architectural character with vigorous silhouettes, steep roofs, pavilions and towers." If the government was looking for a specific model, it need look no farther than the end of Wellington Street: "the external architecture of the Château Laurier ... may be regarded in general outline and character as a worthy suggestion." The government should follow where the railways had led.

The middle of a war wasn't the best time to embark on a major program of government building, however, so work on the plan was put off. Six years later, Borden's government struck another committee to consider the development of downtown Ottawa. This three-man commission didn't agree on much, but they were of like mind on one thing: the château style was the most desirable form for future government buildings. Eight years later, the Department of Public Works came to the same conclusion: "[A]s it is the general consensus of opinion that Gothic should be adopted to harmonize with the Parliament Buildings, being the type of architecture most suitable to our Northern climate, the Deputy Minister [J.B. Hunter] further recommends the adoption of the French Château style of architecture, of which the Château Laurier is a modernized type."

So a hotel had been held up not once, but three times, as the best model for government architecture. This was not so strange as it might seem. The Laurier was operated by the national railway, and the railways had themselves become important symbols of Canada and the Canadian identity, both at home and overseas. To pattern a government building after a style that had been popularized with such success by some of the country's largest, most powerful, and most visible corporations was no bad thing. Furthermore, the style itself—drawing inspiration from the château architecture of France and the baronial architecture of Scotland— gave it a certain iconic impact as well, for it could be construed as symbolic of Canada's two founding European cultures. And then there was the comment about a northern country, something that could have come directly from Bruce Price: the château style just seemed to look right in Canada.

And so Harkin got the CPR's architects to rework the design for the new hotel at Lake Louise to make it more château-like in appearance, and other government buildings adopted the style as well. The Post Office in Quebec's Lower Town (1939), for example, was a throwback to the architecture of the Château Frontenac that inspired it, a small but exuberant bundle of steep roofs, towers, turrets, and gables. Influenced also by the city's château-style Union Station, it said much about the importance of using the style to perpetuate the French character of the Quebec capital. In Pointe-au-Pic, Quebec, the Post Office (1938–39) was a little more restrained, but still had the high-pitched roof that made it unmistakeably château-esque. The inspiration in this case might have been the nearby Manoir Richelieu, owned by Canada Steamship Lines, which had been rebuilt in 1929, after the original building burned down, in an Edward Maxwell–designed château form.

More important, new construction in the government precinct in Ottawa took on a distinctly château character. Perhaps the clearest example was the Confederation Building (1928–31), the style of which grew directly out of the recommendations of the Federal Plan Commission but was further influenced by the people involved in its construction. The project supervisor was Thomas Dunlop Rankin, who had joined the Department of Public Works after a stint with Ross and MacFarlane, the firm that had built so many château-style hotels for the Grand Trunk. Rankin's boss, Deputy Minister James B. Hunter, also suggested that Ross and MacFarlane's "Château on the River," the Hotel Macdonald in Edmonton, would be a suitable model for the new building. As a result, the Confederation Building evolved into a mixture of the Château Laurier and the Hotel Macdonald—in its profile and detailing, the building reminds one of the former, but as in the latter, a central tower is its focal point. Attacked by the architectural press and professional associations as old-fashioned, the Confederation Building nevertheless fit perfectly into government plans for the Wellington streetscape.

In 1937, at the invitation of the prime minister, Mackenzie King, the noted French town planner Jacques Gréber arrived in Ottawa to advise the government on further development in the downtown core. King was keen to turn central Ottawa into another Paris, with broad avenues, architectural gems, and leafy gardens, and wanted the benefit of the town planner's wisdom. Gréber's report also weighed in on architectural styles, his most important recommendation being that the château roofline be retained to provide stylistic consistency within the city. Whether Gréber actually liked the château style or whether he simply wanted to please the man who was paying a lot of money for his opinions is unclear. What did matter was the result: that the style continued to be echoed in official architecture in Ottawa.

For example, when the Montreal architect Ernest Cormier presented his designs for the new Supreme Court building, he envisioned a clean, modern structure with a flat roof. He was brusquely sent away to rework his plans to include a château roof. W.E. Noffke, who had been commissioned to design a new post office, had the same experience; as Mackenzie King recorded in his diary, "the idea is to have something more in harmony with the Château [Laurier]," so Noffke was instructed to re-draw his roofline. Even in the late 1940s, when the East and West Memorial Buildings were being planned for the departments of Veterans Affairs and Trade and Commerce, Public Works was directed to add squat, château-like roofs to harmonize with the other buildings along Wellington Street. That was, however, the last gasp of the château style in Ottawa, and indeed it takes a fair bit of imagination to see the link between the West Memorial Building and the Château Laurier. Yet the link is there, in large part because of Mackenzie King's belief that the château style should be Canada's national style.

THE FACT THAT these buildings together created the national style did not protect them against the ravages of times, or the changing demands of hotel guests. Like the provincial legislatures, the château-style government buildings have been refurbished and brought up to modern standards without altering the exterior character, but the château hotels have been subject to the whims of the travelling public. As long as they remained desirable destinations, they were safe, but not even the fact that they were seen as architectural expressions of the Canadian nation could save them if they stopped paying their way.

That was just what happened to the Fort Garry in Winnipeg. The CNR sold the hotel in 1978, and the new owners couldn't make a go of it. There was a brief test of wills between the city, which threatened to seize the building for unpaid taxes, and the hotel's owners, who applied for permission to demolish the landmark in order to force the city to offer tax concessions. Having the Fort Garry declared a National Historic Site in 1980 did nothing to solve the hotel's problems, and eventually the city did indeed seize the building, which then sat vacant until another purchaser came forward in 1988. Still, the Fort Garry floundered; the mortgage holder foreclosed but, realizing there was little point in trying to sell it again, instead brought in a local couple, Ida Albo and Rick Bel, to attempt to revive the hotel. With new energy and enthusiasm, they raised the occupancy rate from a dismal 25 percent to 80 percent by the late 1990s, at which time the Fort Garry was in the middle of a major renovation program expected to cost some $14 million. After years of uncertainty, Winnipeg's grand old château finally faces a more secure future.

The Hotel Macdonald's problem was not lack of guests but lack of space, and in 1953 a sixteen-storey tower was added. Square and severely functional, it won few fans in Edmonton; legend has it that local photographer Gladys Reeves showed it to a visitor, saying "This is the Macdonald Hotel, and that's the box it came in." The Edmonton *Journal* wasn't much kinder, referring to the mismatched pair of buildings as "a patient mother, sitting quietly on the high bank overlooking the Saskatchewan, with her husky, tall daughter standing close behind." In 1983, the hotel closed for renovations, the owners having wisely decided to demolish the addition and renovate the original building. It reopened in May 1991, now the smallest of the château hotels but with its former charm rediscovered.

And then there were the changes in ownership. In the early 1960s, the Hilton hotel chain offered to buy seven CNR hotels and the Jasper Park Lodge; the federal government declined, fearing the political fallout of selling these national landmarks to a U.S. chain. But the spirit of diversification that had motivated the railway to build the hotels in the first place had passed by the late 1970s and its properties began to be sold, beginning with the Bessborough and the Fort Garry. Ironically, the most interested purchaser was CP Hotels Limited, which managed the hotels in the Canadian Pacific chain. As far as the CNR was concerned, selling out to its long-time rival the CPR—which is precisely what happened in 1986—was almost as painful as selling to a U.S. company. Still, it brought most of the château hotels together under the same management for the first time. In October 1999, CP Hotels acquired Fairmont, a small U.S. chain, and amalgamated its Canadian and international properties into the new Fairmont Hotels and Resorts. Only two of the château-style hotels are now in other hands: the Bessborough in Saskatoon was sold to local interests in 1973 and then bought by the Delta chain in 1989, and the Fort Garry is operated by Albo and Bel.

It might be said that much of Canada's history has taken place beneath the steep roofs and towers of our château buildings. That goes without saying for the Confederation Building and the other government structures erected in the style, but it is true for the hotels as well. Virtually every celebrity, world leader, and royal has stayed in at least one of them over the years—Marilyn Monroe, Charles de Gaulle, Alfred Hitchcock, Princess Grace of Monaco, Marlene Dietrich, Mikhail Gorbachev, the Archbishop of Canterbury, even the canine film-star Lassie—and politicians have called them home for a time. R.B. Bennett didn't rent a house or apartment in Ottawa when he was first elected to the House of Commons, but instead took a suite in the Château Laurier. When he became prime minister in 1930, CNR president Sir Henry Thornton offered to convert some small and hard-to-rent rooms in the Château into a single, seventeen-room suite. Bennett balked at the optics of a government-owned railway spending vast amounts of money on a suite for the wealthy prime minister, but Thornton went ahead anyway, convinced that the hotel would benefit from having the prime minister as a permanent resident. Bennett and his sister eventually moved in, paying a nominal rent of about $13 a day. The same happened at the Château Frontenac, which became the home of Maurice Duplessis, premier of Quebec from 1936 to 1939 and 1944 to 1959. He rented a room on the twelfth floor of the central tower, and often held cabinet meetings there. Like the Laurier, for part of its history the Frontenac became a *de facto* government office.

And more momentous decisions were taken at the Frontenac during the Second World War. In 1943, guests and staff were given a few days' notice to evacuate, and two thousand other travellers found their reservations abruptly cancelled. Locals soon learned that the hotel would be the site for the Quebec Conference of senior Allied leaders, including U.S. president Franklin Roosevelt and British prime minister Winston Churchill. For a week in August, the hotel was filled with high-ranking diplomats, officers, and civil servants (Churchill and Roosevelt actually met and stayed in the nearby Citadel, which was deemed safer than the Frontenac), and some of the most important decisions of the war were taken there: the plan for the Normandy landings was endorsed, Britain and the United States agreed not to use nuclear weapons without mutual consent, and, of less consequence in the grand scheme of history, a plan to build a gigantic ice aircraft carrier from frozen seawater and sawdust was discussed and dismissed. A year later, in September 1944, the entire exercise was repeated as Allied leaders again converged on the Château Frontenac to finalize, among other things, the post-war division of Germany into occupation zones.

Yet château buildings were more than just meeting places for people of fame and influence. Architectural historian Abraham Rogatnik's comment that "almost any Canadian born within a reasonable distance from one of these centres will recall today that nearly all the important landmarks of his life took place or were celebrated—and even solemnized—in his local railway hotel" may apply only to people of a certain social class, but it is true that the hotels became focal points of their communities. In most cities, they dominated the skyline until the skyscraper craze of the 1960s, and even now they remain among the most recognizable landmarks in the urban space. Whether they were drawn from French château, Scottish baronial, or German *schloss* models is ultimately irrelevant. What matters is that these hotels, railway stations, government buildings, and houses combined to give the country an architectural style that is, if not uniquely Canadian, then distinctly Canadian.

MAKING WAR ON CULTURAL POVERTY

The last years of the nineteenth century were heady times for Canadians who could afford a night out on the town. Immense and opulent theatres drew the best actors of the age. Internationally renowned musicians played in lavish concert halls or hotel ballrooms. Every large city, and many smaller ones, could boast an opera house to rival anything that Europe or the United States could offer. In some cities, there was even an embarrassment of riches—the town of St. Marys, Ontario, had so many performance venues that for many years its opera house was used as a flour mill. But the advent of the talking picture palace, radio, and eventually television gradually spelled the end of many of these facilities. The lucky few were converted to other uses; the majority fell victim to the wrecker's ball, the arsonist, or simply urban decay.

That Canada was falling behind on the cultural front was a great concern to Brooke Claxton, a First World War veteran who had returned from the trenches with a heightened sense of nationalism. During the 1920s and 1930s, Claxton had been deeply involved in arts organizations, and after he entered federal politics in 1940 he emerged as the spokesman in cabinet for Canada's cultural community. He began a kind of guerrilla campaign to move the arts closer to the top of the Liberal government's agenda, and eventually pitched an idea to Prime Minister Louis St. Laurent: a commission of inquiry into the state of Canadian culture, carefully couched in terms that would appeal to the more hard-headed members of cabinet. It was not a plan to give the long-hairs and highbrows unlimited access to government money, but a pragmatic response to post-war nationalism, the electorate's growing interest in cultural matters, and, not incidentally, the deepening Cold War. The world, after all, was in the midst of a war of ideas. A country that allowed its culture to languish left itself vulnerable; a strong, vibrant culture, on the other hand, was a fire-wall against the communist menace.

The cabinet, ever aware of the calculus that weighed political advantage against risk, accepted Claxton's idea, and the speech from the throne in January 1949 announced the creation of the Royal Commission on National Development in the Arts, Letters, and Sciences. It would come to be known as the Massey Commission, after its chair, Vincent Massey, whose family's name was synonymous with private cultural philanthropy in Canada and was best known for Massey Hall (1894) and Hart House Theatre at the University of Toronto (1919). Vincent's brother Raymond went to Hollywood, where he specialized in playing rather cadaverous villains, but Vincent preferred a life of public service: he had been Canada's high commissioner to Britain during the Second World War and would serve as governor general from 1952 to 1959. Along with Massey were four other commissioners: Norman Mackenzie, a university president and art patron from western Canada; Arthur Surveyor, an engineer from Montreal with technical expertise in broadcasting and film; Hilda Neatby, a historian from the University of Saskatchewan; and Georges-Henri Lévesque, dean of the Faculty of Social Sciences at Laval University. Together, the five commissioners covered all the bases: region, language, religion, gender, expertise. They would hold a month of meetings in Ottawa in the summer of 1949 before embarking on a cross-country tour to listen to Canadians. All told, they heard from nearly five hundred groups and individuals, representing arts organizations, educational associations, service clubs, universities, government departments—everything from the Arts Centre of Greater Victoria and the Conservatoire National de Musique de Québec, to the Alberta Tuberculosis Association and the Innkeepers of Prince Edward Island.

In June 1951, the Massey Commission published its long-awaited report, one of the most significant in Canadian history. It covered everything from film and television to universities and museums, but it also had some scathing comments about the country's cultural facilities. In short, the commission confirmed what consumers of culture had known for years: that Canada was "singularly deficient" in suitable venues for the performing arts. At the turn of the century, the report noted, Canada had more and better music halls than it did fifty years later; now, to use just one example, "no city in the world of comparable size is so inadequately equipped for the public performance of music as Montreal." Across the country, the story was the same. Performers were having to make do with "inappropriate and incongruous settings, in gymnasiums, churches, hotel rooms, school halls or in motion picture theatres rented for the occasion at ruinous cost." It found much truth in the advice of Robertson Davies's unforgettable character Samuel Marchbanks to aspiring playwright Apollo Fishhorn: "Now what is a Canadian playhouse? Nine times out of ten, Fishhorn, it is a school hall, smelling of chalk and kids, and decorated in the Early Concrete style." Such a state of affairs had produced a cultural depression, and inaction was no longer possible: Canada needed proper facilities if the performing arts were to avoid extinction.

This was not a new idea. Seven years earlier, in June 1944, a coalition of arts groups had lobbied the federal government to fund the construction of community centres across Canada that could be used for the performing arts. It was even argued that, instead of erecting the kind of statues that had sprung up by the thousands after the First World War, cultural centres could serve as living war memorials. This idea, unfortunately, hadn't quite worked out the way arts groups had hoped. In most communities that erected such centres after 1945, the cultural lobby was easily out-muscled by a much more powerful local group: the hockey lobby. So what might have been the Anytown Memorial Community and Cultural Centre became the Anytown Memorial Arena; all too often, pucks and sticks won out over cellos and greasepaint.

But the times were right for the problem to be revisited. The erection of some important concert halls in the 1950s—the Queen Elizabeth Theatre and Playhouse in Vancouver, the Jubilee auditoria in Calgary and Edmonton, the Beaverbrook Theatre in Fredericton, and La Grande Salle in Montreal's Place des Arts, to name a few—suggested that interest in public funding for the arts was growing. Then, it started to dawn on a few people in Ottawa that the Centennial of Confederation was drawing near. Canada had already been awarded the 1967 international exposition, but Expo '67 was intended to show Canada to the world, and the world to Canada; it wasn't really intended to be our national birthday party. However, the federal government was on the case, and on 6 May 1959 a one-day conference on planning for the centenary convened in Toronto. Every manner of idea was tossed around, but one that seemed to stick could have come directly from the pages of the Massey Commission report: a suitable way to mark the Centennial was a cross-Canada program to build a chain of concert halls and theatres.

As planning for the centenary proceeded over the next few years, this seed of an idea gradually took root. A committee dealing with the cultural aspects of the Centennial, chaired by Ellen Fairclough, the first woman in Canada to hold a federal cabinet position, recommended that a national theatre and concert hall be erected in Ottawa as a permanent memorial to the centenary, and that individual communities be encouraged to consider building performing arts centres as Centennial projects. They would have dual value: "The buildings themselves would have a lasting symbolic value, especially if they were clearly identified as federal–provincial projects commemorating the Canadian Confederation. They would also greatly improve the cultural life of the Canadian people."

Even given the attention generated by the Massey Commission, the amount of emphasis on cultural buildings may seem a little surprising. However, economics-professor-turned-cabinet-minister Maurice Lamontagne outlined the reasoning behind it in a speech to the Manitoba Centennial Corporation. He began by referring to Canada's "cultural poverty": there was no feature film industry; performing arts groups were perpetually on the brink of financial ruin, kept alive only by the sacrifices of a few dedicated souls; and Canadian performers lacked the funds or facilities to tour the country to share their work. The consequences of this, said Lamontagne, were dire. As long as we failed to build a strong cultural life, young, talented Canadians would continue to leave the country. He also referred to cultural separatism, with French and English culture growing up in isolation, as one of the prime sources of national tension. It could not be allowed to continue: "Let us make war on cultural poverty in Canada, so that in the future, culture, which will always be an element of diversity, can also become a strong unifying force."

Lamontagne had sounded the trumpets—but how was the war to be waged? The provincial premiers were already onside, having accepted Prime Minister John Diefenbaker's 1959 invitation to join a committee to plan the Centennial observances. They even had a project to discuss. In January 1950, Frank MacKinnon, the principal of Prince of Wales College in Charlottetown, Prince Edward Island, had proposed to the Massey Commission that a performing arts centre be erected in the provincial capital to honour the Fathers of Confederation, who had met there in 1864 to begin discussions that would eventually lead to a union of the British North American colonies. When asked why an arts centre would be an appropriate monument, MacKinnon responded that no community "can continue as a distinct and effective political and economic unit if it ignores its heritage and neglects its culture." The Fathers of Confederation might not have thought much about cultural matters, so it was up to the current generation to commemorate their work by correcting that oversight.

In 1961, MacKinnon secured the incorporation of the Fathers of Confederation Memorial Citizens' Foundation to lobby for a special memorial in Charlottetown. The foundation came up with a plan for a building worth $5.6 million, the cost to be divided between the federal and provincial governments. Diefenbaker was supportive, giving MacKinnon $250,000 to get the ball rolling and pledging that if the provinces paid their $2.8 million, his government would contribute its half. Dief probably thought it was a risk-free promise—who could convince five Conservative, three Liberal, two Social Credit, and one CCF government to agree on anything? Well, Frank MacKinnon and his committee did. In a coast-to-coast whirlwind of cajoling and arm-twisting, they got all ten provinces to agree in principle. It looked like MacKinnon would get his building.

Armed with a grant from the Canada Council, the foundation promptly launched a design competition. Judges sifted through the entries and finally picked a winner, which they announced at a formal dinner at Ottawa's Château Laurier in January 1962. Now, the foundation had a concrete plan for the Fathers of Confederation Memorial Building next to Province House, where the 1864 meetings had been held. The ball was in the first ministers' court—they had to decide how to make good on their pledge. Later that year, at a meeting in Victoria, they agreed that each province would contribute 15 cents per capita, with the federal government providing matching funds, to a total of $5.6 million. Every single Canadian, then, was represented in the proposed building to the tune of 30 cents.

The spirit of special interest couldn't be contained for long. In a speech at the sod-turning for the Charlottetown building in February 1963, Quebec premier Jean Lesage observed that Confederation had achieved many of its goals but hadn't done much to foster unity between the principal language groups. Biculturalism, in his eyes, meant that the French culture must be given more opportunity to assert itself. One way to do so, he thought, would be for the federal government to subsidize a concert hall in Quebec at the same level of funding received by Prince Edward Island. After all, the Fathers of Confederation had met again at Quebec in 1866 to iron out some of the issues that emerged after the Charlottetown Conference. Surely this gave Quebec an equal claim to be considered a cradle of Confederation? The possibility had been mooted at Victoria in 1962—the premiers had agreed in principle to another memorial in Quebec City—and Prime Minister Lester Pearson couldn't deny that Lesage had a point. In short order, cabinet concurred: Quebec would get $2.8 million, the same as Prince Edward Island, for its concert hall, so long as the federal grant didn't represent more than half the construction cost.

That took care of two provinces, but it remained to decide how projects in the others would be funded. The provinces rejected Ottawa's first plan as too stingy, so the federal government sweetened the deal: each province would receive $1 per capita of population (or about $19 million in total) to spend on local projects as they saw fit (although it was stipulated that the projects should be cultural or recreational in nature), as well as a $2.5-million lump-sum grant for "a centennial project of province-wide value." The only catch was that this grant would be reduced by any amounts Ottawa had already pledged. Because of the Charlottetown and Quebec City projects, Prince Edward Island and Quebec would get no further federal money. Manitoba was bidding for the Pan-Am Games, and Ottawa was supporting that bid to the tune of $500,000; if the Games went to Winnipeg, Manitoba would get only $2 million in Centennial special grants. The same held true for Alberta. The cities of Calgary and Banff were working on a joint bid for the 1968 Winter Olympics, and Ottawa had already contributed $2.5 million to their effort. If the International Olympic Committee chose Alberta, the province would get nothing more for the Centennial. Eventually, this harsh condition was dropped in favour of a plan more in keeping with the spirit of cooperative federalism: the per capita grants would be provided, as long as the provinces found $2 in other money for every federal dollar received; a $2.5-million grant would be given to each of the eight other provinces, although the sum could represent no more than half the total cost of a major project; and Ottawa reserved the right to veto any project that didn't meet the spirit of the agreement.

The whole thing had to be hashed out in cabinet in December 1963. Walter Gordon, who had moved from a prosperous accounting firm to become the finance minister, warned that the federal government was headed toward its biggest deficit in history; before agreeing to the deal he wanted to know what the total cost of the anniversary celebrations would be. Diefenbaker reacted with characteristic impatience. Large sums of money would have to be spent, he informed Gordon testily. That was a given. What they were discussing was not how much to spend, but how to spend it. To Gordon, this seemed entirely backward—how could they decide how to spend the money if they didn't know how much they were going to spend? But he was torn. As a passionate nationalist, Gordon could see what the program could do for Canadian identity. The accountant in him, however, didn't like it. Cabinet had already agreed to pay for a national theatre and concert hall in Ottawa—surely that was enough? But Lamontagne held firm. "There was a serious lack of cultural centres in Canada," he reminded his colleagues. Such centres would be essential if national arts festivals were to be mounted in the future and if Canada were to foster a national culture. In the end, Lamontagne's vision won out over Gordon's frugality: the Confederation Memorial Program, as it came to be called, would go ahead.

EXPECTING THAT MANY communities would take the advice of the Massey Commission and the federal government and use their funds to assist the performing arts, the centenary planners in Ottawa were already considering how they might help local committees do things right. In early 1963, Hazen Sise, a Montreal architect and veteran of the Spanish Civil War, was commissioned to draft guidelines on the requirements for a modern performing arts centre. Prominent members of the cultural lobby and urban groups suggested a few changes—such as dropping the reference to elegant lobbies filled with "shimmering women"—and then the document was presented to a June 1964 seminar on the architectural requirements for the performing arts.

In his opening address, Centennial commissioner John W. Fisher marvelled at the fact that there were already forty or fifty performing arts centres being contemplated as Centennial projects, in the provincial capitals and in many other cities as well: "Ten years ago it would have been inconceivable to think that such a development was forthcoming in a country that was known for its wheat, its forests, the Maple Leafs and the glorious traditions of 'La Belle Province.'" In his view, this was because the Massey Commission had convinced the public that "arts had become a vital part of our daily life and not just a hobby of the self-selected few." If Canada's up-and-coming artists were to stay at home rather than stray to greener pastures elsewhere, they had to have better performance facilities that were in constant use, "not as empty shells—but as living edifices which will be in keeping with the idea of these buildings as lasting monuments to the Centennial of Confederation." For the centres would, Fisher was sure, meet the same goals as Confederation: "[T]he Arts could and should serve as one of the most important bridges between our East and West, for all Canadians."

With those inspiring words ringing in their ears, the delegates at the seminar got down to business. The plan was for a string of performing arts centres to serve as the platform for three regional touring circuits (perhaps connecting to American cities), as well as a national, coast-to-coast circuit. But what kinds of buildings were best? The community centres that had been proposed earlier were planned by people with no appreciation of theatre, and in Sise's view were "more likely to constitute a parody of theatrical facilities than the real thing." Instead, the new performing arts centres must have professionally designed facilities for both the performers and the audience. These were covered by a number of highly technical reports, all of which stressed the importance of securing expert assistance. Acoustics, for example, were tricky, and "it has become fashionable for everyone, including people we suspect of being tone-deaf, to have an opinion and to announce it with the assurance of an expert." For his part, Guy Beaulne, long-time director at Radio-Canada and creator of the huge popular radio (and later television) drama *La Famille Plouffe*, was not shy about expressing what many in the arts community only whispered among themselves: that architects often failed in designing performing arts centres because they knew nothing about the theatre. Actors and producers should tell architects what was needed, not vice versa.

Other amenities too were essential in these buildings. They needed works of art that were integral to the architectural design, not just scattered around without rhyme or reason. Lobbies had to be spacious enough to prevent bottlenecks and to provide room for the audience to mingle before and after performances, and during intermission. There should be a coat check, and a shop and restaurant could provide valuable extra income. Even more important was a bar—"Canadians are not exactly a nation of teetotallers," Sise said. "A bar or bars will be welcome and well-patronized. Moreover, they are an *extremely important source of income.*"

Centres would have to be built in a variety of sizes: studio theatres having 299 or fewer seats (these were popular with promoters because they could be operated with a studio licence from the Actors' Equity Association, which allowed the payment of lower wages to actors); repertory theatres having between 850 and 1000 seats; and large halls with up to 2300 seats. In each case, the centre should be located as close as possible to the heart of the city. The flexibility in size was important, not only because larger cities had a much bigger potential audience than smaller cities, but because this flexibility would allow for the broadest variety of performances. Building only immense halls for operas or the symphony would, thought John Hirsch, the first artistic director of the Manitoba Theatre Centre and later artistic director of the Stratford Festival, tend toward "the build-up of a uniquely 'mink-stole' audience."

The commission thought the Ottawa seminar was a great success and was even more gratified when many provinces and communities confirmed that they would indeed spend their money on performing arts centres. Naturally, the major provincial projects were the most complicated, but by October 1964, agreements had been signed with the five provinces that had decided to erect concert halls. The Arts and Culture Centre in St. John's would start construction in March 1965; estimated to cost $6 million, it was due for completion in July 1967. The Centre for the Performing Arts in Winnipeg was slated for the same time frame, although the province estimated that construction costs could climb to $10 million. Quebec's partner to the Charlottetown building, provisionally called La Conservatoire, was estimated to cost $6 million, although more exact figures wouldn't be available until the design competition closed in November 1964. Saskatchewan had elected to build two performing arts centres, in Regina and Saskatoon; both were a little more modest, planned at under $5 million each, but citizens of Regina were about to vote on a $1-million debenture issue that could alter the plans for the centre in the provincial capital. The centrepiece, Ottawa's National Arts Centre, was projected to cost over $18 million, including nearly $4 million for an underground parking garage that seemed, to some observers, extravagant. The best estimate was that it would not be ready for use before March 1969. The national chain of performing arts centres was beginning to take shape.

FIRST CAME THE FATHERS of Confederation Memorial Building, which was in operation long before the ground was even broken for the other projects. Not that the road had been easy. The original design contest had called for a building that was part shrine to Confederation and part theatre, art gallery, museum, and library. This, for Frank McKinnon, was crucial. "It is appropriate that the building be a cultural centre," he wrote. "National greatness is not fashioned by political organization or industrial development alone. The spirit of a nation and the loyalty of its people are based more on tradition and culture." The fact that it had to harmonize with Province House, the Georgian legislative building next door where the Fathers had actually met, was the biggest design challenge. Province House was not very large, nor were the other buildings in the area. The trick, as one architect put it, was to build a large, modern, multi-use facility (it would be the largest, most expensive structure ever built on the Island) that would not overwhelm "the delicate, almost miniature, townscape of the early 19th century."

The judging panel had selected a design proposed by Montreal architects Affleck, Desbarats, Dimakopolous, Lebensold, and Sise, the firm that had been responsible for the Queen Elizabeth Theatre in Vancouver and Montreal's Place des Arts. In his appraisal of the building, architect Douglas Shadbolt noted that it was entirely appropriate for societies to turn away from the age-old practice of erecting columns or pantheons to mark the great deeds of nations and move toward commemorating the past with buildings that had a communal function. What better way to honour "the peaceful wedding of a nation by negotiation and good will" than with a building that celebrated the past while providing the opportunity to celebrate the future through cultural expression? And to harmonize the old and the new, the architects planned to use the same sandstone from Wallace, Prince Edward Island, that had been used in Province House. This, for one journalist, softened the modernity of the new structure. "Naturally it is modern," wrote the *Globe and Mail* a little condescendingly, "but it will contrast with some modern building which seems too obviously planned with obsolescence in mind."

Construction had to be accelerated because the theatre was booked for the annual Dominion Drama Festival, to be held in the spring of 1964.

And while other parts of the complex still resembled a building site that spring, the theatre was in fact ready for its first production, but only just—Mavor Moore, who had taken on the job as the centre's first director, recalled hustling the carpet layers out the back door minutes before the audience came in the front door. But from the lead-off performance of Arnold Wasker's *Chips With Everything,* put on by the North Kamloops Parent–Teacher Association Theatre Wing, the festival was a great success, although not completely without controversy. A local woman had loaned a brass bed for one of the plays, only to see it used in some rather risqué scenes; scandalized, she demanded its immediate return.

For the building's official opening on 6 October 1964, the foundation had invited Queen Elizabeth and Prince Philip, but Islanders didn't quite know what to do with their monarch. Instead of huge cheering crowds, newspapers reported polite applause and small clusters of people who lined the 4-mile route between the Royal Yacht *Britannia* and the Centre to cheer "not loudly or for a prolonged period." One policeman admitted it was probably the quietest royal procession he had ever seen. Restraint was also the order of the day at the Royal Command Performance that officially opened the theatre, if we can believe Scott Young's cheeky article on the occasion. It was a night of Canadian celebrities—Lorne Greene was the master of ceremonies (a big star on U.S. television, Greene had declined his customary appearance fee of $50,000 as a favour to Moore), and Dave Broadfoot, Gratien Gelinas, the Travellers, Les Feux-Follets, Anna Russell, and Yves Letourneau provided the entertainment. Young thought that the audience of "distinguished sable-wearers, mink-wearers, decoration-wearers and possessors of nice bare backs enjoyed themselves," but he couldn't say if the Queen liked Broadfoot's spirited routine about a Scotswoman doing a commercial for acne medicine. At least the crowd was well behaved, observed Young, sitting down when they were told "so that there would not be too much milling around and shouts of 'Hey, Elmer, over here' when the Royal couple hove into view." But he was most struck by the fact that the audience stood in stony silence when the royal party arrived, staring at the Queen "as numbly as if she'd just announced that an earthquake was imminent." Young turned to Peter Jennings, then an up-and-coming journalist, and said, "I'll clap if you will." They both did, and after a few seconds of puzzled silence, the audience joined in. The Queen, Young thought, seemed grateful.

The verdict, not only on the opening ceremonies but on the theatre itself, was almost overwhelmingly positive. In the Montreal *Star,* Peter Desbarats called the complex "a miniature, extremely modern 'Acropolis' in the provincial capital." Douglas Shadbolt liked everything about the theatre—the rich colours and textures, the restraint, the quiet dignity— everything but the angular hanging clouds suspended above the audience seating, which he thought were "a very disturbing feature of this other- wise beautiful room." Canadian comedy icons Wayne and Shuster weren't quite so diplomatic, and called them elephant diapers. Even so, observers admitted that the complex was a huge success. Theatre critic Nathan Cohen saw it as "a symbol of genuine national meaning." Frank MacKinnon, it seemed, had done his work well.

AS THE PERFORMING ARTS CENTRES planned for other cities lurched toward their official openings, Cohen's notion of the facilities as having genuine national meaning became standard rhetoric. It certainly played well in Newfoundland. There, the province had chosen to build its arts complex on the grounds of a fashionable country estate that had been home to successive families of wealthy townspeople. The buildings were being used as an Anglican orphanage when the province bought the property, razed the structures, and began work on the Arts and Culture Centre, as it would be called until someone thought of something better. The govern- ment eventually held a contest to find a new name, but it was a fiasco, leaving the complex with what arts journalist Sheila Gushue called a "prepossessing and rather frightening title."

The design contract for the building, which would include a 1017-seat theatre, art galleries, a Maritime museum, libraries, and meeting space, went to the firm of Cummings Dove Whitten of St. John's. Their layout of the interior space was a triumph, for it brought all the different varieties of artistic expression together in the hopes that patrons' appreciation of one would be enriched by the other. But the exterior design drew mixed reviews from Newfoundlanders. The party line was that "the form of the building is conceived as a strong 'castle-like structure' which the architects hope will give appropriate expression to the qualities of both the people of the Province and the striking local environment," but one journalist didn't quite see the metaphor: "The reddish-brown, supposedly castle-like structure is monolithic and … well, ugly. This sets the right mood—no preconceived ideas and an aura of pessimism. You're prepared for the worst—$7,000,000 down the drain."

But when the centre opened on 22 May 1967, just in time for the Dominion Drama Festival, the praise was unanimous. "The culmination and elegant sanctuary for a proud people's honourable past; a tremendously practical adornment for the present; and a heady inclination of a stupendous future," wrote one journalist enthusiastically. Every element of the building was perfect. The carpets were the plushest in all of Newfoundland. The lighting control panels looked like something out of the Kennedy Space Center. The cloakrooms were gorgeous—"never before in Newfoundland have coats had a more elegant place to stay." In a comment that would have pleased the planners of the program, John Fraser observed that "this building is, in a sense, a living thing. It is going to house not only the art and culture of Newfoundland, but of all mankind. The plays and concerts performed there will continually add to the texture of the structure. It will link Newfoundland's historic inheritance with the nation and the world."

The Festival was a triumph—but then, nothing happened. Queen Elizabeth, the Queen Mother, was supposed to perform the official opening of the centre on 1 July 1967, but instead, the complex was mothballed. "It appeared we had a hopeless white elephant on our hands," wrote Fraser. "The place was locked up, quite empty, and subjected to a series of political football scrimmages." Finally, in September 1967, John Perlin, who had been the local organizer of the Dominion Drama Festival, was named administrator of the centre. He had few illusions as to the task before him and admitted that the complex would not likely pay for itself: "the government has accepted the philosophy that the arts shouldn't have to pay off in profits of dollars and cents." Perlin, along with the new gallery director Peter Bell, got the centre up and running, bringing in everything from local little-theatre groups (rental rates were kept low to encourage use by amateur thespians) to national and international touring companies.

In time, the Arts and Culture Centre gave impetus to the arts in Newfoundland, exactly as the planners of the Confederation Memorial Program had envisioned. The provincial government later built smaller arts centres in Gander, Grand Falls, Corner Brook, and Stephenville (using the Czechoslovakian and Yugoslavian pavilions from Expo '67, bought at fire-sale prices and cannibalized to make theatres). This gave the province what it had never before had: a circuit of modern performing arts facilities. In 1972, the *Mail-Star* gloated that Newfoundland had better theatre spaces than Nova Scotia and admitted that the Spanish castle in St. John's, now that it was getting "a lived-in look," was starting to become more appealing. Most importantly, the complex had become "an arts centre for the people, not a centre for arty people … not merely a decorative institution for a small slice of the population, but a springboard for arts activities throughout the island." The Arts and Culture Centre also had the distinction of being the only provincial hall that actually opened in the Centennial year.

Next was the Manitoba Centennial Concert Hall, which had run into some early controversy over location. When the downtown site was first announced in the spring of 1964, one local complained bitterly that the jewel in the city's cultural crown shouldn't be placed "in a pawn shop area … near the three smoke-belching chimneys of the central heating plant." The government had to agree that the immediate surroundings of the proposed hall didn't look like much at the moment, but promised that the complex would eventually have a magnificent setting. There were few naysayers in sight on 1 October 1965, when the sod-turning for the complex was held. Instead of inviting the usual dignitary with a silver-plated shovel, organizers urged all Winnipeggers to take part, each one receiving a souvenir trowel to use. When Premier Duff Roblin (the grandson of Sir Rodmond Roblin) rang a bell, everyone turned over their own little chunk of earth—everyone from the hundreds of schoolchildren who had been let out of school for the occasion (they mobbed Roblin after the ceremony to get him to autograph their shovels) to city councillor Edith Tennant, and Margaret Konantz, the member of Parliament for Winnipeg South, all decked out for the occasion in black gloves and pearls.

In fact, project head Maitland Steinkopf made every effort to ensure that Manitobans felt a sense of ownership in their Centennial project. The first performance in the new theatre, on 25 March 1968, was a free concert for the workers who had built the centre, and two days later, when Governor General Roland Michener cut a big ribbon as part of the official opening ceremonies, each of the two thousand guests snipped little ribbons that had been tied to their seats, to symbolize the public's involvement in the project. Opening night went off without a hitch—"even the pair of pigeons rumoured to be hidden somewhere in the upper confines of the auditorium refrained from raining any disapproval on the speakers," reported the *Free Press*—even if the refreshments left something to be desired. "It don't matter how fancy you make it," grumbled one local guest, "or how small you cut it, or how much you charge for it—an egg salad sandwich is still an egg salad sandwich." But an undersized sandwich hardly mattered in the grand scheme of things. What counted was that Winnipeg had what is still regarded as one of the finest concert halls in North America.

Delays also occurred in Saskatchewan. In Saskatoon and Regina, the local committees had started construction before tenders for the complete project had come in. Saskatoon hadn't gone beyond excavating a huge hole for the foundation before discovering that the tenders were all around $8 million, almost twice the original estimate. Regina had already gone even further, digging the foundation and erecting the steel superstructure, when it got the same nasty shock—having budgeted $2 million for the project, the city learned that the actual cost would be close to $9 million. One business writer, looking on the two building sites in June 1966, predicted that Saskatchewan could be the first province to complete its Centennial projects—"one of the largest and deepest swimming pools in the country and the other the world's largest set of monkey bars."

Both cities needed to find extra money to fund the projects; the provincial government had announced in 1966 that it wouldn't put up any more cash for the centres. So the city council of Saskatoon decided to use electricity rebates that had previously gone to ratepayers to complete the project. Opening night for the 2003-seat Saskatoon Centennial Auditorium was 1 April 1968, and representatives of all levels of government were there to smile, shake hands, and hear the Saskatoon Symphony

Orchestra perform Orff's "Carmina Burana." Premier Colin Thatcher complimented the city on its shrewd money management ("I wish Regina had done as well," he added), and predicted that the building would "provide a fuller and more complete life for people in this area ... as the focal point of culture and the arts." Then he surprised everyone by pulling out a cheque for $125,000 and presenting it to Saskatoon mayor Sid Buckwold as a gift from the provincial government. Even federal cabinet minister Judy LaMarsh was at a loss for words, but only temporarily. She quickly recovered and wondered aloud to the audience if she had anything in her purse to present. "Would you settle for a comb with three broken teeth?" she quipped.

Thatcher might well have advised Regina's council to accept the broken comb, because the centre in the Saskatchewan capital was still in serious financial problems. The plebiscite to enable the city to issue debentures to pay for the complex had passed by a wide margin, but construction soon stalled for lack of funds. For years, the centre's half-finished steel skeleton dominated the skyline, "an apparent multi-million dollar scheme of futility," as one local journalist put it. Finally, the Thatcher government had no choice but to take over the project to get it done, in six years and at a cost of $7.5 million. The gala unveiling planned for May 1970 had to be postponed because of an electricians' strike, and it was not until 24 August 1970 that the Saskatchewan Centre of the Arts held its grand opening. Only the grumblers noted that the theatre had already been christened (it had hosted two sold-out shows by comedian Bill Cosby, who had been booked long before labour strife killed the first planned opening); everyone else basked in the glory of the occasion. On stage was the world-renowned Jan Peerce and the Regina Symphony Orchestra, under conductor Howard Leyton-Brown, but most guests came to see the building. Everyone who was anyone was there—Premier Colin Thatcher, whose "beaming smile was almost as wide as the stage" (perhaps it was relief as much as glee) and who predicted the centre would be virtually self-supporting in its second year (although the government had already budgeted $50,000 for its projected annual deficit, and some people were wondering publicly if that would be enough), the province's lieutenant-governor Stephen Worobetz (who particularly liked the vibrant orange carpeting), MPs and MLAs—people dressed in everything from white tuxedos to blue jeans. Even the city buses were decorated with black ties for the occasion. Before the evening was over, Thatcher toured all of the committee and meeting rooms, each named for one of the provinces. It was surely only a coincidence, and not a comment on the future of Canadian federalism, that the director's lounge was called the Alberta Room.

Quebec's project moved even more slowly. Within a few months of getting the go-ahead from federal officials, Premier Lesage struck a committee to define the plan, including the kind of complex to be erected, what it should cost, and where it should be situated. That it was to be a theatre and concert hall was never in question, but the committee was deadlocked over a site. Every civic and arts group consulted had a different idea, but Lesage overruled them all: the theatre would be built at the edge of a new complex of government buildings that was to be part of an administrative precinct on what is now the boulevard René-Lévesque, giving the area a magnet to keep people there once the offices had closed for the day.

A national design competition opened in May 1964, and six months later Montreal architect Victor Prus, a Polish Canadian who had designed the Bonaventure Metro station, was announced as the winner. His structure would have three main components: a large concert hall (to be named Salle Louis-Fréchette, after the man who was known in some circles as the National Poet of the French Canadians), a smaller auditorium (the Salle Octave-Crémazie, honouring the writer who was claimed by some to be the Father of French-Canadian poetry—clearly the fact that he got the smaller hall put him firmly in second spot in Quebec's literary hierarchy), and a conservatory. But what to call the entire complex? The committee considered naming it after Quebec cultural greats like Calixa Lavallée, who wrote "O Canada," Canada's first playwright, Marc Lescarbot, or Louis Jolliet, the composer and first organist in the Cathedral of Quebec, and then batted around Théâtre de la Colline (Theatre on the Hill), but discarded that as a little too arrogant. Eventually, the committee chose a name that had the tradition of many great theatres behind it: le Grand Théâtre de Québec.

In January 1966, eighteen months after the Charlottetown centre had opened, Lesage finally performed the sod-turning to get Quebec's project underway. Soon afterward, he was tossed from office by the Union Nationale, and the new premier, Daniel Johnson, decided to review all building projects initiated by the previous administration. Everything was put on hold, including the Grand Théâtre de Québec, which had become *"un lac grisâtre,"* a huge hole filled with muddy water. After looking at other possibilities, the government decided that the original plans should be pursued, and construction started again in September 1967. But still there were delays, with letting the contracts, with labour disputes, and especially with cost overruns. In November 1970, the government appointed Guy Beaulne as the first artistic director and, a few weeks later, finally announced the date of the gala opening. What it didn't announce until much later was the cost, which had ballooned to around $14 million.

On 16 January 1971, not many people were contemplating the cost. Instead, they were looking forward to the festival of four performances, by the Quebec Symphony Orchestra, Les Grands Ballets Canadiens, a choral ensemble, and the band of the Royal 22nd Regiment. Arts columnist Jacob Siskind, in his reflections on the opening concerts, couldn't say enough about the quality of the Salle Louis-Fréchette. For the audience, it was warm, pleasant, and relaxing, the kind of room that instantly made the patron feel comfortable. For the players, it was "one of the most MUSICAL halls we have in Canada, one that will help the orchestra grow into a much finer ensemble." All in all, he thought, the Grand Théâtre de Québec was a remarkable achievement: "[A]ll of Canada will benefit from it."

The capstone of the entire Confederation Memorial Program, although not the last centre to be unveiled officially, was in Ottawa. A national arts centre in the capital had been suggested in the Massey Commission report and again by Fairclough's committee in 1961, not only because of the symbolism of commemorating the centennial prominently in the national capital, but because the city was singularly deficient in concert space. Ottawa had fourteen venues for the performing arts, including three built for sporting events and one for livestock exhibition, but none were suitable for a touring philharmonic orchestra. The best hall in the city was the old Capitol Theatre on Bank Street, which dated from the 1920s and was hardly good enough for a nation's capital. When Zubin Mehta brought the Montreal Symphony Orchestra to the theatre, he could only squeeze three-quarters of his musicians on stage. Consultants hired by the federal government concluded that at least 22 of 32 countries surveyed had better facilities in their national capitals; at least ten Canadian cities were better equipped, and no Canadian city of a similar size had poorer performing arts venues than Ottawa. That was hardly news to the people of the city. They had watched the Canadian Repertory Theatre collapse for want of a decent hall, and many wondered what would go next. According to one concerned citizen, the erosion of Ottawa's cultural life had left the city nothing more that "a great big blob of bureaucracy."

Fortunately, the Centennial Commission saw the wisdom of these arguments and recommended the National Arts Centre as a top priority. Architecturally, the centre was constricted by the Parkin Plan, a long-term scheme for urban development of the capital that emphasized a pleasing vista southeast from Parliament Hill down the Rideau Canal. Anything built in that area, as the centre would be, had to conform to that plan. This meant a low building with very deep foundations, rather than something tall and majestic. In terms of what would go on in the centre, the government took the advice of G. Hamilton Southam, the coordinator of the new complex, that "the National Arts Centre is too important to be left to civil servants," and turned to a series of experts—Louis Applebaum as musical adviser, John Hirsch and Jean Gascon as theatre advisers, Tyrone Guthrie as festival adviser—to help plan programming.

The advisers immediately started making big plans, but the construction process was more protracted, as a wry column by Ottawa *Citizen* reporter Christopher Young observed. The project had started out as a faint wish in the hearts of a few optimists, and then it became a plan, and then a public issue. "One day, to the general amazement, it became a hole in the ground ... eventually so huge that the ant-like men scurrying around in the bottom of it looked scarcely more substantial than the dreams of earlier years." And then the hole was filled in and any further progress closed off from sight, until one day, Ottawans noticed that "hulking grey-brown shapes began to form themselves above ground ... like some science fiction monster in the middle of their town." One passerby commented that the centre's fortress-like appearance suggested "they built it expecting the people of Hull to attack."

Despite doubts about the name (Young observed sourly that "it was named in the pedestrian Canadian style ... couldn't someone please think of a more inspiring name than National Arts Centre? NAC indeed. It sounds like a military headquarters"), the public opening on 31 May 1969 was a huge success. Some fifty thousand people, more than three times what had been expected, swarmed the building and its grounds, although they all had to be cleared out in time for the gala opening that evening. The ceremony went well until public works minister Arthur Laing began to praise the complex engineering that went into the acoustics. At that precise moment, the public address system broke down. There was much nervous rushing about, and it corrected itself in time for the board of the National Arts Centre Corporation to be introduced by its chair, Lawrence Freiman. But then the system acted up again, producing strange feedback noises and making Freiman sound like Mickey Mouse. The ever urbane (and, at that point in his political career, ever unruffled) Prime Minister Pierre Trudeau rescued the occasion with a few well-chosen words. He praised the centre's beauty and, with a nod toward Parliament Hill, expressed the hope that it would inspire Canada's legislators to "improve our performance in that other publicly-supported playhouse across the street."

With over 1.1 million square feet of space, the NAC was the only bilingual, multidisciplinary performing arts centre in North America and was among the largest such complexes on the continent. The centre also had a deeper meaning that was consistent with the goals of the Confederation Memorial Program. Ottawa *Citizen* columnist Audrey Ashley saw opening night of the NAC as "a sign of growth and maturity in what was once continually referred to, rather patronizingly, as 'a young country.'" Hamilton Southam agreed: "Our actors have practised their art for generations in the misery of high school auditoriums.... The building of the Arts Centre is the most tangible sign, and happily not the only one, that the days of penury and exile are over.... That surely is the essential meaning of the Arts Centre."

THE BIG PROVINCIAL PROJECTS were not the only ones realizing the windfall of federal money. Any community group could bring forth a proposal
for a centennial project, the only stipulation being that the lion's share of
the money had to come from other sources. These projects ran the gamut
from curling rinks and public libraries, to published histories of chess in
Canada and of the township of East Flamborough in southern Ontario,
but planners were delighted to see that a good number of communities
recognized the importance of the performing arts and were prepared to
use the money available to erect theatres or concert halls. Indeed, the
dreams of people like Maurice Lamontagne and Ellen Fairclough were
fulfilled, because within a few years of the Centennial celebrations, an
orchestra or theatre company could mount a cross-Canada tour, playing
solely in venues that had been erected as Centennial projects.

Our imaginary company might start in Vancouver's Centennial
Theatre, which became home to the North Shore Light Opera Society
soon after its opening in 1967, although they would have been advised to
use the washroom facilities elsewhere before arriving. It was bad enough
for the audience, but there was only one men's and one women's washroom backstage for the performers. Imagine "a class of little girls in tutus
all rushing to get into one washroom after getting off stage," mused one
arts journalist. Then, after stops at the Centennial centres in Regina,
Saskatoon, and Winnipeg, our company might visit the Western
Manitoba Centennial Auditorium, next to the Queen Music Building at
Brandon University, a project that had a little controversy attached to it.
The report of the first meeting of the Manitoba Centennial Commission
noted that, in addition to the centre in Winnipeg, the province had also
committed to funding the auditorium in Brandon. This was "apparently
a special deal between the Premier of the Province and Brandon, and one
gets the impression that in retrospect it is being privately regretted." But
Brandon got its 877-seat theatre, which remains in use by the university
and local theatre groups.

Our troupe might just be able to squeeze into the Centennial
Auditorium in Cartwright, Manitoba, built in 1967 and improved in
1970 using a $409 grant from the province's Centennial committee,
before moving on to Centennial Hall, in London, Ontario. Ever quick to

sniff out the possibility of grants, London's deputy city clerk had written to the Centennial Commission in 1963 with a proposal to erect a concert hall and auditorium costing about $3 million. On 21 June 1967, the 1854-seat Centennial Hall held its official opening. Londoners would later complain about the flat floor (which made for more difficult sight-lines than a sloped floor) and the long, narrow design (which meant that most people sitting in the balconies had to crane their heads to one side to see the stage), but in 1967 Centennial officials regarded the hall as a huge success. The city had kept the cost down to $855,000, of which the federal program contributed $163,000. "The architect has done a wonderful job, as has the builder," wrote the regional director to his supervisor; the "money has been well spent."

Then it is on to Toronto's St. Lawrence Centre for the Arts, which had been designated as the city's primary Centennial project. In April 1966, the *Toronto Star* reported that all the money for the centre was in place and that people could expect a grand opening late in the Centennial year. But six months later, Toronto mayor Phil Givens said that funding issues had pushed the project back, and when construction tenders came in at figures higher than anyone had expected, many city politicians and journalists were sure they had heard the last of the St. Lawrence Centre. That's when members of the Toronto Arts Foundation came up with a scaled-back design, and in May 1968 Toronto city council gave the go-ahead for the project. It finally opened on 2 February 1970, three years after the Centennial. It may have been late but, just like the Arts and Culture Centre in St. John's, the St. Lawrence Centre had a huge impact on the local arts scene. When it opened, there were six theatres in Toronto; a decade later, there were thirty-six, a boom that many credited to the existence of the centre.

Our troupe's next performance might be in a much smaller venue in Whitby, east of Toronto, where the old Ontario County Court House, originally built between 1852 and 1854, was transformed into the Centennial Building, home to the Whitby Modern Players (later the Whitby Courthouse Theatre). The thespians of Whitby had been a peripatetic group. After the town hall they had called home for years was demolished, they played in church basements, high school auditoria, even the Whitby Psychiatric Hospital. When the Centennial grant plan was announced, Whitby jumped on the bandwagon and the Court House was converted into a theatre space—using lights made of sockets set in 5-pound jam tins and seats scavenged from a demolished movie theatre in Hamilton.

Next, after the National Arts Centre and the Grand Théâtre de Québec, might be a stop at the 571-seat Centennial Theatre at Bishop's University in Lennoxville, Quebec, opened on 14 January 1967. Originally created to serve the needs of the university's drama department, the theatre soon expanded to serve the community, launching its first major season in 1975, The Cultural Series, which included classical music, dance, mime, theatre, and jazz. From there, it's on to the Charlottetown centre and then, a grand finale at the Arts and Culture Centre in St. John's. Our troupe has completed its triumphant, cross-country tour, and all without playing in a single church basement or high school gymnasium.

The fondest hope behind the Confederation Memorial Program was that the centres would endure as living reminders of the Centennial. So how have the buildings fared in the forty years since Canada's one hundredth birthday? Have they achieved the broader goal of fostering a national culture? In 1966, Hamilton Southam had expressed concern that, unless the program was managed correctly, Canada would be left with a string of beautiful auditoria that were little more than white elephants. Happily, Southam's fears were unfounded, although the Centennial performing arts centres have certainly experienced some growing pains.

Charlottetown has perhaps suffered the most, in part because many of the provinces that had pledged to support the Fathers of Confederation Memorial Building (now the Confederation Centre of the Arts) eventually wriggled out of their financial commitments. In June 2004, the centre celebrated its fortieth birthday, but slow ticket sales that season resulted in a deficit of about $250,000. Not for the first time, the Confederation Centre would ring in the new year with a shutdown and temporary layoffs. After a decade of rave reviews and sold-out shows, the National Arts Centre too fell into a slump. Seven CEOs came and went in the 1990s as the NAC drifted, all the while losing its audience. In 2000, the NAC was finally jolted into action and came up with a five-year plan to recapture its national role, put greater focus on educational activities, and, not incidentally, make more money. By 2006, predicted the plan, "the original magic and excitement of this organization" would be recaptured: "The NAC's best years are still ahead of us." The Grand Théâtre de Québec (which enjoyed international fame in 1984 when it played host to the Shamrock Summit, featuring the Reagans and the Mulroneys on stage singing "When Irish Eyes are Smiling") was continually improving its facilities to provide a better experience for performers and audiences, but one of the costs was escalating ticket prices—a seat that had cost $5 in 1972 had gone up to $65 in 1996. Arts administrators are generally uncomfortable with high ticket prices, but are also aware of public sentiment that the users of theatres should pay most of the costs. "Why should my taxes fund a concert hall that I never go to?" is a typical question aired in public meetings or letters to the editor.

Still, as so many of the major players behind the Confederation Memorial Program pointed out, one should think not of covering deficits but of making investments. The program had never been simply about building venues for ballets and symphonies; it had been about fostering a national culture to help bind the country together. Together, the centres constituted a public works project that was, in its motivation, little different from the trans-Canada airway or highway—a project of national interest in which the country as a whole should be involved and whose social utility was more important than its cost. As Maurice Lamontagne put it, the centres "are going to play in the cultural field ... as positive a role as that played in the economic field by the railways built by our great-grandfathers." These structures were all about bringing Canadians together through the arts. Southam predicted that "when high school students in Regina are moved to laughter by Molière played by young French-Canadian actors from the National Theatre School in Montreal, and when music lovers in the Eastern Townships give a standing ovation to a talented pianist from Toronto—then English- and French-speaking Canadians will not only understand each other better, they will have learned at last—and not too soon—to admire each other." Maybe things haven't quite worked out that way yet, but it remains a noble goal.

HOW YOU GONNA
KEEP 'EM DOWN
ON THE FARM?

A MOVEABLE POST OFFICE

We live in an age of near-instantaneous communication. If we don't get a response to an email within a few hours, we start to wonder whether something went wrong with the transmission. With text messaging, a few seconds' waiting for a response can seem like an age. Internet chat rooms allow us to converse, for all intents and purposes, as if we were face to face. But what if we had to wait months or even years for a reply to an urgent inquiry? What if we had to wait days in hopes of seeing a passing traveller who might be willing to carry a letter on to the nearest port? What if our mail came, not to a convenient in-box on our computer, but to a rural post office that might be a dozen miles away?

For most of Canadian history, this was the reality. For centuries, letters and packages, now dismissively known as snail mail, represented the only link between people, and it was a link they treasured more than we can imagine. In 1809, the Canadian painter William Berczy wrote to his wife of the joy their letters brought him: "What greater pleasure could I have when I am far from you, than to take advantage of the happy and marvellous invention of transmitting thoughts on a sheet of paper over any distance imaginable." The kind of communication that many of us have all but discarded as old-fashioned was, for our ancestors, a kind of minor miracle.

The first letter written from Canada probably came from the pen of Charles de La Tour, an early governor of Acadia, who wrote to King Louis XII of France on 27 July 1627; however, an official postal service didn't begin in this country until 1693, when Louis de Baude, Comte de Frontenac, the governor of New France, commissioned a messenger to carry letters from Montreal to Quebec. At the same time, travellers were often willing to carry private correspondence with them as they moved around New France. Everything, of course, depended on the seasons. Small vessels plied the St. Lawrence between Montreal and Quebec in the spring, summer, and autumn, and all types of travellers could be found on the colony's roads, so there were many ways for correspondence to circulate. But in the winter months, much of that movement ceased. Whether you lived in one of New France's major cities or on an isolated seigneury in the backcountry, winter all but cut you off from the outside world.

Communication with Europe was also dependent on the shipping season. At Quebec, it typically opened in late April and continued until November, and the speed of the mail was governed by the crossing times. The eager correspondent could have a batch of letters ready for posting as soon as the first ship left Quebec in the spring; the trip to France took a little over a month, and then, if the recipient was equally prompt, a reply might be sent back on a ship departing France in late May. But against the prevailing winds, that crossing took over two months, so the reply would not reach Quebec until late July. If all went well, it might just be possible to send a follow-up letter and get a reply to that before ice closed the port of Quebec for the season. But that was a best-case scenario. Much more typical was the experience of fur trader and explorer Alexander Mackenzie, who found that doing business across the ocean demanded a degree of patience that is almost inconceivable today. A single transaction, which involved sending the order, the goods, and the payment back and forth across the Atlantic, could take as long as forty-two months from start to finish.

Aside from the royal messenger and the occasional government courier, much of this postal traffic was unofficial. Not until 1734 was the first official mail route opened in Canada, the post road between Montreal, Trois-Rivières, and Quebec, and the correspondence was delivered by a messenger on horseback. Twenty years later, in 1755, the city of Halifax became the site of Canada's first official post office. This bureau functioned largely for outgoing mail: the sender left a letter and the fee of one penny, and the letter would be given to the first ship captain bound for the city of the addressee. Effectively it was a branch of the British post office—every purchase, from an office clock to an ink pad, had to be approved by officials in London—and the service remained unreliable. It wasn't uncommon for military or government officials to find piles of letters sitting in the Halifax post office, simply because no one had bothered to send them on. Much of the blame was put on the British postal officials, so the Halifax office took to making decisions first and telling London later. In 1785, for example, the local postmaster opened a post office in Annapolis and began a service to Halifax once a fortnight, choosing to not tell his superiors in London until the new service was well established.

The more important connection after the British conquest of New France was between Halifax and Quebec, because it was essential to link the major cities of the new colony with the Maritimes. On 10 January 1784, the first trial mail sleigh left Quebec, arriving in Halifax on 29 February and returning to Quebec on 24 April, almost four months later. The mail got through, but at a price—the Post Office lost over £100 on the venture yet was determined that it could be made to pay in time. In October 1787, the regular service began (once a fortnight in the summer, monthly in the winter), with the Post Office modestly predicting it would make a £75 profit on each trip. It seems incredibly slow to the modern mind, but for eighteenth-century Canadians the trip by sleigh or cart must have seemed blindingly fast—three and a half days from Halifax to Annapolis, two days to St. John, two days to Fredericton, then anything from ten to fourteen days to Quebec. If everything went like clockwork, a letter mailed in Halifax would reach Quebec in under three weeks.

Slowly, other areas were brought into the postal network. Digby, Nova Scotia, was linked to Halifax in 1810 by a mail cart that left the Nova Scotia capital every Tuesday afternoon; if conditions were good, the trip took about forty hours. Prince Edward Island, which had been trying since the 1770s to get an official service so as not to rely on private couriers, finally received regular postal service between the island and Pictou, Nova Scotia, in 1816. More post offices opened in Nova Scotia— twenty new ones up to 1830—and road improvements between Quebec and Halifax gradually reduced the travel time to eleven days in the summer and fourteen in the winter.

Increasingly, public discontent began to focus on equity. Both the service and the cost depended entirely on where you lived, for there was no uniform postal rate throughout British North America. When the British post office first established the postal rates for Canada in 1765, a letter that was to travel up to 60 miles cost four pence, up to 200 miles cost eight pence, and every additional 100 miles cost another two pence. These rates were repealed in 1801, but the British government forgot to include Canada in its new postal legislation, so for the next three decades, we had no official postal rates. In practice, local authorities took it upon themselves to set their own. To send a letter from Halifax to Truro, for example, cost 4½ pence to mail, but the very same letter going to Sydney cost 11½ pence. Such disparities became especially galling after 1840, when the British government introduced a uniform postal rate for all letters travelling within the British Isles but never thought to apply it to the colonies.

In 1849, Britain decided to bow to complaints and transfer responsibility for postal service to colonial governments. Two years later, in July 1851, this change came into effect, and with it came a uniform postal rate for the British North American colonies (except British Columbia and Vancouver Island, where a patchwork of services provided by the Hudson's Bay Company, express couriers, and private riders was responsible for moving the mails): three pence—or five cents in the decimal currency that the colonies would adopt a decade later—for any standard letter weighing up to half an ounce (previously, the same letter had cost, on average, eighteen cents to mail). According to Canada's new postal regulations, letters in urban centres would be delivered by carriers, a service that cost both the sender and the recipient an extra half-penny each, on top of the regular postage. Many people grumbled at the additional charge and opted to have their mail held at the post office, where they could pick it up at their convenience.

By this time, the colonies were dotted with post offices and way offices (set up between post offices), which were only opened after a petition to the government. A community's success depended on a number of factors. The Post Office was a great source of patronage, and having a friend on the government side who could twist some arms in support of your petition never hurt. But petitions were also judged on the public service that a post office would potentially provide. If an area was well populated by people who were likely to write letters (literacy rates of the local population were taken into account—one rough-and-ready method was to count how many people had signed the petition with an *X*) or if the government thought that a post office might draw settlers, the petition was likely to succeed. Interestingly, the potential cost versus revenue of a proposed post office was rarely a deciding factor. The post office existed to extend civilization, not to generate revenue for the government.

If a petition succeeded, the post office usually went into the shop, office, or home of a loyal party man and provided a full range of postal services, from selling stamps to dispensing postal money orders. The way office, on the other hand, was simply an intermediary. The letter writer would pay two pence to have the letter delivered to the post office, where the usual postage rate would be charged as well. The farther one lived from the post office, the more way offices a letter had to pass through; if it had to go through three way offices, the correspondent had to pay two pence to each way office operator, as well as the regular postage rate. Thus for people living in a town or village with a post office, mailing a letter was relatively cheap; the more remote your farm, the more expensive it became.

Neither the postmasters nor the way office keepers were particularly well paid—the real advantages lay in the fringe benefits. They could send a certain number of letters annually without charge, something that was a real boon to a businessman, and were also exempt from other civic duties, such as militia service or jury or inquest duty. These perks were not to be sneezed at, and postmasters and way office keepers were keen to retain their positions. They had to provide a reasonable level of service, though, because a few complaints from the public were often enough to have an office-holder removed.

The linchpin in the network was the post rider, who had to battle bad roads, extreme weather, and wild animals to get the mail through to its destination. The rider on the Matapediac route, between the St. Lawrence and Baie de Chaleurs in northeast New Brunswick, faced a 96-mile trek that was difficult in the summer, but positively perilous in the winter, when horse was exchanged for dogsled or showshoes. There were only three or four shelters along the entire route, and more than one rider perished in the performance of his duties. Furthermore, postal authorities kept a careful eye on them. All delays had to be explained, and a fine or dismissal awaited the post rider whose excuses failed to mollify his superiors. His other responsibility was blowing the post horn two or three times as he neared a post or way office, so that a new horse could be made ready and the mail assembled for delivery to the next office. Locals didn't hesitate to complain to the authorities if the rider failed to sound his horn in time for them to get their letters ready.

In the decade before Confederation, the postal services expanded dramatically as the population grew. The 1865 report of the postmaster general of Canada West revealed that since 1851, the number of post offices had grown from 601 to 2197, the miles covered by post routes from 7595 to 16,309, and the number of letters posted from 2.1 million to 12 million. Service was improving even more in the cities. Montreal and Toronto had both seen the installation of receiving boxes at major intersections, where people could drop letters for pickup by postal couriers. Things got even better after Confederation. As of 1868, the uniform postage rate went down to three cents per half-ounce letter (in 1899 it would drop further, to two cents for a 1-ounce letter). The postal service in Canada was so efficient that it even became a carrot to be dangled before the eyes of British Columbians and Prince Edward Islanders to convince them to join Confederation. As a contemporary ditty in British Columbia went,

You want the mail
You want the rail
You want the cars to hie on
Come join us and we'll thread the land
With passage-ways of iron.

Perhaps the greatest innovation of the era was free household delivery in urban centres. In the early days, practices varied. Halifax had adopted free delivery in 1851, but in other cities, a letter carrier collected a cent or two from the homeowner for each letter he delivered to that address. In some cities, the carriers were paid a salary and the fees were remitted to the Post Office. Elsewhere, letter carriers were not paid but kept the delivery fees as their wage. In 1874 this started to change. Beginning with Montreal on 1 October 1874, free home delivery came to most of Canada's cities: Toronto, Quebec City, Ottawa, Hamilton, and St. John in 1875; London in 1876; Winnipeg and Kingston in 1882; Victoria in 1888; Vancouver in 1895. The change was made, postal officials said, to improve the service for city dwellers: "large numbers of letters which, under the old system, would have either remained at the post office for several days, until called for, or have failed of delivery altogether, are now delivered promptly to addressees. The facilities for the interchange of local correspondence have been notably increased, [and] a great amount of travel to and from the Post Office saved the public." The program was an immediate success. In its first year, the number of pieces of mail delivered to homes on a weekly basis almost tripled, growing again in 1880, when the Post Office raised the fees it charged for postal boxes to encourage people to kick the deeply ingrained habit of picking up their own mail.

This, of course, laid bare the basic inequity of the Canadian postal system: rural Canada was getting the short end of the stick where the mail was concerned. People in rural districts had always paid more to send their letters, but the introduction of the uniform postal rate had gotten rid of that disparity. Now, the government had admitted that it was a waste of time for the city-dweller to walk three blocks to collect their mail at the post office, but no one seemed to care about the farmer who had to walk several miles to collect his.

Many people believed that inequities like this were behind the worrying trend of rural depopulation. Rural life was, by its nature, isolating, and the postal service, which had always been about keeping people in contact, was doing nothing to reduce that isolation. City folk got their letters day in, day out, whatever the season, but what farmer could afford to waste half a day during harvest time to collect the mail? How often during the winter were concession roads too blocked by snow to permit travel? Any number of circumstances could intervene to prevent country dwellers from collecting their mail for days or even weeks at a time. And it wasn't just about personal letters. It was bad enough to go for days without knowing if a letter had arrived bearing the latest news of an ailing parent or sibling. What about the newspapers that weren't picked up? How long might a farmer go without finding out that the government had fallen, or the monarch had died, or the country was at war? And what business opportunities were lost under the current system? Shopping by catalogue had grown enormously as postal services expanded, but again the farmer was disadvantaged. On Monday, he might decide to buy a scythe from the Eaton's catalogue. If his order could be mailed that day, the purchase would go through. But if he didn't have time to travel to the nearest post office until later in the week, perhaps by then he had decided that he really didn't need a brand-new scythe and the sale was lost. The new catalogue business was all about giving shopping opportunities to people outside the cities, but the postal system wasn't working to the benefit of either retailers or rural consumers.

The *Globe* was one of the first newspapers to raise this matter, coming out in favour of rural mail delivery in an account of the U.S. experiment with it in November 1899. The newspaper concluded that the impact in the United States had been entirely positive. By substituting one moveable post office for several stationary ones, the government had realized considerable cost savings. Postal revenues had gone up because farmers could subscribe to newspapers and magazines and have them delivered to their doors. Municipalities had diverted money to improving their roads, because good roads were a prerequisite to the awarding of a rural route. The value of farms along routes had even increased, as mail delivery reduced rural isolation and made farming a more attractive proposition.

All of this led the *Globe* to declare that rural mail delivery should come to Canada: "With the injurious cityward tendency so strong, anything likely to make life on the farm more attractive is worthy of consideration."

In a 1903 editorial, the newspaper was even bolder in its claims: the service would bring a kind of enlightenment to rural districts. The time when people would journey to the post office and meet "once a week to ask for letters and talk over ancient news" should pass. With home delivery, "the people in the rural districts are in close touch with the doings of the outside world from day to day. The farmer reads the morning newspaper at noon, and before evening all the members of his family are familiar with the world's history for the previous day. This freshness lends an interest unknown, and prevents the narrowness of vision frequently resulting from the isolation of rural life. Every family is entering more fully into the intellectual life of the world."

The Reverend Calvin McQuesten, a Presbyterian minister who wrote a feature called The Tatler for the Montreal *Herald* (he also edited a women's column under the pseudonym Nina Vivian), tried to push the government in the same direction. "Thousands of young men," he wrote, "are dissuaded from entering into agricultural life not so much by their aversion to hard manual labour, as by a dread of the isolation which it involves." If they had the contact with civilization that rural mail delivery afforded, they might well decide to take up the country life. But "being compelled to go for days at a time without seeing a daily paper ... just because there has not been time to hitch up and drive to the post office for the mail, is a condition of life too horrible to contemplate." Naturally, rural groups agreed. The annual meeting of the Dominion Grange, an agricultural lobby group that was imported to Canada from the United States in 1874, never failed to urge upon the government the need to establish rural mail delivery. In 1901, the group predicted that such a service would be a cure-all for the ills of rural society: "There is nothing that would stimulate, give more pleasure, add more comfort and attractions of farm life to both old and young than free rural mail delivery."

Yet only a few politicians took much interest in the matter. A Liberal official in the riding of South Oxford, in southwestern Ontario, told a party convention in 1900 that it was impossible for city folk to imagine the inconvenience of having to make a 2- or 3-mile trip to the post office every day during the busy season and urged his own government to adopt the U.S. experiment. In January 1901, the Quebec *Chronicle* reported that Postmaster General William Mulock was looking into the question of rural mail delivery and had sent Toronto's assistant postmaster to Washington to study how the Americans were faring. Mulock wasn't afraid of new things where postal matters were concerned—among the innovations that came during his tenure were electric stamp-cancelling machines for letters, the special delivery service, the world's first Christmas stamp, the Imperial Post (under which a letter could travel between any two places in the British Empire for two cents), and the regulation that allowed Canadians to send picture postcards—so he shouldn't have feared a new service like rural mail delivery. But, despite the favourable verdict from Washington, Mulock couldn't get over the cost. Later, he revealed his personal opinion that the U.S. statistics had been fudged to make the system appear cheaper than it really was. So, when the matter came up for discussion in Parliament, his reply was firm: Canada was too sparsely settled and lacked the financial resources to make rural mail delivery work.

The matter refused to die, and in March 1905, a debate in the House of Commons quickly emerged as a battle between the parsimonious minds in the Post Office and MPs who represented rural districts. The latter were well aware of rising dissatisfaction within their constituencies, coming largely from the perception that they were being treated unfairly in comparison with city dwellers. Haughton Lennox, the Conservative member for South Simcoe, led the charge, unleashing on Mulock a barrage of statistics about how the system worked in the United States and how it might reasonably be attempted in Canada. But beneath his charts about costs per mile of delivery route were precisely the same points that the *Globe* and Reverend McQuesten had made: rural mail delivery, something that people in the cities had been enjoying for decades, "will bring increased comforts to the home, and make the contrast between city and rural life less marked than it is to-day. It will tend to encourage farmers' sons to stay upon the farm, and thus add to the general prosperity of Canada, by giving them facilities now denied." Conservative MP Joseph Armstrong of Lambton East then took up Lennox's argument, accusing the government of "legislating and catering to a large extent to the cities, towns and corporations of our country, and sadly neglecting the rural districts." Would it not be too much to ask, wondered Armstrong, for the government to put aside a few thousand dollars to test rural mail delivery, to see how it might work in Canada? At that, the ears of backbenchers suddenly pricked up. Money for a trial run? Surely that should be in *my* constituency! One by one, they got to their feet. West Kent would be the ideal place for a trial. Brockville is the obvious choice. The riding of King's is willing to be the guinea pig. Prince County would happily host the test. South Essex trumped them all—if the government saw fit to award that constituency, it would pay half the cost of the trial run.

Mulock, however, was having none of it. In his opinion, rural mail delivery was "one of the wildest schemes the United States had ever embarked upon." From an initial outlay of $40,000 in 1897, when eighty-two trial routes were set up in twenty-eight states, the costs had exploded, to the point where the U.S. post office's deficit had ballooned from a mere $2 million to over $14 million, all thanks to rural mail delivery. The Canadian Post Office, on the other hand, had a modest surplus, and Mulock didn't intend to divert that hard-won surplus into a service that would drain his department's coffers. Not that he didn't have every sympathy for the plight of the rural population (he himself represented the rural riding of York North). It was simply a matter of setting a precedent. If he gave delivery to one rural district, even on a trial basis, he would soon face calls to extend it to every other district. Those calls would become irresistible, and soon Canada would be bearing the costs of a delivery system that far outpaced those in the United States. Mulock was willing to share with the House any information he received from his U.S. counterparts on the subject, but he would go no further than that. For one farmer in southwestern Ontario, that wasn't nearly far enough.

GEORGE WILCOX was a practical man who valued facts and figures. His was the clear-sighted pragmatism of the pioneer, inherited from his ancestors who had emigrated from England to New England not long before the American Revolution, and from his father, who had moved to Oxford Township in southwestern Ontario in 1839. As he tramped from the family farm to the nearby village of Springford, Ontario, to collect his mail, the numbers ran through his head. Every year, he walked 800 miles to pick up his mail. He had friends who travelled 16 miles a day, or 2500 miles a year. Collectively, the people of Canada's rural districts covered a total of 10 billion miles each and every year, just to collect their letters and newspapers from village post offices. He kicked a stone ahead of him and paused—well, maybe that last number wasn't quite right, he thought, but the general rule held true. In Michigan, where he had worked a plot of land bought on speculation in 1902, the mail came to the farmer rather than vice versa. Free rural mail delivery had saved the U.S. farmer untold time that, in Canada, was wasted in trips back and forth to the post office. Wilcox returned to Oxford Township in 1905, a zealous missionary with a cause. His mind was made up: he would bring to the farmers of Canada the great gift of home mail delivery that their neighbours south of the border enjoyed.

On a cold morning in December 1905, he started out on another walk to the post office, just as he had done hundreds of times. But this trip was a little different. Clutched in his hand were letters to newspaper editors— in Woodstock, Ingersoll, Tillsonburg, Hamilton, and a half-dozen other cities—all singing the praises of free rural mail delivery. These were the first salvoes in George Wilcox's offensive against the Canadian Post Office. He began by describing his situation in Michigan, where he had paid $25 in taxes on his 160 acres, a sum that was sufficient to permit the government to send the mailman to his gate six days a week, excluding holidays. In Oxford County, on the other hand, the taxes were three times higher but every farmer had to hitch up the team and drive "three or four miles to a post office after the mail that has been lying there like as not for a week or more, and is all ancient history." What was worse, the city dweller in Canada "has his mail delivered at his home or place of business, or both, three or four times a day, and the bill is paid by the Government with the money that for the most part comes out of the farmers' pockets." For Wilcox, the issue was more than one of equity—it was about extending the benefits of civilization to the very people who were creating Canada's prosperity: "Are the people and their descendants, who out of a dense forest, made this Eastern Canada what it is to-day to be forever deprived of a great and important service that immediately removes farm life from its isolated and lonely position into interesting, constant and quick intercourse with the wide world?"

Wilcox's first letter was widely reprinted in Ontario newspapers, and as he carefully pasted the cuttings in his scrapbook, he decided that persistence would pay off. He started to amass a formidable arsenal of facts and figures and continued his letter-writing campaign. In a letter to the Hamilton *Spectator* in February 1906, he imagined the publication and delivery of a small farm newspaper. The typesetters scurry to take the latest agricultural market news from the wire service and set the figures into columns. The plates are quickly fitted on the printing press, which begins to crank out newspapers, folded and addressed, at a rate of two hundred per minute. Bales of newspapers are hustled onto delivery wagons and sped to the railway station, where iron horses speed through the country-side like "rushing, screaming tempests" to a hundred rural post offices. The day's news is vital to the success of the farmers to whom the papers are addressed (a price change of a few pennies a pound for hogs could mean a tidy sum for the farmer with fifty animals), so the publisher had done everything possible to make the process quick—under two hours from print shop to country post office. And then … the newspapers sit. One addressee might find a few hours the next day to make a trip to the post office, but for the subscriber in the back concessions, it might be a week before the burden of farm work freed him for half a day to travel into town. By then, the late-breaking market news was out of date and of no use to anyone. The bustle of activity in the publishing house, as likely as not, has been for nothing.

Wilcox's letters were always like this—he alternated between whimsical scenarios that revealed his wry sense of humour, and hard facts and figures. The following spring, he wrote to the London *Free Press* that Ottawa collected an average of $64 per family in taxes each year, while rural mail delivery would cost no more than sixty-five cents per family annually, surely a small investment to bring the comforts of the city into the country. The Post Office had generated a surplus of $1.5 million the previous year—what possible argument could be raised against using a few thousand dollars of that surplus to test the U.S. system in Canada? In fact,

Wilcox argued, the surplus would pay for most of the service, for he had calculated that the country would need 2500 rural mail carriers (as opposed to the 36,000 in the United States) at a cost of $700 each, or a total of about $1.8 million annually.

As the letters flowed forth from Wilcox's pen, he was starting to win more allies in Parliament, and they in turn were beginning to put pressure on the government. Now, they faced a new postmaster general—Mulock had moved on, yielding the portfolio to Rodolphe Lemieux from the Quebec riding of Gaspé, one of Canada's many constituencies that were entirely rural—but not a new policy. Lemieux made it clear that government plans did not include rural mail delivery. The solution, instead, was to increase the salaries of rural postmasters and build more rural post offices. Lemieux then made the mistake of trying to defend his policy by citing dubious evidence, in this case the opinion of the San Francisco *Argonaut,* which he called a "very high-class U.S. publication," that rural mail delivery would continue to be ruinously expensive in the United States. Wilcox, whose command of the minutiae on the subject was better than anyone's, was more than a match for the postmaster general, and he promptly laid bare the conceit in a letter to the press. The *Argonaut,* far from being a high-class publication, was a journal of little consequence: of the eighteen major papers in the San Francisco area, it ranked dead last in terms of circulation, and its statement that Canada had already instituted rural mail delivery and was rapidly expanding it (a statement that Lemieux had carefully avoided quoting) destroyed any credibility it might have. Later, Lemieux was backed into stating that the government would be willing to establish a post office every 2 miles, if the population warranted it. This seemed so close to a post-office-at-every-farm scheme that critics of the government couldn't imagine how it could be any cheaper than free rural delivery.

By now, Wilcox and his allies had a new weapon. Sir Wilfrid Laurier's government had been elected in 1904, and would soon have to face the voters again. Shrewdly, supporters of rural mail delivery began to transform it into an election issue. Individual Liberal MPs had already urged their government to commit to the service—now Liberal riding associations across western Ontario began to pass resolutions in favour of rural delivery and to urge their MPs to get on board. As Wilcox wrote pointedly to the Woodstock *Sentinel-Review,* "all these people have votes and memories, facts that should have been taken into account by people who get up on platforms and preach harmony and good feeling, and the beauties of Democratic institutions, and not be treated as a joke and consigned to the realm of executive committee oblivion."

Wilcox's next step was to try to interest the leader of the opposition, Robert Borden, in the matter. Borden was a city man, a former mayor of Halifax, but Wilcox thought he might see the electoral advantage of championing rural mail delivery and so he sent him a thick sheaf of newspaper clippings on the subject. Borden was noncommittal at first, replying that "the time is hardly ripe for the immediate establishment of a rural delivery system," but as he searched for issues that would offer voters a clear alternative to the governing Liberals, he kept coming back to Wilcox's idea. Finally, in August 1907, he made rural mail delivery part of the Conservative Party's election platform. "It would be a great economic saving," he later told a crowd at Woodstock, Ontario, "for one man to deliver mail to the houses of two hundred people instead of the two hundred people having to hitch up and drive to the post office."

Wilcox, by his own admission, was shocked. A staunch Liberal by inclination, he had always assumed that his own party would one day see the wisdom of the service and adopt it themselves. To find that "Mr. Borden had actually stolen my Free Rural Mail Delivery plank" and co-opted it for the hated Conservatives was a bitter pill, but he took the matter in stride. Borden had succeeded in making rural mail an election issue, and Wilcox thought this just might force the hand of the governing Liberals. And so he redoubled his efforts. In May 1908, Wilcox wrote an open letter to Lemieux that combined a mass of statistics about the U.S. experience of rural mail delivery, with a fanciful description of the day when the service would come to this country: "then Miss Canada will joyously behold the spectacle to the Free Rural Mail Delivery Man driving up to her mail box at her gate, and she will say to herself what a fool I have been to have tramped millions and millions of miles to and from the country post office when the outlay of a few paltry dollars would have instituted this great convenience years and years ago."

Finally, with just over a month to go before the federal election, the government decided that the time was right to pull a plank out from under Borden's feet. A brief notice in Canadian newspapers stated that Lemieux intended to institute rural mail delivery immediately so that "farmers will be able to get their mail at their door without the necessity of sending after it to the village post office." Wilcox immediately wrote to Laurier to urge upon him the need for a major public announcement: if the Liberals made a loud and unequivocal commitment to rural mail delivery just weeks before the election, it just might sway those country voters who were toying with throwing their votes to Borden. Laurier was quick to see the wisdom in this and invited Wilcox to a giant Liberal Party meeting at Niagara Falls on 15 September 1908 to hear Lemieux deliver the grand announcement. Laurier was there too, and Lemieux took the opportunity to introduce him to the gentleman from Springford. "This is our old Rural Mail friend," he said cheerfully as he pushed Wilcox toward the prime minister.

The details of the Liberal plan came out over the next few days. The first trials would be held over routes that were currently served by mail wagons: instead of carrying all the mail to three or four post offices along the route, the wagon would make deliveries at dozens of boxes along the way, at the end of each lane. In addition, families living on side roads could place boxes at the nearest intersection with the main road, and receive delivery there. For the moment, the Post Office didn't expect to need additional personnel or equipment. The farmer, however, had to buy an official postbox for $3 (the government sold them at cost); mail would not be deposited in any other kind of box. After the initial trial period, any group of people could apply for a route to serve their area. They simply had to submit a sketch of the proposed route, and it must avoid detours— the carrier would not detour down a side road simply to serve a single customer.

On the tenth of October 1908 the scheme that George Wilcox had long fought for—"the latest word in luxury for farm life"—finally came to pass. On that afternoon, a red mail wagon, driven by Captain W.R.

Ecclestone, left the Hamilton postal terminal to travel the first rural delivery route established in Canada. There were thirty-seven customers along the route to the village of Ancaster, but no letters were collected until the twenty-fifth box, owned by a wizened old farmer named Walter Vansickle, at the junction of the Dundas and Ancaster roads. Vansickle, who had simply come out to check his mail, found himself in the middle of a ceremony attended by a smattering of local farmers and a handful of local dignitaries, including George Ross, the chief superintendent of post offices for the Dominion, and Adam Brown, a long-time Hamilton member of Parliament. Sadly, no one had thought to invite George Wilcox.

THE LIBERALS WON the election of October 1908—rural mail was only one of a number of issues in what was a nasty campaign—but then came the accusations that the Post Office Department seemed remarkably less interested in rural mail delivery after the election than it had been before. The Dominion Grange was also suspicious, wondering how a measure that the government claimed would be impossible until Canada's population topped twenty million "became suddenly feasible on the eve of the general elections." And the authorization of new routes did seem rather slow. Granted there was reluctance to start new routes in the winter, but there was no denying that demand for the service was uneven: only fifty routes in total had been established in the six months after the first trial, despite the Post Office's estimate that 4500 potential routes existed across the country. In western Canada, none at all had been authorized, because of the distances involved and the poor state of many roads. Nova Scotians had not submitted a single request, which the Toronto *Star* put down to the fact that "the rural population is content with the soap-box or tomato-can service, whereby the stage driver dumps the family mail in the aforesaid receptacle, receiving in return a bag of apples per year, or horse feed, or perhaps a merry smile." In western Ontario, on the other hand, prosperous farmers thought nothing about forking out $3 for a mailbox to allow them to enjoy all the comforts of the city; more routes had been established in George Wilcox's heartland than anywhere else in Canada. And the newspaper predicted that demand would grow. The winter was a slow time for the farmer, and it was a nice break from the monotony of the season to drive to the post office, collect the mail, and spend a few hours passing the time. Once spring came and the demands of farm work returned, calls for rural routes likely would increase.

This is precisely what happened. By the summer of 1909, the number of routes had doubled, and by the following spring there were 339. Persistent calls continued for expansion. William Chisholm, the Liberal MP for Antigonish, Nova Scotia, argued that, in spite of the improvements, "the people of the rural communities are not being dealt with as generously as they should be ... you must do what is necessary to make rural communities more comfortable and to make life in farming districts more bearable if you wish to retain your rural population. The boys and the girls go away because they have not the conveniences at home." From across the floor of the House of Commons, Conservative Martin Burrell, of Yale–Cariboo in British Columbia, agreed: "It is the cry in Canada that we want rural population, and if we want to develop that class of our population we must certainly give the fullest consideration to those scattered communities which are laying the foundations of their future homes, and who are cut off entirely from their old connections and associations." Reluctantly—a postal official admitted in 1910 that his department still regarded the service as experimental and had "held in check as much as possible the applications for delivery"—the government began to relax the restrictions, and by 1913, there were 72,000 boxes along almost 1400 routes, 600 of them established that year alone. The Post Office reported that the "constant clamouring for rural mail delivery ... shows no signs of abating and the indications are that the time is not very far distant when the system will, at least as far as Eastern Canada is concerned, be complete."

As the rural routes expanded, Wilcox couldn't resist the occasional I-told-you-so. During the First World War, he wrote to several papers to remind them of how things might be had his campaign not succeeded: "[E]very day during this titanic conflict that is dragging thousands and thousands of our fairest sons and daughters into the very jaws of death, anxious mothers and fathers, wives and sweethearts, brothers and sisters, and the people generally, would, in the aggregate, be travelling 500,000 miles and more to and from the post offices of Canada for the latest news from the battlefields athwart the sea." In fact, the thirst for letters and news from the battle fronts probably did have something to do with the huge growth in the system during the war. By 1918, the number of routes had more than doubled, and rural carriers were now delivering to more than 173,000 boxes across Canada.

Before long, the mail carriers had become part of the fabric of rural life, often serving their particular customers for long periods. In October 1933, in Pictou County, Nova Scotia, Hugh Munro won the contract for the rural route running from the village of Scotsburn. He also ran a barbershop and sang in the church choir, but that didn't stop him from faithfully delivering to his customers along Rural Route #3 for over forty years. In 1943, Francis Young began delivering the mail on a 40-mile route between Powassan and Commanda in northern Ontario, first by horse and buggy and then, when the roads improved, by truck. A favourite with the locals, and not only because he was willing to deliver groceries and supplies between farms along with the mail, Fran was a fixture on the route for forty-two years. In Prince Edward Island, the rural route out of Elmira was contracted in 1929 to Neil Cheverie, who ran it until he died. His son George then took over, followed by George's younger brother Pius, who started on the route in 1945. Every weekday, Pius collected the mail at the Elmira railway station (if the train didn't arrive, he had to ride the 10 miles to Souris to collect the mailbags), and started out on his 20-mile round trip to the eastern tip of the island. For most of the year, he travelled in an open buggy, but for the winter Pius built himself a sled with a small hut on it; sliding windows on each side allowed him to reach the mailboxes and still keep out the worst of the cold.

By the time Pius Cheverie retired from his route in 1985, after his family had served the people of the Elmira area for nearly sixty years, the job of the rural mail carrier had changed. The horses and buggies had been replaced by sedans and minivans, and the carriers were finding it increasingly difficult to cover their costs. As independent contractors rather than government employees, they received no benefits, and increases in the price of gas meant that their take-home pay could drop dramatically without notice. Because they received a lump-sum payment for each route regardless of how many hours it took to complete it, many of them earned less than the minimum wage for their work. To add insult to injury, they had to bid for their routes, and the early Post Office was renowned for its miserly contracts with rural mail carriers. Later came accusations that Canada Post kept the bidding process closed so that they could force contractors to underbid themselves in order to keep their contracts. "We know you've had the route for twenty years," went the argument, "but we've got someone who will do it for a thousand a year less—can you beat that?" Whether or not the other bidder actually existed was often a topic of hot debate among carriers.

Over the years, various attempts were made to improve the conditions for rural mail carriers, either by classifying them as government employees or allowing them to form a collective bargaining unit, but Canada Post always held firm on the basis that anything but the status quo would be ruinously expensive. Finally, in 2003 the Canadian Union of Postal Workers (CUPW) and the Organization of Rural Route Mail Couriers won the battle. As of 2 January 2004, rural mail carriers became unionized employees of the Canada Post Corporation, with all the benefits and rights that went along with CUPW membership. One wonders what Hugh Munro, Francis Young, or Neil Cheverie and his kin would have thought of that.

Ironically, the arguments that rural mail carriers faced in the 1990s were the same ones that George Wilcox had battled against in the early 1900s. For Wilcox, providing a service to the public was the ultimate goal; for the Post Office, nothing was more important than the cost. And in one respect, Mulock and Lemieux had been right all along. Rural mail delivery was never a money-maker. Rural routes certainly increased postal traffic, which in turn boosted revenues for the government, but they never reached the point of paying for themselves. The Post Office economized by paying rural carriers scandalously low wages, but few cost savings were realized through closing small post offices—the number actually peaked in 1911 before falling off slightly in 1921 to a level that would remain stable until the 1950s. Instead, when Post Office deficits became more frequent after the mid-1920s, Ottawa became increasingly reluctant to authorize new rural routes. In 1921, just thirteen new routes were added, and none at all in 1923 and 1924, when the number of boxes served by rural mail carriers stood at just over 200,000.

A number of factors were behind this slowdown. In the first place, most people who wanted rural delivery now had it—few areas in the country were without the service. And because the long-term trend toward rural depopulation continued, the electoral muscle of the countryside slowly weakened. As rural Canadians became a weaker voting block, they became less able to influence the federal government. Finally, there is no question that the federal government in 1908 was backed into starting rural mail delivery, and that Lemieux and Laurier were reluctant converts. In considering rural mail mainly from a financial perspective, Lemieux resembled his cabinet successors from later decades, who would look first and foremost at the bottom line in evaluating any new service: rural mail delivery didn't pay, so rural mail delivery shouldn't be encouraged. By the mid-1920s, this attitude was the norm, and was evident in the restriction of rural routes.

Until then, however, successive governments had always regarded the social benefits of the postal service as paramount; a deficit in the Post Office Department was acceptable so long as broader social goals, such as allowing Canadians to stay in touch with one another, spreading knowledge through newspapers and periodicals, or reducing rural isolation, were achieved. Wilcox and his allies in Parliament, clearly, were much closer to contemporary understandings of the postal service than the cabinet ministers they battled. They realized that rural mail was a means of bringing country dwellers, who made up the majority of the population in 1908, into the national fabric, of giving them the kind of conveniences that city people enjoyed. They were interested in compensating for Canada's geographical challenges by establishing an efficient communications infrastructure. After all, what were the consequences for the nation if more than half its population lacked ready access to newspapers and magazines, were unable to take advantage of the growing business of catalogue shopping, and were reluctant either to stay in or move to rural areas because of the isolation for which they were so notorious?

George Wilcox lived to the age of ninety-one, his constitution perhaps strengthened, ironically, by the thousands of miles he walked to collect his mail in the years before rural delivery came into being. For the rest of his life he would be known as the Father of Canadian Rural Mail Delivery, but he never let that honour affect his essential humility. By ending one factor behind rural isolation, his efforts had played a role in bringing the country together. In his own way, George Wilcox was a nation-builder, but he preferred to see himself as a servant of the public: "As I look back upon the trail I travelled, not always on the beaten path, there is a satisfaction in the contemplation that during the journey I tarried by the way and done some things that has already made the going easier for thousands and thousands of my fellows, and will, I ween, as the years go by for millions yet unborn."

CALLING RURAL CANADA

f Alexander Graham Bell had had his way, we would all be answering the
telephone with a cheerful *"Hoy hoy"* instead of "Hello." But Bell quickly
lost control of his invention. This was partly his own fault—like many
inventors he was interested in the realization of an idea, not the commercial outcome. And his idea was the possibility of transmitting human
voices by mechanical means. Through the early 1870s he laboured, and by
1874 he had succeeded in transmitting the sound of a musical instrument.
Then, on 10 March 1876, the breakthrough. With his assistant, Thomas
Watson, working in another room of the Bell family home in Brantford,
Ontario, he transmitted the first audible phrase ever sent over metal wires:
"Mr. Watson, come here, I want you." With that peremptory command,
the telephone was born.

Keen to move on to other projects, Bell registered the necessary patents,
and then promptly turned over his rights in the telephone to others. The

National Bell Telephone Company was established in the United States, but to develop the Canadian market, Bell gave 75 percent of his Canadian patents to his father, Melville, a teacher, who conscripted family friend Thomas Henderson, a Baptist minister, to help deliver the miracle of the telephone to Canada. Neither of them knew much about the technology, but they were keen as mustard and appointed enthusiastic agents to help them bring telephony to interested Canadians, either by leasing them the equipment or selling it to them outright, in which case buyers still had to pay monthly fees for line use. Bell and Henderson also knew a public relations opportunity when they saw one. One of their first sets of phones linked the office of Prime Minister Alexander Mackenzie with the residence of Lord Dufferin, the governor general. Mackenzie, a dour Scots stonemason who came to office mainly because Canadians wanted a break from the brilliant but dissolute John A. Macdonald, hated the device. Dufferin didn't particularly care one way or the other, but his wife had taken an interest in the telephone and wanted it kept. Melville Bell shrewdly re-dated Dufferin's rental agreement so that the governor general became the proud owner of the first telephone lease in Canada.

The new technology slowly spread through Canadian cities. In 1878, the Hamilton District Telegraph Company opened the first exchange in Canada, with eight lines and forty telephones, and the following year, Melville sold the Dominion Telegraph Company a five-year licence to operate Bell's system in Canada. But competitors were cropping up, and telephone salesmen—some honest, some not—were criss-crossing the country hawking telephone sets. The environment was quickly becoming an uncongenial one for the elderly teacher and the Baptist minister. In Prince Edward Island, Henderson sold just nine telephones, seven of them to the railway; in New Brunswick, only one customer expressed an interest in Bell's product. Melville decided to sell his Canadian patents, but the asking price of $100,000 was beyond the reach of any local suitors. In the end, the buyer was none other than National Bell—and thus Canadian telephony became owned by Boston interests.

National Bell immediately trolled around for someone to run its Canadian operation and soon settled on an insurance man named Charles Fleetford Sise. The aggressively capitalist grandfather of the radical socialist architect Hazen Sise, who had played a leading role in the Confederation Memorial Program, Charles had a bit of a checkered past: he had commanded a Confederate blockade-runner during the U.S. Civil War and had later acted as private secretary to Jefferson Davis, the president of the short-lived Confederate States of America. In 1880, when there were about six hundred telephones in the country, he came north to Montreal. The Bell Telephone Company of Canada soon had a federal charter, something that happened remarkably quickly—just three months from the bill's introduction in the House of Commons to Royal Assent. Later, when Bell began to use the power that came with its charter, critics would charge that political influence had been at work in the speedy passage of the bill. In reality, few members of Parliament in 1880 thought that the telephone would amount to anything.

In fact it did, and lines came to dominate Canadian cities. At first, the companies either piggybacked them on telegraph poles or negotiated roof privileges—telephone lines were strung over the roofs of houses, with the homeowners receiving free service in exchange. When citizens started to gripe at the number of wires draped over their rooftops, telephone companies ran pole lines along city streets, but this was no better. Streetscapes were soon clogged with poles, some with eight or ten cross-arms, and thick networks of wire running overhead. What was worse, the telephone was clearly not the miracle that early promoters had promised. The first wires were iron, which created a problem known as induction—with the telegraph, telephone, and electrical systems all using the same kind of wire, the interference between lines made it all but impossible to use the telephone at certain times of the day. In some cities in the 1880s, the sound quality and delays for connections led to as many people dropping telephone service as were picking it up.

The problem, as far as Sise was concerned, was competition: too many companies were in the game and they were getting in each other's way. And on principle, Sise didn't like competition. He wanted the field free for his company and was determined to go to any lengths to get it. He began buying up small telephone companies and telephone branches of telegraph companies. Some acquisitions were easy, but when a competitor did refuse to sell, Sise was ruthless. At their first meeting, the company's

Canadian managers decided that the way to deal with opposition was to kill it; if a company wouldn't sell out to Bell, it would be crushed, even if that meant cutting rates and running at a loss. This was the fate of stubborn independent companies in Dundas, Peterborough, and Port Arthur, Ontario. When they refused to sell, Bell simply offered free service to the townspeople; the competing firms soon collapsed, leaving Bell to take over at its normal rates. If all else failed, Bell turned to enforcing its legal patent protection, and not just against rival companies. In January 1881, the company issued warnings that only its service was "entirely FREE FROM RISK OF LITIGATION." Few people doubted that Bell would haul some unfortunate subscriber of a rival company into court as a way to demonstrate the wisdom of signing with Bell.

It was the fate of a small firm in Sherbrooke, Quebec, the Dominion Telephone Company, to become a symbol of what was wrong with Canadian telephony. Established in 1882 by a Mr. Webster, the company did well for a time by offering a rate ($17—a little over $300 in current values—for a home telephone) that was considerably lower than Bell's. Such a situation was intolerable for Bell, which immediately offered free service for the first year of a three-year contract and forced Dominion into bankruptcy. The difference between Dominion and the other companies that Bell had crushed was that Dominion had tried to bring telephone service to the rural districts around Sherbrooke, a concept that hadn't yet occurred to many people in the business. But some were starting to wonder why rural Canadians were being deprived of this most modern of conveniences at a time when country dwellers still made up more than half of the nation's population. In Manitoba, Ontario, and Quebec in 1904, there were fewer than 2000 phones in rural areas, but more than 64,000 in towns and cities. To put it another way, in the cities, there was one telephone for every 22 people; in the countryside, just one for every 1246 people.

The time was ripe for telephones to start moving into Canadian farmhouses. In the first place, once Alexander Graham Bell had solved the problem, it was really quite easy to make a telephone, especially after *Scientific American* published detailed plans of Bell's invention. You could make a decent device out of a cigar box and some piano wire, and a

Quebec jeweller received a patent for a telephone that used a bunch of knitting needles as the core. Such attempts were not always successful—a Victoria newspaper reported a failed attempt to build a set of telephones using copper wire, two spools of thread, some tins and nails, two tooth-powder boxes, and a couple of empty champagne bottles—but plenty of other home-built sets worked as well as anything that could be leased from Bell. Furthermore, it wasn't difficult to put up a telephone line. As an early manual from one equipment supplier put it, "[T]here is really no more trouble in building a telephone line than in building a good wire fence." And in fact, a good fence could serve perfectly well as a telephone line, as the manager of a ranch near Medicine Hat discovered in 1896. He purchased a pair of telephones and placed one in the ranch, the other in the railway station, connecting them via the wire fence that ran along the CPR rail line. To the astonishment of the locals, the device worked perfectly.

This do-it-yourself trend was possible because, despite the threatening advertisements, few people knew or cared about patent laws. Indeed, Bell's cherished patents were soon under attack. Mr. Webster of Sherbrooke launched the first challenge, and through the 1880s and 1890s, the courts gradually whittled away Bell's patent protection. In 1893, when the company's U.S. patents expired, telephone equipment flooded the market. Independent companies didn't even have to deal with Bell anymore.

As a result of the ease with which telephones could be installed, the 1890s saw a mini boom in rural telephony. Many of the early networks were established by doctors or merchants for business reasons. Dr. Alexander Beatty lived in the village of Garden Hill, north of Port Hope, Ontario, but his patients were spread out over the surrounding townships. In an emergency, it could be a full day before a member of the most distant of the families drove to Garden Hill, picked up Dr. Beatty, and delivered him to see the ailing individual. The good doctor was a progressive man, so he decided to take advantage of the most modern technology and start his own telephone company. He purchased a switchboard for the parlour of his home, four telephones to be installed at strategic locations within a 10-mile radius of Garden Hill, and enough wire to connect them all, and the Beatty Telephone System was born. The enterprise was strictly non-profit—Beatty or his wife operated the switchboard, the doctor made any necessary repairs to the board, and the local farmers were encouraged to fix faulty lines themselves. At first the system served only his medical practice, but as time passed, more and more people in the countryside around Garden Hill asked to be hooked up. By the time of Dr. Beatty's death in 1946, it served more than two hundred customers with 100 miles of line, all of it operated by members of his family. In Quebec, Dr. T.J. Demers's rural telephone company was so successful that he eventually gave up his medical practice to devote all his time to the business. He began with a small company and then bought la Compagnie de Téléphone de Bellechasse, which had been languishing since receiving a provincial charter in 1893. Demers quickly built it into a booming system of fifteen hundred customers and 1200 miles of pole line connecting Rimouski, Matane, Montagamy, and Rivière-du-Loup, profitable enough that he soon drew the attention of Bell. When Bellechasse tried to increase its customer base in Lévis, Bell threatened to prosecute the company's customers for patent infringement. Neither Demers nor his customers were frightened, and the Bellechasse continued to operate successfully for years.

In 1884, the North-West Territorial Council, which governed the vast region between Manitoba and British Columbia, built lines out of Saskatoon and Edmonton, and invited farmers along the route to link up; residents had to supply the poles, and the government would supply the wire, insulators, telephones, and labour. Once the lines were in operation, anyone who was connected could use the line for 15 cents per call. Even municipal governments got into the telephone game. In 1900 Neepawa established the first municipal telephone system in Manitoba. Bell threatened to cart away all its equipment in retaliation, but the municipal system had the last laugh. Within a few years it had two hundred customers, while Bell's subscriber list had dwindled to just twelve.

Yet these rural independents served only a fraction of Canadians living outside of the towns and cities; the vast majority of them had no access to telephone service and little hope of getting it in the foreseeable future. The rural question was starting to loom large, and supporters of rural mail delivery often argued that the combination of postal service and the telephone could keep young Canadians from deserting the country for the conveniences of the city. The arguments were both economic and social, as a column in the *Globe* demonstrated: "[R]apid adoption of the telephone in rural districts … tends still further to relieve the isolation, which is the only objectionable feature of country life, and to bring the farmers into more immediate touch with commercial and general affairs … it has a practical and commercial value greater in most instances than its actual cost.… It saves both himself and his help many useless trips to ascertain the condition of the market or to receive or deliver goods. The actual time of men and horses wasted in fruitless errands that could be avoided by a telephone connection is often of more monetary value than the cost of the service.… In the extension of this modern convenience to rural districts the enterprise of telephone corporations has not played a very important part."

Here, the *Globe* had gotten at the crux of the matter. On the matter of rural mail delivery, the federal government had been the bad guy, for dragging its feet and depriving rural dwellers of a service that could dramatically improve their way of life. With telephone service, there was a new villain: the Bell Telephone Company of Canada. It was conspiring to deprive the majority of Canadians of the wonders of modern telephony by refusing to serve rural areas and by doing everything it could to crush those independent companies that tried to do so.

And the company made it quite clear that it had little interest in serving the rural customer. There was no use arguing that the telephone could help end rural isolation, because no one at Bell in those early years accepted that the telephone had a social function. The men who ran the company saw the telephone first and foremost as a business device, which meant that, almost by definition, its use should be confined to the city. The idea of using a telephone as a means of personal contact between distant neighbours was entirely foreign to Bell's ethos at the time. The company did more than simply ignore the telephone's potential as a tool for social interaction; it actively discouraged such use as frivolous and wasteful. "'Visiting' on the phone in order to gossip tied up party lines," declared Sise.

More important, he believed, rural telephony was simply bad business. As Sise later said publicly, the company decided to "give preference to the needs of a larger number rather than to a lot of farmers' lines. There is a much better return from the expenditure of money on that work than there will be from the expenditure of the same money on smaller lines." Privately, Bell officials were even more hard-nosed, actively discouraging the construction of rural lines. In 1904, when new technical specifications for farmers' lines were issued, a regional superintendent said bluntly that it mattered little to Bell for "it is not intended to make a special effort to secure this class of business at present." To critics, this was the real face of Bell: the urban, central Canadian monopoly that was wilfully and callously withholding service from farmers. Despite the fact that the company had been declared a public utility (an amendment to its original charter called Bell's operations "a work for the general advantage of Canada"), Bell had made a business decision not to serve rural Canadians, the majority of the nation's population.

Then in 1905 came a landmark court decision that would cement Bell's character in the minds of its harshest critics. The company's charter gave it the power to erect telephone poles wherever it wanted, on municipal or even private property, without the permission of the property owner, but for years municipalities had tried to get this changed. Finally, a case launched by the City of Toronto made it all the way to the Judicial Committee of the Privy Council, which ruled in Bell's favour. For critics, this was the final insult: the company now appeared untouchable. The only alternative was to try to rein it in through the federal Parliament. By now, the rural lobby had been joined by other groups, which began to talk of telephone regulation or even nationalization. At Bell headquarters in Montreal, those were bad words, and the directors must have glanced around uneasily as the vultures gathered.

First among them was William Findlay Maclean, a loose-cannon Conservative member of Parliament and the editor of the yellow newspaper called the Toronto *World.* "As least loved as any man in public life," according to historian Robert Collins, Maclean hated all forms of government privilege, from free railway passes for MPs to pensions for former cabinet ministers. Maclean had a nose for smelling out corruption, and he was certain he had found it in Bell's cosy relationship with the federal government. He thought it a little suspicious that the railways minister,

A.G. Blair, who consistently opposed any telephone reforms in the Commons and who defended Bell's exclusive arrangements with the railways, was also president of New Brunswick Telephone, which counted the Bell Telephone Company of Canada as one of its major shareholders. No wonder, Maclean mused, that Bell always seemed to get protection from the federal government. Prime Minister Wilfrid Laurier, himself a close friend of many Bell directors, simply responded to the charges by calling Maclean a communist.

Nevertheless, Laurier could not brush off the two hundred municipal governments that presented petitions protesting Bell's power to erect poles wherever it chose. Reluctantly, in March 1905, he established a parliamentary inquiry, known simply as the Telephone Committee, to look into the whole question of telephones, including the extension of service to rural Canada and Bell's treatment of independent companies trying to serve rural customers. The committee chair was to be the postmaster general, William Mulock, an appointment that cheered Bell's critics. In 1903, he had proposed government aid to establish rural telephone cooperatives, a measure that had been killed in cabinet by none other than A.G. Blair. Mulock was known to be sympathetic to the nationalization of the telephone system (he couldn't understand why it was any different from the postal system, which the government had been running for decades), a position that had been influenced by the British telephone expert Francis Dagger. Dagger, the guru of the anti-Bell forces, had immigrated to Canada in 1899 to work for Sise, but quit within a year, disillusioned with Bell's practices. Thereafter, he preached his gospel to anyone who would listen: municipalities should own and operate all telephone exchanges, and the federal government should own all long-distance lines and regulate the entire system.

Mulock, however, was just one member, and Sise was immediately on his way home from a European holiday to organize an intensive lobby of the rest of the committee. Soon, he received the welcome news that six of the fifteen members were "rather friendly" and that two more were "within reach." Bell should have no problem, Sise was told, securing a sympathetic majority on the committee. Still, the evidence seemed to confirm what the rural lobby had argued: that country dwellers were disadvantaged under the current system. One expert testified that rural telephony had been "absolutely neglected and discouraged" because it was less profitable than serving cities. Indeed, of the 96,000 phones then in use in Canada (70,000 of which were owned by Bell), only 2566 could be classified as rural.

Rural lobbyists believed they had mounted a strong and convincing case, but then the unseen hand of Bell began to act. The arm-twisting of committee members had continued, and on 30 May 1905, the federal government announced that Mulock had been called to England mysteriously on government business. His replacement revealed where his own sympathies lay by effusively thanking Bell for hosting the committee at a company reception and opining that they probably couldn't make any recommendations, given the huge mass of evidence submitted. In the end, this was precisely the conclusion the committee wrote when it met for the last time in July 1905. Their report, which might have been a ringing endorsement of the expansion of rural telephony under government ownership, instead consisted of three immense volumes of turgid prose and contradictory evidence from which no conclusions at all could be drawn. Mulock soon resigned from cabinet, pleading ill-health. Journalists wondered in print how someone too ill to sit in the House of Commons could so soon thereafter take a position as a chief justice of the Ontario Supreme Court; they would have been even more suspicious had they known that Mulock would live another forty years, to the ripe old age of one hundred. In fact, few people doubted that political influence had been at work, and privately, Sise himself took credit for the chairman's departure from the scene. And then, in the election that followed, who took Mulock's constituency, and eventually his seat in cabinet? None other than Allen Aylesworth, who had been Bell's legal counsel during the committee hearings. Even by contemporary standards, this was political jobbery at its worst. Critics had long suspected that Bell benefited from friends in high places (in fact, various MPs did receive small retainers from the company, with promises of more if they defended the company in Parliament)—and those suspicions were now validated.

By any measure, the outcome of the 1905 hearings looked like a victory for Bell, but it did change the telephone landscape and eventually forced

Bell to give ground on some fronts and declare unconditional surrender on others. The very fact that the committee had been struck at all convinced the company that it would have to be more forthcoming in connecting independents (but not rivals) to its long-distance lines. Bell also responded with a public relations offensive: a series of advertisements, called Telephone Talks, published in Canada's newspapers. They were aimed at convincing the Canadian public that Bell wasn't so bad after all and that it really was interested in providing service to people in rural areas. "Material inducements are offered to every rural section which may require telephone service," one such ad claimed. "We are ready to encourage and assist any group of farmers who wish to avail themselves of the plan which has been so successful in some parts of the United States [where farmers could build their own systems and connect to Bell for a small monthly fee per subscriber]. We do not wish it to be understood, however, that the above is the only plan upon which we are prepared to furnish service to farmers."

This new, apparently rural-friendly Bell, combined with a resurgence in the lobbying efforts of those who saw the telephone as an antidote to rural isolation, ushered in what might be called the golden age of rural telephony. Bell's monopoly was apparently broken and the telephone liberated from the grip of the central Canadian megalith. For much of its history, Bell controlled most of the telephones in Canada, except for one period: from 1906 to 1921, the majority of telephones were operated by municipal systems, small rural independents, farmers' cooperatives, and private companies. For Bell's harshest critics, those were heady days.

The situation varied across the country. In Ontario, where Bell had a strong presence, the provincial government introduced legislation in 1906 making it easier for rural independents to operate: any group of farmers could establish a company and apply to their local council, which would construct pole lines and levy a charge against the properties that benefited. The result was rapid growth in the number of independents operating in Ontario. By 1910, when the Ontario Railway and Municipal Board— established by the provincial government in 1906 and the precursor to the Ontario Municipal Board—was made responsible for telephone companies, there were some 460 companies, most in small towns and rural areas;

eleven years later, the number of independents in the province peaked at 689. Many of these systems were founded by small, loosely organized groups of farmers who put up their own money to build and operate the system, contributed their own labour to keep construction costs down, and provided poles from their own woodlots. Such systems were never intended to expand beyond the use of founding farmers, but most of them eventually did. Typical was the Southwold and Dunwich Telephone Association in southwestern Ontario, established in 1906 with a single line between Bert Clay's fishing business in Port Talbot and J.O. Lumley's general store in Iona. At first, they couldn't afford poles so they simply strung the telephone line on fence posts and trees. Anyone along the line could become a subscriber, as long as he accepted responsibility for the maintenance of his own section of the line. Four years after its founding, the association reported having two hundred customers; by the early 1920s, three hundred. The Southwold and Dunwich remained in operation until 1964, when it sold its 440 telephones to Bell.

Similar growth occurred in the Maritimes, where Bell exerted varying degrees of stock control over the provincial companies. A manager of the Nova Scotia Telephone Company had told the Telephone Committee that about thirty independent companies were operating in the province but— in a comment that echoed what had been said about rural mail delivery in the region—that locals were tight-fisted when it came to the new technology: "[T]he farmers apparently did not want 'phones or to put it another way, were not prepared to pay for the service." He noted that the company had built 10 miles of line out from Pictou to a prosperous farming district and offered phones at $15 a year; even at that low price, they had great difficulty getting subscribers, and in one case found a group of farmers sharing one phone, each of them paying $1. In New Brunswick, after the opposition leader made the extension of rural telephone service an election issue, New Brunswick Telephone announced plans to encourage farmers to connect: if they built their own pole lines and bought their own telephones, they would then be connected to the company's lines. This was cheaper than the company building new rural lines itself and, in addition, relieved the pressure to serve rural areas. The Telephone Company of Prince Edward Island also faced demands for expansion that, because of its precarious financial state, it could not afford to meet. The company dealt with these requests the same way it had been doing since the 1890s: by allowing locals to build their own systems and connect to the long-distance lines, in exchange for an annual fee. The upshot was a proliferation of firms such as the Sturgeon Rural Telephone Company (1922), with two customers, and the Southern Rural Telephone Company (1924), with six. By the end of the 1920s, fifty-six of these small companies were serving 1394 rural customers, who used nearly one-third of all telephones on the Island.

In Quebec, Sise and other Bell officials had long argued that the conservative francophone farmer was opposed to the expansion of telephone networks—a comment that said more about cultural stereotypes than the attitude of French Canada. In fact, there was more independent telephone activity in Bell's home province than the company wanted to admit. In 1904, the province's sixteen independent companies supplied nearly a quarter of Quebec's telephones, and in the interwar period, there were nearly two hundred independents, most serving rural areas. Clearly, the Quebec farmer wasn't as conservative as Bell imagined.

The real changes, however, took place on the Prairies, a region that Bell had targeted as a potentially lucrative market. Sise had great plans, and in the 1880s and 1890s the company engaged in an aggressive program to build exchanges in the growing towns of Manitoba and the North-West Territories. Only in Edmonton was Bell beaten out by an independent, and in 1889 Sise could report that the company was making good progress in the West and that he was hopeful of further growth. In fact it was not to be, and ironically, Bell itself was partly responsible for the frustration of Sise's hopes. The company demonstrated a remarkable ability to offend western Canadians. The problem may have started in the 1880s, when a Bell agent suggested that it would be years before Edmonton amounted to anything. If there was one way to offend Westerners, it was for an Easterner to tell them their city was nothing more than a backwater. Then, in 1892 Bell applied to the territorial legislature to have its charter enacted there. The government of Manitoba had agreed to this a decade earlier, but after watching the wrangles going on in central Canadian cities over pole privileges, the North-West Territories council fought the provision that Bell could run a pole line on any street, with or without a municipality's permission. Opposition was so strong that the bill died, but in 1903 Bell again gave notice that it wanted an ordinance from the territorial legislature allowing it to exercise the "powers and privileges" of its charter. Here was another misstep—the words *powers and privileges,* particularly when used by a central Canadian corporation, were to a Westerner like a red flag to a bull. Even worse was the fact that the bill was introduced in the legislature by R.B. Bennett, who was identified with the CPR and other hated eastern monopolies. Any way you looked at it, Bennett's bill was doomed. His other experience with the telephone around the same time was just as unhappy. He owned one of the first cars in Calgary, but crashed it into a telephone pole and never drove again.

Bell remained blithely undaunted by these setbacks and was determined to continue expanding in the West. If people were suspicious of its intentions, then the company would have to work twice as hard to win their affections. And Bell did expand dramatically, bringing telephone service to many rural areas. A new long-distance line was built to connect Edmonton and Calgary, as was a loop line running east from Lethbridge to bring those farming areas into service. The Calgary and Lethbridge city services were modernized, and so was the system in Winnipeg. In all, the number of Bell telephones in western Canada between 1905 and 1907 increased by 157 percent, a growth rate higher than anywhere else in the country. Such growth represented a significant expenditure, especially since each telephone required about $150 in capital investment.

All this should have been enough to convince skeptical Westerners but it wasn't, for Bell still couldn't resist treating them like petulant children in need of adult supervision. When the company wrote to the town of Wetaskiwin, saying that it was about to establish a telephone system there, the town council replied, Don't bother—we already have a municipal system that serves our purposes quite well. Bell's response was not to congratulate them on their enterprise and bow out gracefully, but to restate the powers of its federal charter and inform the town that it would be installing a system whether the council wanted it or not. The result of episodes like this was that Bell's construction projects drew nothing but scorn. The modernization of urban exchanges only moved the Calgary

Herald to wonder if Bell was paying enough taxes to the municipalities; the loop line from Lethbridge was greeted with the sour observation that it had taken far too long; and the Wetaskiwin fiasco caused the Red Deer *Advocate* to complain about the avarice Bell exhibited in ignoring the will of municipalities. The bottom line, as C.W. Peterson, secretary of the Calgary Board of Trade, wrote in May 1904, was that the rural West was being shafted by the central Canadian monopoly: "The telephone I believe is the most useful of the many modern devices for rendering farming easy and profitable ... in every instance we have been blocked by the Bell people. That we are being damaged, directly and seriously by the attitude of the Bell Company, I am certain."

Bell could hardly have missed the signs that its western fortunes were sagging. When Sise visited Edmonton in 1904 to investigate the possibility of buying the municipal system, he was greeted with the headline "Killing Competition Object of Bell Officials." He probably also saw a copy of a pamphlet issued by the Telephone Committee of the Union of Manitoba Municipalities, provocatively entitled "Shall the People Own Their Own Telephones or Shall They Contribute to the Octopus?" There was no doubt about it—the rumblings over government ownership of the telephone system were spreading through Bell's promised land.

Such rumblings were felt first in Manitoba, where rural municipal systems complained that they were being prevented from connecting to Bell's long-distance lines. In January 1905, a government committee recommended looking into the possibility of public ownership of telephone systems. Then came the disappointment over the conclusions of the Telephone Committee in Ottawa. Anyone who had doubted Bell's political influence, and the ease with which the company wielded it, could have no doubts anymore, and the pressure grew for governments to step in and curb Bell's unbridled power. In November 1905, the premier of Manitoba made a public commitment to government ownership of long-distance lines and municipal ownership of exchanges, with telephone service provided at cost. The new government of Alberta acted quickly too, earmarking a chunk of its first budget for preliminary work in establishing a government telephone system, starting with an experimental Calgary–Banff line.

Again Bell responded aggressively, hoping to convince western governments of its goodwill. In Manitoba, it offered to provide Bell equipment to independents and farmers' cooperatives where it wasn't economical for the company to operate and to expand long-distance lines to under-serviced rural areas. Alberta got a new express line between Edmonton and Calgary and a new line from Calgary to the rural district south of the city. But once again the company made a tactical error. When the provincial government rebuffed its offer to divide up the Alberta market, Bell announced in a fit of pique that it would go ahead with plans to build a competing system in Edmonton. The newspapers raged that this was a declaration of war. One cabinet minister brought up Bell's charter again, calling it "the most pernicious and iniquitous piece of legislation that has ever been perpetrated upon people claiming to be free." For Sise and his board of directors, the day of reckoning was at hand, and it came in February 1906.

On the 14th of that month, the Alberta government announced that it would take over the entire telephone system in the province, owning all long-distance lines and municipal exchanges and building rural lines wherever the farmers wanted them (Manitoba introduced a similar bill two weeks later). It was left to John T. Moore, the member for Red Deer, to add the rhetorical flourishes. Referring to it as Emancipation Day, he took up the call of the rural lobby and observed that "the policy will go farther to dispel the feeling of isolation and loneliness peculiar to the life of the frontier." Warming to the topic, he threw all restraint to the wind. It was Valentine's Day, he noted, and the announcement was a "valentine to the beloved people of Alberta." From love he quickly turned to a war metaphor: Charles Fleetford Sise "may be a Napoleon but unfortunately Alberta has a Wellington and today the Bell Telephone Company meets its Waterloo." In sum, Moore predicted, a new day had dawned for Albertans: "[L]ife in Alberta will be worth living insofar as the telephone will accomplish that purpose.... Many instances of insanity and even suicide might have been averted if the tension of solitude had been broken by messages of cheer and comradeship.... [W]e hail the advent of this new era, which will witness ever increasing thousands of our people being bound together by cords of copper and steel."

Alberta and Manitoba both took the leap the same month, but then their paths temporarily diverged. In Manitoba, with an election in the offing, the government's new powers sat idle. The ruling Conservatives and opposition Liberals searched for an election issue that was politically popular but relatively safe, and both fastened on the telephone: the government campaigned on its act, while the Liberals stumped a plan that would bring the entire system, phones, exchanges, wires, poles, and all, under the direct control of the province. What was common to the two campaigns, though, was the amount of Bell-bashing, with both sides implying that Manitobans were "paying tribute, in the form of exorbitant charges, to the limitless greed of a conscienceless octopus."

In truth, both sides acted shamelessly, politicizing the issue with misleading and alarmist predictions. Government members made outrageous promises that telephones rates would be half Bell's or less, while the so-called expert they hired maintained that, under the government's plan, every farmer in Manitoba would have a telephone for $1 a month. (After the election, more than a few MPs and at least one cabinet minister admitted that they didn't know anything about telephones, and that they had as good as lied to the voters.) There was a minor setback in December 1906 when a municipal plebiscite revealed that less than half of the province's municipalities actually *wanted* to own and operate telephone exchanges, but the government blundered on regardless. When they won the provincial election of 1907, the Conservatives chose to interpret the results as a vindication of their telephone policy. The problem was with those municipalities, 67 out of 122, that had no interest in building their own exchanges. Faced with their reluctance, the government had no option but to adopt the opposition's platform: the Manitoba system would be entirely government-run after all.

Alberta, in contrast, wasted little time in getting its system up and running. The provincial government first offered to buy Bell's entire operation, but when that offer was rejected, it created Alberta Government Telephones (AGT) and immediately started to make good on its promise of building rural lines and offering rates that were 30 percent lower than Bell's. Again, the widespread loathing of Bell became clear. When Bell started to build rural lines, it got nothing but criticism; when AGT did it, the newspapers could barely contain their glee. The Lethbridge *Herald* gushed that "every farmer in Alberta will be in a position to possess a phone in his home.... [T]ry to find a case in Alberta where the Bell people have been interested enough to erect lines along the concession roads in order that the men who are the bone and sinew of this province could be provided with one of the great advantages of modern times," while the *Albertan* expressed confidence that rural depopulation would come to an end: "[E]very successful farmer in the province will be able to possess a telephone that will help to keep the boy on the farm. He won't need to be jealous of his city friends."

Sise was starting to see the writing on the wall. All around him, his hard-won western gains were being eaten away. The once-profitable system in Red Deer was down to just ten customers, while the AGT system there had topped two hundred. In Manitoba, the provincial government had announced that it was building an exchange in Winnipeg to compete with the Bell system there. Sise thought he might be able to deal with the government in Edmonton, but realized that the situation in Manitoba had become too politicized and that there was little hope of saving the company's operations there. He concluded that he may as well strike a deal and at least get some money out of the province. On 30 December 1907, Bell reached an agreement with the Manitoba government to sell its system (which by then was up to fourteen thousand subscribers and 2500 miles of pole line) in the province for about $3.3 million, a transaction that immediately doubled the provincial debt and committed Manitoba to unknown costs in the future. In January 1908, the Alberta government began negotiations that concluded when Bell agreed to sell its system for around $675,000. Then, in May 1909, the Saskatchewan government bought Bell's assets in the province for $369,000. Sise's great dream of a western empire had blown away like prairie dust.

In acquiring the Bell system in Manitoba, Premier Rodmond Roblin proudly announced that "whatever profit there is in the operation of the telephone system from this time on will belong to the people of Manitoba rather than to a private company." Stirring words, but successive governments in each of the three provinces would ultimately discover that there would be no profits on rural telephones, only ever-growing operating deficits.

In Manitoba, despite promises that the system would be run on sound business lines, the Manitoba Telephone Commission (MTC) immediately became an irresistible source of patronage and influence-peddling. Because the Conservative government relied on rural votes, it forced MTC to extend rural lines even where there wasn't demand; wherever there was a political opponent to be placated or friend to be won, MTC put up unnecessary and unprofitable rural lines, built exchanges, or extended free services. One MP forced the commission to buy a huge number of poles from a constituent, despite the fact that the MTC already had a surplus of poles. Nevertheless they were eventually put to good use. In 1910, the Manitoba *Free Press* reported that the government had been "fishing for votes with telephone poles." Just before the provincial election, railway cars full of telephone poles were unloaded at Woodbridge, and it was intimated that the area would be connected right after the election; local labourers were even hired to take poles out to the proposed route of the line. The electors of the district duly voted for the government candidate, and then two weeks later, teams of workmen came and took all the poles back to Winnipeg.

And then there was the question of rates. Far from bringing the dollar-a-month telephone to Manitoba farmers, the MTC was forced to raise rates to avoid financial disaster, only lowering them in 1909 under pressure from the legislature. The government continued to claim that the commission was running a surplus, but their accounting practices were tailored to ensure that the books always looked good. After three years, the number of telephones in the province had more than doubled, to nearly 30,000, including more than 7000 in rural areas, but in 1911, the government finally had to admit that something was amiss with MTC. Estimates suggested that, far from generating annual surpluses, the commission had run up a debt of some $300,000, largely because line construction was costing as much as 30 percent more per mile than it should. Local suppliers of food, accommodation, horses, and equipment, it seemed, regarded the arrival of an MTC construction crew as a licence to jack up their rates, confident that the government would pay their bills rather than pick a fight with a rural voter. In fact, everything about the system continued to grow: the phone rates went up (rising by over 150 percent by August 1912); the network expanded to triple the size it had been when the government took over; and, most important, the deficit ballooned, totalling some $650,000 for the MTC's first seven years in business. Something had to give, and ultimately it was the government. Beset not only by the telephone debacle but also by the chaos surrounding the construction of the provincial legislature, Roblin's Conservative government opted to resign in May 1915.

The situation was hardly better in Alberta. As soon as the province took over the system on 1 May 1908, the public works minister, W.H. Cushing, immediately reduced rates by about 8 percent and set out to double the size of the rural system by the end of the following year. AGT's policy was simple: it would connect any farmer in the province, so long as that connection didn't involve the construction of too much new pole line. AGT built 1500 miles of line in 1911, and in 1912 nearly doubled the progress shown in all previous years, increasing wire mileage by 96 percent and the number of customers by 88 percent. The system would double in size again by 1914, and by 1924, it was nearly five times larger than in 1912.

As in Manitoba, though, all was not right. The growth rate seemed too good to be true, and indeed it was. Soon, the opposition began turning up embarrassing details about the work of AGT. The line to the village of Pibroch had cost $1400 to build, but generated just 40 cents a month in revenue. In 1913 (an election year) government bought 125,000 poles, but 47,000 remained on hand, fuelling speculation that it too had been using telephone poles to fish for votes. Nor could this rampant growth be sustained forever, especially since AGT was putting no money aside for depreciation. Like many telephone systems of the period, the company lived in a fantasy world in which a telephone line, once constructed, worked perfectly forever. A high-priced consultant from Chicago told the government that it had to raise its rates, stop expanding rural lines on demand, and create a reserve fund for repairs and replacement of the system. Given the rhetoric that had come to surround rural telephony— cheap phones for farmers—the first two were non-starters, but at least the government agreed to put aside some money for repairs.

It took the First World War to slow AGT's expansion. By 1916, demand had collapsed, and the government built only 10 miles of rural pole line that year, just 3 miles the next year. The government would, however, allow farmer-built lines to connect to government lines if they met certain standards. This policy led to a boom in what were called mutual telephone companies (soon there were as many as sixty), like the Fairview Mutual at Dunvegan, in Peace River country. The Fairview offered its customers an unusual service: each morning, they would be alerted by nine short rings and an operator would read the latest war bulletins.

After the war, with whispers of wrongdoing still emanating from the opposition, the government finally agreed to bring in outside experts to examine the operations of AGT. Their conclusion was that the system offered good service and that its equipment was well constructed, admirably standardized, and well maintained. It was, after all, the largest rural system in North America, with 20,000 miles of line and twenty thousand customers, all maintained by a mere twenty-five men. However, they couldn't offer a clean bill of health because of AGT's appalling accounting practices, which were putting the utility on a collision course with financial ruin. One of the consultants likened the company to an aircraft instrument panel with nothing but a fuel gauge: the pilot had no way of knowing whether he was spinning, upside down, or about to crash. This, they warned, was the future facing AGT. It might not happen tomorrow or next week or next month, but sooner or later it was inevitable that the utility would crash.

Their prescription left a bitter taste in the mouth of the government: rural revenues would have to increase by a staggering 157 percent if the system were to survive. The provincial government was certainly not going to punish rural voters for mistakes made by the previous administration, but it did agree to raise rural rates by about 30 percent, hiking the charges across the system at the same time to cover what they knew would be a perpetual shortfall in the rural sector. Back in Montreal, Sise may well have felt satisfied that he had been proven right.

The housecleaning was soon to get more intense. In 1921, the United Farmers of Alberta swept to power with a message of zealous reformism and progressivism. And Verner Smith, the new minister in charge of AGT, started hacking away at the deadwood with a vengeance. He was astonished to find that an AGT official had put his car, which he had named "Charlotte" for accounting purposes, on the company payroll and was collecting an extra $100 a month on behalf of Charlotte Ford. He also discovered that one of the Liberals' last acts in power was to embark on an orgy of telephone-pole buying, scooping 400,000 poles from constituents and party supporters, enough to last the utility for a generation. He immediately started selling them off to bring in much-needed cash, and for years, AGT poles could be found in the strangest places: carrying lines in Saskatchewan and throughout the U.S. Midwest; in mines in British Columbia, where they were used as pit props and railway ties; as sleepers in the Edmonton street railway; and even propping up the fences in the buffalo compounds at Elk Island and Wainwright national parks.

Once they got into power and had a look at the books, the UFA's long-time election promise of an expanded rural telephone network at low rates had to be jettisoned. Rates started to climb, but any gains the utility made were wiped out by the brutal winter of 1924–25. Freezing rain coated wires with so much ice that they were as thick as a person's arm; hundreds of poles collapsed under the extra weight. When it wasn't the sleet it was the plunging temperatures, which caused the wires to snap in hundreds of places as they contracted in the cold. Damage was estimated at $140,000, or one-third of the utility's entire reserve fund.

That spring, Verner Smith had some hard decisions to make. Telephone rates in the province remained low (they were 32 percent higher in Manitoba, 95 percent higher in Saskatchewan), but he simply couldn't raise them to the point where the rural system would be self-supporting. Ironically, AGT was saved by the Depression. In 1929, the system had 62,000 telephones, nearly a third of them in rural areas, but by the end of 1933 was down to under 40,000. Its own rural revenues were vanishing even more quickly than farmers' profits, but when AGT looked at how the province's eighty-nine mutual telephone companies were doing, it got a shock. They were actually holding their customers, and for one simple reason: their rates were lower because their standards were lower.

Primary-school scribblers instead of heavy hardcover ledgers, meetings in a farmer's kitchen instead of an opulent boardroom, no generous salaries for directors, and a mend-and-make-do maintenance policy. When an AGT pole rotted, the utility had to send a work crew out to replace it with a brand-new pole; when one of the mutual's poles rotted, someone simply lashed the telephone wire to the nearest fence post and service carried on.

Quickly running out of room to manoeuvre, AGT made a decision: the entire rural system would be sold off at 5 percent of book value, to any existing mutual or to any group of locals that wanted to start up a mutual. Of course, AGT couldn't admit that the decision had been taken solely for financial reasons. Instead, the government rationalized by arguing that better roads, more travel, and the radio had all but eliminated rural isolation, making telephones "little more than a social convenience." This was partly true, but also more politically palatable than saying that the United Farmers of Alberta couldn't afford to provide telephone service to farmers anymore.

The first of the new mutuals took over on 1 April 1933, twenty-five years after Bell had been banished from the province. New companies cropped up like prairie roses, with names that were just as colourful: The Passchendaele Mutual (honouring one of the bloodiest battles of the First World War), The New Deal, The Quints (to recognize Canada's newest sweethearts, the Dionne quintuplets), The Hammer, The Gilt Edge. All of them bought their equipment for next to nothing—the Sunset Mutual Telephone Company purchased a system worth $10,683.33 for only $425—and most of them immediately prospered. The Sunset more than doubled its customer base; others more than tripled their subscribers. By the end of 1936, there were some six hundred mutuals in the province, and AGT was all but out of the rural telephone business. Ironically, it was this withdrawal that saved rural telephony in Alberta. Under AGT, the number of rural telephones had dropped below 8000; by the end of 1936, it was back up to 14,500.

After selling off operations in Manitoba and Alberta, Bell rid itself of its Saskatchewan plant as little more than an afterthought. In any case, Saskatchewan was the smallest of the three, with only 3250 telephones, and there was little sense in retaining it between the two government-owned systems. In the end, Saskatchewan made all the right decisions in putting together its rural system. Premier Walter Scott confided to a colleague in Edmonton that it was suicide to build rural lines on demand the way AGT was doing and opted instead for a more cooperative system. In 1908, on the recommendation of Francis Dagger, the government passed legislation allowing rural residents to form cooperatives to provide phone service; the government's role would be confined to offering free poles and technical service, owning large municipal exchanges, and retaining responsibility for all long-distance lines. The following year, the Department of Railways, Telegraphs, and Telephones acquired Bell's assets in the province and soon bought five other local systems. These acquisitions were all careful and prudent, and they helped the system expand almost as fast as Alberta's but at a fraction of the cost. In three years, the system grew from 20 exchanges to 93, and the number of customers rose to nearly fifteen thousand. By 1912, there were 337 rural companies, 5 municipal systems, and 15 independents built by private enterprise. Typical of the new firms was the Benson Rural Telephone Company (1912), run by farmer shareholders, each of whom bought five shares at $25 a share. A year later, it had 43 miles of pole and forty-one telephones. It never got much bigger—peaking in 1915 with forty-nine subscribers—but Benson Rural served the district well and faithfully for many years.

Unlike in Alberta, the expansion of the Saskatchewan system didn't slow down during the war. In the 1917–18 fiscal year, when AGT had all but stopped adding to its rural plant, Saskatchewan added 204 new rural systems, 11,000 more pole miles, and 11,614 new subscribers. By 1920, it had more miles of pole line than any other province, and only Ontario and Quebec had more telephone subscribers. By 1927, Saskatchewan's 1198 small rural telephone companies represented almost half of the national total. Not that there weren't growing pains—a post-war audit found that the company's accounting practices were just as bad as anyone else's, but because of the efficient way in which the system operated, the controversy never amounted to much. Thus for most of the century, the Saskatchewan Telephone Company remained the only unregulated system in Canada.

CONTROVERSIES ASIDE, the rural lobbyists had done their work well. In a couple of decades, rural Canada had gone from a few scattered sets to one-third of farms connected. This was nothing like the level of penetration that existed in Canada's cities, but given the physical obstacles involved it was a remarkable achievement.

The construction of a rural telephone system began with the construction gangs. By the 1920s, the erection of telephone lines had become routine, a far cry from the situation in May 1881, when the first line between Hamilton and Toronto was put up at a rate of three-quarters of a mile per day. At that time, there were no specialized tools and the only way to deal with hard ground was to blast a hole for the pole. The instruction manual told workmen to cover the charge with a boulder, but the first time they tried it, near the village of Waterdown, the boulder rocketed into the air and came down on a farmer's prize sow. The foreman found himself with the unexpected expense of paying for the farmer's loss.

AGT, when in its expansionary mood, built lines using gangs of specialized workers. First, a district was surveyed and the pole lines laid out. Then, the hole-digging crew went in; they got 50 cents for a 5-foot-deep hole, plus 5 cents for every extra foot. Once all the holes were dug, the five-man pole crew went through and sunk the poles, each man getting 5 cents a pole. They were accompanied by the liner, who made sure all the poles were lined up true; the anchorman, who got $5 to set the anchors; and the roofer, who was paid 10 cents for sawing a point on the top of each pole. Next came the wire gang, which set all cross-arms for a quarter apiece, strung all the wires, installed the telephones, and put the lines into service. They worked at a terrific pace; the record at the time was set near Provost, Alberta: 114 miles of pole in fourteen working days.

Once in service, the line still had to be maintained. The South Flaxcombe Telephone Company in Saskatchewan paid its repairman 40 cents an hour plus $1 a day for his horse to keep the telephones working. He rode around the district with his safety belt and climbing spurs, a roll of wire tied to the saddle, and a bag of tools hanging from the horn. Perhaps his most frequent job was to replace the glass insulators that carried the wires, for they proved irresistible to a man armed with a rifle or a boy armed with a rock. He also had to change people's batteries (the common battery system, which eliminated the need for each phone to have its own battery, came to Canada in 1900 but took much longer to get to rural districts) and replace the receiver caps, which often became damaged when people realized they came in handy as cookie cutters or teething rings.

The image of a rattled parent using part of the telephone as a teething ring makes us realize what a novelty was the telephone. Rural mail delivery was simply an improvement on a service that already existed; a device that allowed you to talk to a neighbour who might be miles away was a new-fangled contraption of which many older Canadians wanted no part. Of course, the telephone had at one time been new to all Canadians, but certain stories, true or not, tended to attach themselves to the supposedly backward country dweller. One Saskatchewan farm girl remembered an old fellow who was terrified by the box on the wall. He had never wanted one in the house in the first place, but the family insisted. Invariably, when it rang, he would quickly back away from the apparatus, staring in terror at the disembodied voice coming from the handset. And there was the one about the elderly farmer who insisted that a kink in the line would cause the call to turn right around and go back to where it came from. Another supposedly hung bags of camphor on the receiver cord when talking to an adjacent farm that was under quarantine, in the belief that germs could be passed along the lines. This recalls an ugly episode during the Montreal smallpox epidemic of 1884, when an angry mob surrounded the Bell building, intent on torching it because they believed the disease was being spread via the company's lines.

Even people who were excited about getting a telephone had to be taught how to use it, so companies typically distributed rules of etiquette to their customers. At an early meeting, the North Flaxcombe Rural Telephone Company in Saskatchewan established its code of conduct: anyone who refused to stop talking after five minutes was fined 25 cents; business calls had priority over social calls (a rule that would have warmed the cockles of Charles Sise's heart); the use of profane language could draw a $5 fine, which had to be paid before the person could use the phone again; and there was to be *no* listening in, or "rubbering."

Rubbering was the distinguishing feature of the rural telephone world, thanks to the party lines that the companies used. With the party-line system, a number of telephones were connected to a single line. When the operator directed a call, the telephone rang in the house of everyone who shared that line. One long ring meant that everyone should pick up the telephone, to be informed of some local emergency or upcoming event. If you heard your distinctive ring—a typical telephone number might be 10r15, which meant that you were on line 10 and your signal was one long ring followed by five short rings—you knew the call was for you. But any other curious person on the same line could pick up her receiver as well and eavesdrop, or rubber, on your call. Nowadays, most people would regard this as an intolerable invasion of privacy, and the party-line system did have its drawbacks. Alberta tried to keep the number of subscribers on each line to fifteen, but some lines had more than twenty telephones connected, a practice that meant, as one farmer wrote to the Edmonton *Journal,* "the ringing is going on night and day to such an extent that a telephone is a torture, not a convenience." It was also hard to sort out your own ring from the dozen others on the line. "A typical number," wrote the same farmer, "is one long three short one long two long and three short," a combination that demanded a good deal of concentration if you were to hear it correctly. And when one person was on the line, no one else could use it, which could be a real annoyance if people ignored the five-minute call limit. One Alberta farmer recalled trying to get two neighbours off the party line so that he could make an emergency call. Finally, in desperation, he picked up his receiver and said forcefully, "Mrs. Wishart, I smell your bed burning." Immediately, "there was a screech on the other end and everybody hung up and got off the line."

People were more bothered by the practical inconveniences of the party-line system, however, than by concerns over privacy. Rubbering was a kind of meeting over the telephone rather than an invasion of privacy. It was an early version of the conference call that allowed half a dozen neighbours to exchange advice, and interjections were not always unwelcome. Dr. Beatty was known to spend his idle hours listening in on his neighbours' calls; far from resenting his intrusion, many came to appreciate his sage, if occasionally unexpected, advice. As one possibly tall tale went, two farmers were negotiating a sale over the party line. "John, 26 cents a pound is my final offer," declared one farmer. "Wellington, I'll have to think about it" came the reply. In the brief pause that followed, a third voice piped in: "Take the offer, John, you can't beat the price."

The party-line system was part of what made the telephone so important in reducing rural isolation, particularly for farm women. In an area where her closest neighbours could be spread over a dozen square miles, a farm wife couldn't often drop her chores for an hour's walk to a friend's house for coffee and conversation. She could, however, pick up the phone and spend a few minutes chatting as a welcome respite from the drudgery of farm life. The rural telephone lobby may have been overstating the case when it claimed that extending service would prevent suicides on the farm, but travel writer Thomas Wilby, who saw his share of rural isolation while driving across Canada in 1912, was closer to the mark when he called the telephone "the safety-valve of Prairie life."

MOST OF THE NEARLY 2400 small local telephone companies set up to serve rural Canada have long since disappeared. In 1975, of the nearly 700 independents that had once served half of Ontario's rural population, just 40 remained; the rest had been sold or merged. Some fell victim to demands for regulation. When the Ontario government required rural companies to incorporate, many decided to sell out or merge with other systems rather than face the legal costs and hassles of becoming a corporation. Outside of Alberta, where the number of independents grew in the 1930s, the Depression killed a few more—in July 1932 telephone companies in British Columbia were losing an average of forty customers a day— as did the Second World War, which made it hard for small companies to get the material and skilled workers to maintain their systems. And then there were natural disasters. A heavy winter storm could deposit up to seven tons of ice on each span of wire, bringing down hundreds of poles and putting an entire system out of operation in a matter of hours. The need to rebuild after a storm was often the last straw for a small independent, particularly if it already had been wrestling with the costs of much-needed upgrades to the system. For it was modernization, especially the move to direct-dial service (as opposed to the old method, in which the operator connected the call), that finally killed the small rural telephone company. Many cooperatives had never put aside much in the way of a reserve, and the costs of improving were often far higher than the total value of the system. Simply put, it was easier and cheaper to sell out than to upgrade.

As much as it probably hurt to admit this, the times had changed, and a small farmers' cooperative telephone company was becoming a thing of the past. A wire fence couldn't carry dial service, let alone the touch-tone line or dial-up internet access that was to come. A single repairman on horseback couldn't serve hundreds of customers. And a cooperative couldn't handle the costs of upgrading. Facing a bill of $500,000 to bury its lines as a prudent safeguard against storm damage, the Kindersley Rural Telephone Company had two options: try to raise the money itself or sell out to the government system, which in 1968 had changed its name to SaskTel. For the pragmatic farmers whose grandfathers had started the company, there was only one answer, and in 1977 Kindersley Rural turned over its assets to SaskTel. It wasn't the only rural to do so. In 1982, SaskTel wound up a program that saw some seven hundred rural telephone companies voluntarily assimilated into the provincial system.

In the decades after the Second World War, the remaining holes in the rural telephone network were filled by big utilities rather than by small independents. In Alberta, the government decided that the province's telephone system was not adequate for a wealthy, upwardly mobile province. Reluctantly, AGT got back into the rural telephone business and embarked on a policy to put a telephone in every farm, which meant taking over the mutuals, although none would be expropriated, and entering into another ambitious construction program. This time, however, AGT decided to bury the telephone lines as they built, a process that was much quicker and more efficient than the old-fashioned method. During the great boom period of the early twentieth century, AGT crews had put up 20,000 miles of pole line during a ten-year period; by the 1960s, crews were able to bury 64,000 miles of telephone cable in a ten-year period. Farmers found that their telephones were connected, quite literally, overnight. On the evening of 26 July 1968, in the area around Drayton Valley, AGT had 60 farm telephones; when the residents awoke the next morning, 406 telephones were in operation. What happened in Drayton Valley happened across Alberta, and by 1975, the government had finally more than filled all the gaps in the rural system—there were 65,000 farms, and 69,000 rural telephones.

The changes would reshape the Canadian landscape. Thomas Wilby and Jack Haney had used telephone poles to help them navigate across the prairies in 1912, but through the 1960s and 1970s the old lines continued to be pulled down. When Kindersley's lines were buried and the old poles removed, it represented the end of an era. One local regarded the new prairies with a hint of sadness: "Gone were those symbols which spelled the end to pioneer isolation; gone was the dimly-seen lifeline which saved the lives of people who were caught far from home in the fierce storms of winter; gone were the favorite perches of generations of sharp-eyed prairie hawks and owls." When microwave towers started replacing other pole lines, the step certainly represented progress, yet it seems unlikely that a microwave tower will ever inspire the kind of poetry drawn forth by the old junction pole:

> *Ghost-like it stands, in the pale half-light,*
> *Pathetic, mute, and alone,*
> *Ugly and warped, it's tamarack wood,*
> *Weathered hard as a stone;*
> *But it seems to embody the duty it serves,*
> *With a dauntless strength of its own.*

Now that the poles are gone, it's easy to forget the vital role that the small rural independents and the lines they maintained played in the development of Canadian telephony. When the big corporations or the provincial governments either couldn't or wouldn't serve thousands of rural Canadians, cooperatives and mutuals blossomed across Canada to meet the need. Their equipment may have been outdated and their maintenance procedures often left something to be desired, but they were responsible for connecting a whole generation of Canadians, and they kept them connected until the pressure on corporations and governments became impossible to resist. And even if, in many places, the original infrastructure no longer exists, the system upon which it was grafted continues to serve Canadians. Like landing fields along the trans-Canada airway, many rural telephone lines have disappeared, but the system they helped build remains.

SWITCHES CONTROL EVERYTHING BUT THE CHILDREN

Electrify everything that could possibly be electrified—that was the mantra of urban Canada in the late nineteenth century, when cheap electricity became a reality. Streetlights were popular; in fact for the first few years, urban newspapers were known to print daily reports on how bright the streetlights had been the night before. And as the hydro movement stormed through Canadian cities, it brought with it every form of electrical appliance that the truly modern household deserved, from vacuum cleaners and ranges to irons and toasters. Public transit was electrified, the rich could install electric elevators in their homes, and hydro made possible a revolution in entertainment with the coming of the moving picture palace. Before long, cities were ablaze with brightly lit store windows, automobile headlights, electric street lamps, and illuminated signs.

Of course, there were no electric streetcars or cinemas in rural Canada, but hydro did have one characteristic that the mail and the telephone did not: it was something you could provide for yourself. Getting a telephone meant hooking up to an existing system, but it was possible to electrify a farm without help from anyone. Within certain limits, every farmer could become a power supplier. All it took was a small gasoline engine and an electric generator, both of which became available in the early twentieth century. The generator was belted to the engine to produce energy for immediate use, or to be stored in batteries for later. When larger engines and generators became available, groups of farmers could pool their resources and buy a combination to share for heavy work, like filling a silo or threshing grain. Around the same time, the Delco "lighting plant" came to Canada; an engine and generator together, it eliminated the troublesome task of hooking up and unhooking the two. Within a few years, the plants were available in automatic models: the engine would start up when the batteries were low and then shut off when they were fully charged.

If farmers realized the possibilities of supplying their own power, so too did the owners of small water-powered saw, flour, or planing mills. It was simple to hook a belt to the waterwheel and connect it to an electric generator. Of course, the business of the mill came first, and during working hours the waterwheel powered the saws and planers, but after hours, the mill owner could distribute hydro to whoever wanted it: the belt was moved to the generator to provide power for local customers. Typically, electricity was available from six o'clock to midnight, although many mills also turned on the hydro on Monday mornings, the traditional time to do the washing, and might even be persuaded to power up for special events. One was even generous enough to turn on the juice for an hour each day at lunchtime, so that people could listen to the news on their radios. For most rural people, this kind of hydro was quite sufficient. They owned few appliances, so there was little hardship in being without power during the day. Some balked at the cost, though: the people of Breadalbane, PEI, which acquired hydro in 1917 when a mill converted, thought the monthly rate of $1.50 was nothing short of extortion for six hours' worth of electricity a day.

And it didn't take long for rural Canadians to realize other problems in these sources of hydro. Gasoline-powered generators were fine for lighting and small appliances, but their limitations became clear as soon as the farmer tried to operate a new machine that was a bit too powerful for his old equipment. Even under normal circumstances, operating one piece of electric farm machinery meant making sure that everything else was turned off, to avoid overloading the equipment. The mills had their own problems. They depended on water for their power, either fast-running streams or outflows from dams. But because the flow of any stream changed with the seasons, so too did the amount of power available. Dams offered a more consistent supply, but when they washed out (as they did frequently), they took the hydro with them.

There was only one solution. If rural Canada were to enjoy the same access to reliable hydro that most cities enjoyed, it would have to move to power supplied by larger generating units, what was known as central station power, the same kind of electricity that was available in urban areas. After all, just as it had been with mail delivery and telephones, the issue was that of equality. Why should modern conveniences be denied to the majority of Canadians because of where they chose to live? The answer seemed self-evident. In fact, it was a little more complicated.

HARRY SLATTERY'S *Rural America Lights Up,* written in 1940, paid tribute to the progress of rural electrification in Canada, singling out the province of Ontario as the pioneer in North America. Before 1910, the situation there was much as in other provinces: a mix of small private companies, big urban utilities, and rural residents who met their own needs and those of their neighbours as best they could. But once Adam Beck, the cigar-box manufacturer, municipal politician, and tireless champion of publicly owned electric utilities and rural electrification, "switched on" the town of Berlin (now Kitchener), Ontario, in October 1910 to usher in the era of public power in the province, interest in rural areas grew rapidly. Soon, the Hydro-Electric Power Commission (HEPC), established by the Ontario government in 1906 to build transmission lines to carry electricity from private generating facilities to the province's cities, was surprised to find itself swamped with requests from dozens of townships and municipalities for cost estimates of providing them with electric service. Taken aback, the commission had to ask itself a tough question: did it want to try to serve dispersed rural customers before consolidating its urban services, which were much easier and cheaper to operate? Whatever Beck's fellow commissioners might have thought, for Beck himself there was only one answer: the commission couldn't resist the challenge. To do so was to admit that it wasn't up to the task of bringing electricity to Ontarians. And so in 1911 revisions were made to the Power Commission Act that allowed rural residents to apply to their township council, which would then determine whether it was possible to provide a hydro connection to that area.

The legislation was easy enough, but no one at the HEPC was under any illusions about the obstacles involved. First and foremost was the cost. Initial estimates were that a mile of primary transmission line would cost $512 to build, but when the construction crews actually got to work, the real costs were more than $1200 per mile. Attempts to trim expenses by having farmers provide free labour in hauling and erecting poles, and free board to work crews, didn't go over well in the back concessions. Also, consumption patterns were very different than in the city, where the average householder tended to use roughly the same amount of power week in, week out. Farmers used power sporadically. The lights were on every evening, but the large farm machines for threshing grain or cutting wood, which consumed more power, were used only a few times a year. This was an inefficient use of power—farmers would be paying year-round for a service that they used to its full potential only a few days out of the year. In hydro parlance, rural customers couldn't support a high load factor, which brought with it lower rates; the low load that they did support meant high electricity rates.

The HEPC's response was quite different from what we are used to today. Now, it's all about conservation—turn down the thermostat, install light timers, buy high-efficiency appliances. In short, do anything you can to cut power consumption. A century ago, hydro's message was the opposite: farmers were told that the only way to get cheaper power was to use more. If something could be plugged in, it should be, and the more often, the better. The more electricity they used, the higher the load factor; the higher the load factor, the lower their rates. And the commission went to great lengths to show them how to use more power.

The 25th of June 1912 was a red-letter day for the people of Beachville, a small farming community in southwestern Ontario: they would get a first-hand look at the marvels of electricity. The HEPC had rented the Methodist church's driving shed and had festooned it with cedar boughs, bunting, and coloured lights. Inside was an astonishing array of electrical appliances—water pump, fan, washing machine, stove and range, vacuum cleaner, coffee percolator, soldering iron, kettle, tea samovar, water heater, griddle, grill, curling iron, cigar lighter, chafing dish, toaster—all of which were demonstrated for the 1700 curious locals who filed through the building. Roast beef, potatoes, toast, tea, and coffee were prepared before their eyes, without a single flame being lit, and served to anyone who wanted a sample. Outside the building, a gaggle of farmers watched in awe as an electric milking machine milked a cow and an electric cream separator provided cream for the coffee.

Two months later, the show moved to the Canadian National Exhibition in Toronto, where a model farmhouse and barn were set up to demonstrate the same appliances. The exhibit was such a success (the HEPC took a gold medal for the effort) that the commission decided to send it out on the road. The household appliances went to half a dozen fall fairs and agricultural exhibitions, while specially constructed wagons took the show to farms across southern Ontario. At each stop, hydro officials made toast, tea, and coffee, milked cows, threshed grain, filled silos, and demonstrated a dozen other chores that could be lightened with electricity. They may not have known it at the time, but the people who came out to ogle what was affectionately known as the Power Circus were seeing the beginning of a revolution.

There was more to it, though, than Beck's travelling hydro road show. A research division worked on inventing or adapting European farm equipment to make it cheaper and more useful to Canadian farmers. Sales agents targeted small rural industries—brick factories, butter plants, flour mills, quarries—that could be convinced to use large quantities of electricity and help the rural system achieve lower rates. The commission even turned seven privately owned farms into experimental farms, fully equipped with all sorts of electrical appliances, with new gadgets being added as they became available. All this was intended to show the rural community that electricity had a greater variety of uses than most people realized.

Unfortunately this ambitious public relations program never really had a chance to succeed. The First World War quickly sucked up all available labour and materials, and governments decided that there were better ways to fight the war than encouraging farmers to add electricity to their farms. As a result, in the 1910s the campaign for rural electrification in Ontario stalled. If you were lucky enough to live near a transmission line or a municipal system, you could get a hook-up with a minimum of expense; but for the vast majority of farmers, electricity remained unaffordable.

Once the war was won, though, hydro engineers started to think about how the cost problem could be solved. Their solution, which came into effect in August 1919, was the Rural Power District (RPD). If a number of farmers in one area applied for hydro service, they could be organized into a Rural Power District, typically a region of about a hundred square miles. Hydro officials would get a list of farms and their values from the township clerk, determine the farmers who were most likely to want electricity, and call on them personally with their sales pitch. Then, the commission prepared estimates for serving 100 percent, 75 percent, 50 percent, and 25 percent of the farms in that RPD; rates were based on the cost of bringing power to the boundary of the district and distributing it to individual customers. A number of classes of service were created, like Hamlet Lighting, Farm Lighting, Light Farm Service, and Heavy Farm Service; everyone in the same class paid the same rate, regardless of where they lived in the RPD.

There were a few catches. Each farmer had to sign a twenty-year contract, unlike the city dwellers, who signed annual contracts. A farmer who had been connected to an independent system was not immediately compelled to join the RPD, but he could be at any time. This was more than just an administrative change. A good many farmers had been getting cheap power from private companies for years, only to learn one morning that they had to join a new RPD and pay ten times as much for their electricity. The only alternative, they were told, was to go without.

The biggest problem, however, remained the cost of hook-up: stringing wires to bring electricity from the transmission line to the farm, buying a yard transformer to convert it to household current, and wiring the home and barn. Most farmers, no matter how much they wanted power or how low the rates were, simply couldn't afford these initial costs, which could reach well over $1000. In April 1921, the HEPC responded with the Hydro-Electric Power Extension Fund, which would pay half of the construction and maintenance costs of extending primary lines to Rural Power Districts. The first lines, 175 miles' worth at a cost of $22,000, went up in October 1921, bringing hydro to 1065 new rural customers. Two years later, an aggressive construction campaign had brought the number of rural customers, both on farms and in hamlets, up to 14,010. But the HEPC didn't stop there. In April 1924, new legislation committed the government to paying for half the cost of secondary lines (at about $800 a mile to install) as well as primary lines (at about $1200 a mile). This time, the utility carefully stipulated that the grants did not apply to farmers who bought their power from other suppliers.

The expansion looked good—but it wasn't all it seemed. Most of the hook-ups were concentrated in the prosperous rural areas around London, Windsor, Waterloo, and Niagara, where the cream of the rural customer base had plenty of money to pay for the service. Elsewhere in the province, rural Ontario was in the grips of a post-war depression that saw agricultural revenues drop by more than a third between 1919 and 1922. In times like those, what farmer could come up with $1000 to pay for the initial connection and equip his house and barn with wiring and electrical appliances? It wasn't that they didn't want electricity. On the contrary, a special government commission found that the demand for hydro remained high. In its fifty-four public hearings, the commissioners were told that the unavailability of hydro was behind all sorts of ills, from the inability to find farm labourers and the reluctance of young women to marry farmers, to the *cri de coeur* of one farm woman: "You can have no conception of what bitterness of feeling is developed in the mind of the countrywoman when her sister from the city comes out and begins to dilate on the comforts enjoyed in city homes." Even so, the spread of hydro through the back concessions proceeded at a snail's pace.

When the Great Depression gripped the province in the 1930s, taking the average annual rural income as low as $922 in 1932, the HEPC had to work hard to hold on to its rural customers, much less sign up new ones. The commission responded with a rash of new initiatives to make rural hydro more attractive: the twenty-year contract was dropped in favour of an initial contract of five years, with annual renewals after that; cash advances were offered to farmers for wiring their homes and barns, building secondary lines and transformers, and purchasing grain grinders; the service charge for the most common rural service, which had been as high as $4.10 a month, dropped to a dollar a month; and for three years, electricity for washers, sanitary system water pumps, and radios was free.

The HEPC also embarked on a public relations blitz that dwarfed Beck's Power Circus. Its direct descendant was the Hydro Display Coach, which visited fall fairs and agricultural exhibitions. A large trailer would pull into the fairgrounds, and well-groomed young men in good suits would bustle around, connecting every manner of electrical appliance to a portable generator. And then, to the amazement of fair-goers, these men would demonstrate how modern technology would replace the tools that had been handed down through generations of farm families: an electric vacuum to replace the broom and dustpan, a range instead of the wood-burning oven, a refrigerator for the old icebox. The demonstrators had charts and graphs to show that a few pennies a day could save hours of back-breaking labour and demonstrated that a single electric light fixture provided better light than half a dozen kerosene lanterns. It was all marvellous, the audiences thought, if a little bewildering.

There were other enticements as well. A mail campaign sent pamphlets to every farm in the province, and articles were commissioned for publication in farm journals; HEPC even offered to purchase ad space in journals that published editorials in favour of rural electrification. Appliance manufacturers also advertised heavily, pointing out that the price of their products was dropping dramatically: the farmer who balked at an $85 washer in 1930 could buy a much superior model for only $57 in 1939, for example. And then there were the personal visits. Hydro officials called on 77,000 farms in 1935—farmers who were already signed up were shown how to increase their power usage, while the other 40,000 were encouraged to get on board. Toward the end of the 1930s, as the province turned the corner and left the Depression behind, this sales campaign began to show some dividends. Between 1929 and 1939, the number of rural customers served by the HEPC rose from 37,179 to 110,361, over half of the new contracts being signed in the last two years of the decade.

Ontario was leading the pack in rural electrification, with over 37 percent of farms having electricity (either central station power or power from local sources), but other provinces weren't far behind. In British Columbia, the B.C. Electric Railway Company had about seventeen thousand rural customers, roughly half of them farmers; nearly 36 percent of the province's farms were wired. Nova Scotia showed virtually no progress until 1937, when the government's Rural Electrification Act introduced subsidies to cover part of the cost of transmission line extensions into rural districts. After that, development increased dramatically, and by the beginning of the Second World War nearly a quarter of the province's farms were electrified. Not far behind were Quebec, where the provincial government was committed to the notion that people should stay on the farms and in 1936 brought in subsidies to pay for half the cost of rural line extension, and New Brunswick, where by 1941 nearly 20 percent of farms were electrified.

Meanwhile the process had barely begun in other provinces. In Alberta, the only rural extensions were purely incidental to the work of Calgary's hydro company in building its urban network; of the province's more than 100,000 farms, only about 500 had electricity. Of Prince Edward Island's 12,000 farms, only 644 were wired. Even the provinces that had been active in promoting rural electrification had little to show for it. Manitoba had established a Public Utilities Commission in April 1912, in part to determine whether the province should develop a publicly owned power system to give everyone in the province, urban and rural, the same access to hydro. The government established a special commission in 1919 to bring power to areas not served by the Winnipeg Hydro-Electric System or the Winnipeg Electric Company, but a decade later a committee reported that farmers had been reluctant to embrace electricity because they weren't convinced of the direct economic benefits—just eighty farms were being served with electricity through the Public Utilities Commission. In 1929, the province legislated subsidies to cover half the cost of rural line extensions, but even that didn't make much of a difference. By the end of the 1930s, only 500 out of the 59,000 farms in the province had central station power, and even then, they paid much higher rates than did people in Winnipeg. The province of Saskatchewan established a Power Resources Commission in January 1927, in part to look at the possible extension of hydro through the countryside. But despite the active support of the agriculture minister, Charles Hamilton, who looked to rural electrification to end some of the drudgery of farming, a 1928 report concluded that there wouldn't be enough consumption in rural areas to justify the high costs of a building campaign. Not surprisingly, in the province hardest hit by the Depression, electrification was almost non-existent.

Ironically, then, it was on the prairies, where governments had been so keen to get into the telephone business to bring one of the comforts of the city to the farm, where progress was slowest. Alberta (probably still skittish after its disastrous experiment with rural telephones) and Saskatchewan trailed all other provinces in rural electrification, and even then, most of the power on the prairies was supplied by small wind and gasoline generators operated by the farmers themselves. Counting only those that had central station power, by 1939 less than 1 percent of farms on the prairies had been electrified.

THE SECOND WORLD WAR was both good and bad for rural electrification. In practical terms, the conflict was even more damaging than the Depression. The transmission system relied on copper, steel, and aluminum, all of which were essential war materials. Add to that the shortage of skilled labour and it seemed unlikely that government would give rural electrification a high priority. In October 1941, Ottawa confirmed this. Despite provincial suggestions that agricultural productivity could be boosted by continuing with rural electrification programs, the federal government announced an end to rural extensions because of a shortage of materials, particularly electrical transformers. The regulations were relaxed a little in the middle of the war, but not by very much. In August 1942, even Ontario's premier, Mitch Hepburn, who had requested a line extension to power his farm's new milking machine, was turned down.

Yet in ideological terms, the war was the best thing that could have happened for rural electrification. Not long after the declaration of war, the federal government began to consider what Canada should look like after the fighting stopped: what should its priorities be? how should post-war Canada be different from pre-war Canada? what parts of its infrastructure had to be developed? Anyone who knew anything about history knew that war was always followed by economic downturn as war industries saw their fat government contracts dry up. This led to unemployment, reduced consumer buying power, and, almost inevitably, recession. So in pondering these questions, the government had to keep in mind the need to cushion this expected blow; anything that could be done to provide jobs until the post-war civilian economy geared up again should be considered seriously.

Government committees to do just that sprang up like weeds: the Cabinet Committee on Demobilization and Re-establishment in December 1939; the General Advisory Committee on Demobilization and Rehabilitation in August 1940; the Cabinet Committee on Reconstruction, with its four subcommittees on agricultural policy, post-war employment, conservation and natural resources, and building projects; and all of the provincial reconstruction committees. They were charged with examining every aspect of Canadian life, to determine what would be most important to Canadians once the war was won. From their deliberations, it was hoped, would emerge a blueprint for post-war Canada.

It was obvious that people wanted a better country. During the First World War, they had been promised, once the enemy had been beaten, "a land fit for heroes," but that utopia had never materialized. On the contrary, post-1918 Canada was even more mean and grasping than pre-war Canada had been. If the committees learned one thing, it was that Canadians weren't about to be cheated again. They had high expectations—"If the government can spend billions of dollars for prosecuting the war, there is no good reason why the government cannot spend equal sums to help maintain the standard of living in times of peace," stated one report. People wanted better housing, social amenities (such as the performing arts centres that would come in the 1960s), educational improvements, more generous programs for veterans, more accessible health care, additions to the transportation infrastructure (a trans-Canada highway loomed large in many reports). The wish list went on and on.

Prominent on most lists was rural electrification, for a number of reasons. The war had pushed farm incomes up, so that the installation and appliances that had been beyond reach in the 1930s were now affordable. Not only that, but after a decade of depression, the drudgery of farm work was a lot harder to bear when the money and the technology that could reduce it were readily available. But at the root of it all was the common belief that rural electrification would make Canada a better place to live— and wasn't the war being fought to build a better world? And so in the 1940s, people who had tuned out the sales pitch of hydro commissions and electricity boosters in the 1930s started to listen.

During this period the idealized image of the electrified farm emerged in full flower, as a mixture of hard science and futurism. Hydro engineers had studied the experience of electrification on U.S. farms and could quote chapter and verse on how any given piece of equipment made the farmer's life easier. Just one kilowatt hour of electricity could pump as much water as a farm labourer could pump in two days. In a henhouse in winter, when the long periods of darkness typically cut egg production in half, electric lights could increase yield by as much as 90 percent. Electric brooders installed in a hog farm could keep new-born piglets warm and dramatically reduce their mortality rate. Hydro companies were quick to provide statistics on the most common appliances used on farms—block heaters and small shop tools in the barn, washers and irons in the house—and could tell the prospective rural customer the exact cost of operating each appliance on a weekly, monthly, or yearly basis.

More than the statistics, however, it was the vision of the dreamers— who focused less on the barn and more on the home—that stirred the public imagination. Adam Beck had once conjured up a picture of women "working at ease in cool, bright kitchens; of children studying their lessons in well-lit rooms; of farmyards flooded with light; of barns humming to the whirr of electric motors and of stable lanterns hung up to gather cobwebs all across Ontario." In short, rural electrification was the route to domestic bliss. "If you are devoted to your wife the first thing you will do for her is to get her a power washer, then get her an electric iron," wrote one hydro booster. "If you have money left see that she has water pumped into the house." And it didn't stop there. The modern farmer would soon fill the home with every labour-saving device known to science—sandwich toaster, tie presser, cigarette lighter, electric screen door, ice cream freezer, motion picture machine, potato peeler, shaving mug heater. A Manitoba committee even wrote in 1942 of one farmer who gleefully reported that he had installed an electric guitar, amplifier, and high-powered microphone in his house. That probably wasn't what Adam Beck had in mind, but it did allow the farmer to amplify the signal from his radio and broadcast programs across his back forty for the benefit of neighbours who hadn't yet seen the light and embraced hydroelectricity.

The Huron *Expositor* put it all together in a 1942 editorial that captured the promised utopia of the modern electrified farm. "The wider use of electricity after the war will bring revolutionary changes in farming to make it much easier and more attractive to the younger generation," the newspaper predicted. Instead of rolling out of bed before dawn to tend his poultry, the farmer could get used to "waking the chickens an hour earlier with bedside buzzers." He could enjoy a leisurely breakfast, prepared by his relaxed and good-spirited wife on the latest of appliances, and could be sure that all his food and utensils were safe, thanks to their electric sterilization lamps. Then it was off for a comfortable ride on his blissfully quiet electric tractor. Even the country smell of old-fashioned fertilizer was gone, made obsolete by electric high-frequency soil treatments. All the hay he cut that day was stored in the loft using whisper-quiet electric conveyor belts. There wasn't even the sound of a mouse to disturb his reverie, because electrical extermination equipment had rid the farm of all kinds of pests, from rats to cockroaches. His workday done, he could return to his farmhouse, flip on the radio, and read the day's newspaper under his new reading lamp. On the electrified farm, he could live "the life of Riley."

The picture was certainly appealing, and the various reconstruction committees heard all about it. But because hydro was a provincial responsibility, the complaints were loudest in those councils. In Saskatchewan, the Reconstruction Council's report was blunt: the provincial government had done everything wrong in terms of rural electrification. The

Saskatchewan Power Commission (SPC) had been too cautious in extending hydro, failing to encourage farmers to get connected even though more than 2000 farms could be hooked up to existing lines. As a result, of the 15,000 farms in the province with electricity, fewer than 300 of them enjoyed central station power from the SPC; the vast majority used old wind- or gasoline-powered generators, which couldn't handle the more powerful farm and household appliances that would soon come on the market. Once the war was won, concluded the council, the government had to do better. "The widely expressed desire for electrification in the post-war period cannot be ignored," it stated, nor could farmers be expected to pay the full costs of hook-up. After all, people in urban Saskatchewan didn't pay to be connected—to treat people in the rural areas differently would be discriminatory. It was not a matter of choice, concluded the council. The government had an obligation to extend rural electrification, with generous subsidies if necessary, or risk losing the next generation of potential farmers either to the cities or to other provinces where farm life had been modernized with hydro.

Across the provincial boundary to the east, the Manitoba Electrification Enquiry Commission began work in June 1942 and was no kinder to its government. Its surveys of farmers revealed that 83 percent were interested in getting electricity, and even the majority of those with their own generators said they were keen to switch to central station power when it became available. Despite this, the government had failed in bringing hydro to the countryside and had to start planning immediately so that a program of rural electrification could begin as soon as the war was over. The commission should aim to electrify 1000 farms in the first year, bring hydro to every hamlet with more than twenty people within five years, and have 25,000 electrified farms within ten years; over the long term, bringing hydro to the vast majority of the province's 59,000 farms was "entirely feasible and practical." The costs would not be insignificant—to install the transmission line and transformer at one farm would cost $673.27 at minimum, and the farmer would have to spend hundreds of dollars more on wiring and appliances—but the costs of inaction were even greater.

Across the country, the story was the same: provincial governments had done too little to bring the comforts of electricity to the farm, and if the nation's agricultural economy was to survive in the post-war era, more effort had to go into making farming an attractive occupation. And so provincial governments actually took seriously the reports of the various provincial reconstruction councils. The Manitoba report became the basis for an intensive five-year rural electrification plan laid out in the throne speech in February 1945. The province of Alberta established test areas around Olds, Swalwell, and Vegreville in 1943 and 1944 to experiment with various ways to bring power to isolated farms, while the Nova Scotia Power Commission was given a new Rural Electrification Act in 1945 to complete the work started in 1937. In British Columbia, after the hydro commission got the green light for an expanded program of rural electri-fication, the government introduced a bill that allotted $10 million to bring electricity to rural areas of the province. The same thing happened in Ontario, where, on 30 March 1945, the government announced its Five-Year Plan for Postwar Rural Hydro Development. The most ambi-tious of the provincial programs, Ontario's aimed to bring hydro to 58,000 new rural farm and hamlet customers, at a cost to the province of nearly $45 million. Taken together, these various programs would reshape rural Canada. While it might not be made a land fit for heroes, it would at least be well lit.

WHEN THE WAR ENDED in 1945, governments had to live up to their promises, and, much to everyone's surprise, they had a favourable economic climate in which to do this. The economy didn't collapse when the war ended; on the contrary, Canada's gross national product, which had grown dramatically during the war, continued to grow afterwards. Standards of living rose with wages, there was full employment, at least in a statistical sense, and the country enjoyed the most sustained boom period it had seen since the days of Wilfrid Laurier. In times like these, no government could turn its back on plans for rural electrification.

Because of its head start, Ontario was the first province to reach the goal of supplying power to all farmers who wanted it. The five-year plan had called for 7300 miles of new transmission line to hook up 58,000 farms, but targets were exceeded in each of the five years. By 1950, there were 136,251 new rural hydro customers (representing 62.5 percent of the province's farms) connected to 13,223 miles of new line. By 1956, parts of rural southern Ontario had reached 95-percent coverage, and the government calculated that only 19,246 farms remained unserved. Most of them were in northern Ontario, where greater distances and lower loads made it more expensive to supply hydro, but that didn't stop Ontario Hydro chairman Robert Saunders from promising to "blanket the northwest from the Fort Frances and Rainy River farm areas, through to Kenora and north to Red Lake" with hydro. It was a tall order—one study revealed that to serve 761 customers in northern Ontario would require the construction of 766 miles of line, at $9,000 a mile—and it would take years for the north to be fully serviced. Even so, in 1959 a survey revealed that the vast majority of the province's farms had hydro, and fully 98 percent had an electric washing machine. The modern farmhouse in Ontario had become, as one observer noted, a place "where switches control everything but the children."

At the other end of the scale was Saskatchewan. With the lowest rate of rural electrification, that province had the most work to do. And instead of getting right on with construction, the government of Tommy Douglas, which had swept to power in 1944 after spending its time in opposition demanding that hydro be nationalized to allow its mass production and provision to rural areas, got on with more studies. In the summer of 1945, Saskatchewan commissioned Professor David Cass-Beggs of the University of Toronto to examine the problem, but his report was more than the government had bargained for. He said that the province's entire power system had to be overhauled, primarily by constructing larger power plants and integrated networks. As for rural electrification, he said, it made little difference: the bigger problems had to be corrected whether or not the province decided to bring hydro to its farms. He did say, however, that farmers shouldn't bear the cost of extending hydro; if they did, rural electrification would never be self-supporting.

The government's response, after four years of doing almost nothing on rural electrification (in fact, one of the main cabinet supporters of the program resigned when a government official expressed his opinion that people should move to the towns and leave the countryside to the jackrabbits), was the 1949 Rural Electrification Act. Beginning with the assumption that the province's main agricultural product, wheat, didn't benefit greatly from the introduction of electricity, the act then stated that rural electrification was not a major factor in the farm economy. For that reason, any program should be developed on a self-supporting basis; and, because government policy was to encourage people to move to more compact communities, the emphasis should be on powering towns and villages rather than individual farms. The province's contribution for any one extension would be limited to $300, leaving the farmer to find the other $1200 needed to wire a farm. To the government, it was a reasonable response to a difficult situation. To critics, it was a cop-out, a hastily drafted measure intended to help the Douglas government's re-election bid.

Douglas was indeed returned to office, but the SPC was unable to meet even the modest targets (1200 farms in 1949, 2400 the following year) that the legislation envisioned. In 1951, after introducing new procedures for extending service, the commission finally met its yearly goal—but then got the shock of its life. In the midst of another election campaign, Douglas announced that, if he were re-elected, 40,000 farms and all towns would be electrified by the end of his government's next mandate. At SPC headquarters, there was consternation and confusion. Was that 40,000 new farms, or 40,000 in total? Surely Douglas meant the latter, because the former would be virtually impossible to achieve. With a sign-up rate of 65 percent, some 60,000 farmers would have to be canvassed to get 40,000 willing to pay for hydro extensions. Even so, the policy still meant adding 7000 farms a year, as well as every town in the province, and erecting as much line in four years as the commission had built in the preceding twenty-five. The goal, thought the SPC, was "tremendous almost beyond belief."

Incredibly, by hook or by crook (and by shovelling more money at the problem, in higher construction subsidies and signing bonuses to farmers willing to be connected), the SPC did manage to meet the target that the politicians had set for it: by 1956, Saskatchewan had 40,000 electrified farms, or 47 percent of the province's total. Still, it lagged behind its neighbours, Alberta with 55 percent of farms electrified and Manitoba with 80 percent, so in 1957, when the government created the Royal

Commission on Agriculture and Rural Life, a special report was requested on farm electrification to determine how to bring the province up to par.

The report contained little new in the way of conclusions. Rural depopulation was getting worse. Because travel was easier, people were more aware of the conveniences that existed in the cities; if they couldn't get them on the farm, they were more likely to move to the city. There was also a built-in inequality in the system: urban customers didn't pay the construction costs of bringing lines to their homes, but rural customers were expected to, and as a result, farmers had every reason to feel like second-class citizens. And those costs remained substantial: a minimum of $500 for a yard transformer (the farmer in Manitoba paid $65), $400 to wire the farmstead, and $600 for appliances (in Manitoba, the power commission sold appliances at cost plus 10 percent). The report also identified practical problems that stood in way of rural electrification in Saskatchewan: the province relied on more expensive coal or diesel generation, rather than cheaper water power; nearly half of the province's population lived on farms, so compared with other provinces, there were relatively fewer urban customers to subsidize relatively more rural residents; with the largest average farm size in Canada, at 550 acres, farms were more dispersed, and therefore more costly to service. This last factor meant that the SPC had to build more miles of line than in any other province and that there would be fewer customers per mile of line—less than a fifth, for example, of what there was in Quebec.

For all that, however, the report recommended that rural electrification be expanded. The economic benefits were great, but the positive social effects would be felt first. "Social contacts are broadened, and some of the differences between farm and urban living disappear," the report concluded. Hydro "will improve the home atmosphere, help to provide time for reading and leisure and so develop a more satisfied rural population." It was no longer a matter of providing a luxury: "[T]oday electricity is as common a necessity in rural life as is water on the farm."

And so the process of powering up rural Saskatchewan continued. A year after the report was presented, the government's program of rural electrification on a massive scale ended, with 51,027 farms connected to the electricity grid by 50,300 miles of rural transmission line. The total cost had been $47.5 million, of which the farmers themselves paid $25 million. Next came Operation Complete Coverage, launched in 1959 to bring in any last farms that wanted power; about 10,000 farms were electrified under this program, bringing the coverage rate to about 75 percent. After that, connections continued sporadically at a rate of one or two thousand a year, reaching 66,000 by 1966. By that time, the province that had started dead last in the rural electrification race was being consulted by other countries on how to provide power to rural populations.

Through the 1960s and 1970s, the impetus was to fill the service gaps in rural Canada. In 1960, the BC Power Commission informed the provincial legislature that three years' work should finish the task of rural electrification, but in 1966 the government was still fielding pleas for service from isolated areas. A typical request came from the people of Otter Valley: "[W]e should be entitled to the conveniences of electricity. In this day and age power is not a luxury." Their concerns could have come out of a petition from fifty years earlier: children whose eyes were failing because their schools lacked electric light; farmers who couldn't use modern irrigation systems to improve their crops; produce and household food that regularly spoiled for want of proper refrigeration. The response of the area's electricity supplier, West Kootenay Power, could also have come out of the 1920s: it was reluctant to extend service to isolated areas if that service could only be subsidized by higher rates for customers in other areas.

At the other end of the country, the government of Newfoundland took a proactive role in encouraging private utilities to service rural areas. The isolation of coastal communities, many unconnected even by roads, made the provision of hydroelectricity in rural Newfoundland a nightmare. In fact, not until September 1958, when most provinces had powered up over half of their rural population, did the provincial government sign an agreement with Newfoundland Light and Power to build lines where it had not been economical to do so previously. In November, a similar agreement was reached with the United Towns Electric Company, and a third was signed in October 1959 to extend service on the Bonavista Peninsula. By 1964, these three agreements had resulted in the construction of 611 new miles of rural transmission line. Though this might not sound like much, to anyone who knows the remote communities that were connected—Hare Bay, Musgrave Harbour, New World Island, Ship Cove, and dozen of others—the line was a considerable achievement. Yet it wasn't good enough for Premier Joey Smallwood, who in February 1965 promised to provide power to fifty-four more rural communities by 31 March 1966. Five years later, in January 1971, the province finished up a $35-million program to bring electricity to about four hundred communities. By that time, less than 1 percent of the province's homes lacked hydro.

IN 1942, Manitoba's Electrification Enquiry Commission reported that rural communities in the United States held ceremonies for the communal burial of kerosene lamps, to celebrate their conversion to electricity. Perhaps the same celebrations occurred in Canada—as one farmer told the Saskatchewan reconstruction council, "[A]nyone knows that doing chores by a smoking lantern is no fun." But lightening the workload was only part of the benefit and shouldn't obscure the fact that electricity, as much as rural mail delivery or the telephone, dramatically reduced the isolation of rural residents, especially women.

Six years earlier, Laura Kaulback Slauenwhite had left her farm at Falkland Ridge, Nova Scotia, to work as a housekeeper in the tiny rural hamlet of New Germany. There's no question that the house's electricity helped her with her chores, but there was one other appliance, something that was unavailable before the hydro age, that she appreciated: the radio. Still coping with the early death of her husband, in uncertain health herself, and frequently depressed at her family's declining fortunes, she took refuge in the radio, her diary revealing how much she valued the contact it provided with the outside world. "Listened in on an Anglican Church service this evening from Halifax. Heard a splendid sermon"—"We heard the late King Edward's farewell speech at six this evening ... we get all that is going over the radio"—"Listened to the radio broadcast of the proclamation of the new King George VI. It was very thrilling as it came right from London and was real clear"—"Had a church service in the evening and lots of Christmas music ending up with a spelling bee from Cincinnati"—"Listened to the radio a half hour. Heard the good news of the Bluenose beating the American boat"—"Am alone with the radio for company." For Laura and countless other rural residents, electricity, whatever else it did to ease their work, opened a window that provided a much-needed diversion from the stresses and insularity of the rural world.

Back in 1910, when Laura Kaulback was just a child, the Toronto *Globe* published an editorial on the evils of rural depopulation. "The cities are like great vampires," the newspaper stated. "They are constantly drawing away the best blood of the country places, and they send back in return not people but goods. They take brain and brawn; they give up only their lifeless products." For people like George Wilcox, Alexander Beatty, and Adam Beck, the answer was close at hand: something as simple as mail delivery, as commonplace as the telephone, as prosaic as electricity could thwart the vampire cities. As the *Globe* put it, "With the … introduction into the country districts of city comforts and city pleasures, it is possible that the next generation may see an exodus back to the land. When it comes it will be a boon to the nation." Unfortunately the cold statistical reality tells us that mail delivery, telephone service, and electrification did little to end rural depopulation. These services certainly made life on the farm more pleasant and comfortable and perhaps they slowed down the exodus to the cities a little, but it continued nonetheless. The 2001 census revealed that nearly 80 percent of Canadians live in urban centres, a figure that would have horrified the rural lobby of the 1920s, which had been so disturbed when the 1921 census showed that fewer than half of Canadians lived in country districts. Still, the fact that these great initiatives failed to achieve one goal doesn't mean that they were ill-advised. On the contrary, the lesson to take from these experiments lies in their success in achieving another, equally important, goal: to ensure that all Canadians enjoy the same access to services, no matter where they live. Achieving that goal is inherent in the building of a nation.

ICONS OF
A NATION

CASTLES OF THE NEW WORLD

Prairie giants, sentinels of the west, Gibraltars of the plains—grain elevators have been called many things over the years, but the best description came from Walter Herbert, a publicity man for the Canadian Wheat Pool, who wrote an article for the *Canadian Geographical Journal* in 1933. Herbert contrasted elevators with the fortresses of the old world, "massive piles of masonry, fortified and menacing" that cast "nasty and foreboding shadows" over the landscape and its history. Grain elevators were different; they were "fortresses of peace, storehouses of plenty, essential links in a chain of peaceful trade and commerce ... one of Canada's offerings to the goddess of progress." For Herbert, the contrast called to mind a phrase that implied the superiority of North America over Europe and also affirmed the significance of the grain elevator: they were Castles of the New World. Herbert wasn't impressed by them aesthetically, dismissing them as "stark and rather unbeautiful ... a bit drab and ugly," but he understood their importance to the towns they dominated and to the nation as a whole. They were vital links in Canada's economy, structures on which the entire grain trade, and so much more, depended. And like many other building blocks of the nation, they could trace their roots back to the earliest European presence in North America.

The list of European imports to the new world is long, ranging from gunpowder and iron tools to syphilis and Christianity. One of the most beneficial, though, was wheat. The French settlers at Port Royale (Annapolis) planted a small crop in 1605, and in 1616 Samuel de Champlain wrote of wheat being cut at Quebec and shipped to France (probably a few stalks that were decoratively bound for display purposes). In the early days, however, wheat was grown primarily for consumption, not export. When it could, the colony of New France shipped wheat to Cape Breton, Newfoundland, or even France, but this was a risky business. The trick was exporting just the right amount, so that the colonists themselves didn't go hungry. Once in a while, the authorities got it wrong, and the settlers hovered on the brink of starvation until food arrived from France.

By the eighteenth century, the agriculture of the colony was established enough that it could regularly export wheat to the West Indies, which emerged as New France's primary market. But the trade was terribly vulnerable to outside events. Healthy exports of perhaps 80,000 bushels annually dropped to almost nothing during the Seven Years' War, picked up again after the British conquest of New France to peak at 460,000 bushels in 1774, and then plummeted during the American Revolution, when Canada lost its hold on the West Indies market, never to regain it. In 1789, flour had to be imported from Europe, and the following year, exports of wheat from Quebec were banned altogether, so that the colonists themselves could be fed. The end of the revolution in the Thirteen Colonies brought some temporary stability, but then the French Revolution and the Napoleonic Wars started the roller coaster again. Wheat exports from Lower Canada ranged from 126,000 bushels in 1802 to a mere 107 bushels in 1811, and then the combined effects of the wheat midge, which appeared in Lower Canada in 1829, and the rebellions of 1837 to 1838, which stopped wheat exports to Britain entirely, took the fight out of Lower Canadian wheat farmers. Some years, they were unable to produce enough wheat to meet domestic demand, let alone the export market.

By this time, however, wheat had started its move west. The first spring wheat was sown in the Niagara district in 1780, and within a few years, farmers there were petitioning the governor for aid in transporting it to markets in Montreal. Transportation costs were high, sometimes up to one-third of the value of the product; at those costs, it was impossible to make a viable export trade. As transportation improved, though, so did Upper Canada's wheat economy, which quickly outpaced that of its neighbour: in 1860 Upper Canada was producing almost ten times as much wheat as Lower Canada. Yet the experiment with wheat was short-lived. Through the second half of the nineteenth century it became clear that land in Upper Canada could be devoted more profitably to other crops, and wheat acreages slowly declined, just as they had in Lower Canada decades earlier. Wheat continued its march westward.

The first Europeans to put down roots in present-day Manitoba were the Selkirk settlers, who in the early nineteenth century took up land along the Red River, near the site of Winnipeg. Their first wheat crop was sown in 1812, but in those early years, more often than not, their grain fed the grasshoppers rather than the farmers. What the grasshoppers didn't eat, the floods washed away, and it was the early 1830s before the struggling colony was able to start producing a regular surplus. Only then did the export of wheat become a possibility.

On a raw day in October 1876, R.C. Steele of the Steele Briggs Company of Toronto trundled into Winnipeg on a lumber cart. He had come from St. Paul, Minnesota, and he was in a hurry. Ontario's seed grain crop had failed, and Steele needed 5000 bushels of seed wheat for immediate transport to Toronto. He had no time to lose—a freeze would put an end to river navigation, and to his buying trip. Messrs Higgins and Young, general merchants of Winnipeg, undertook to supply the seed, but despite scouring the countryside, they came up with only 857 bushels. Steele took what he could get. He bought the grain at 85 cents a bushel and sent it up the Red River by steamer to Fisher's Landing, and from there by train to Duluth, where it was forwarded to Toronto, at a total freight cost of 35 cents a bushel. The tiny shipment involved only a few dozen farmers but represented the first wheat to be exported from western Canada.

Larger shipments soon followed. In October 1877, Manitoba sent its first wheat to Britain, via St. Paul, Minnesota, and in 1884 delivered the first export to Britain over an all-Canadian route: rail to Port Arthur, boat to Owen Sound, Ontario, and then rail and ship to Glasgow. By 1887, the export trade had really started to boom; in that year, 4 million bushels of wheat were inspected and graded at Winnipeg. It was already becoming clear, however, that the expanding wheat trade needed a better system of handling the product. In the early days, grain was shipped either loose or in bags, and neither method was particularly efficient. Filling and emptying grain bags was costly and time-consuming; in 1910, a farmer could spend $28.75 for one hundred standard grain bags from the Eaton's catalogue, and loading a single rail car from a track-side warehouse could take an entire day. More often, grain went in open wagons to a railway siding, where it was shovelled by hand into the cars. And this was an even slower process. The average wagon carried 100 bushels of grain, the average railway car as many as 2000. That meant a lot of trips back and forth between farm and platform. Depending on how close the farmer was to the railway line, it could take up to a week to load a single car, at a time when the farmer could ill afford to be away from his fields. People who worked in the wheat economy knew that if the trade was to grow, bulk shipping had to come. The day was fast approaching when wheat would be king—and, as Walter Herbert said, the grain elevator would become its castle.

If farmers had their way, those castles would have looked very different. Many growers preferred smaller, simpler flat warehouses that they could build themselves, along the railway lines and close to their farms. Such buildings would provide the most basic of storage, allowing farmers to store their crops in separate bins until they had enough to fill a rail car. For the railway barons, though, such a system was wasteful and inefficient—"a curse to the country as well as to the railway," the CPR's William van Horne called the warehouses. Eyes firmly fixed on the bottom line, the railways demanded larger structures that could load rail cars much more quickly, and therefore less expensively.

Of course, the CPR had no intention of going into the elevator business itself. Instead, the railway encouraged private companies to build them along its lines and used the millions of acres of land that the federal government had granted it as an incentive to builders. Any company that would erect a standard type of grain elevator with a capacity of 25,000 bushels and a mechanical means of loading and unloading grain would get free land along the railway line. If that wasn't enough, the company would also get a monopoly: the railway guaranteed that its cars would accept grain from no one but the elevator operator, not even the farmer who grew the wheat. That was enough for dozens of entrepreneurs across the West. They jumped at the railway's offer and started to build.

Canada's first grain elevator, a 25,000-bushel structure in Niverville, Manitoba, had already been built, in 1879, but it was a round, squat building, quite unlike the typical elevator that is so recognizable today. The first of those elevators, built on a U.S. design, went up in Gretna, Manitoba, in 1881, and was operated by A.W. Ogilvie and Company, which had been in the flour milling business in eastern Canada since 1801. The first in Saskatchewan, at Indian Head, went up in 1883, and Alberta's first was built at Strathcona in 1896. Thousands more were to follow. "Nothing is better calculated to assist in the prompt development of this country than the extension of a good elevator system," announced J.A. Mitchell, the president of the Winnipeg Grain and Produce Exchange, in 1892. A revolution was coming to western Canada.

The prairie vistas would be changed by the appearance, in hundreds of communities, of the country elevator, also known as a "house" and sometimes referred to as a line elevator because they were usually built in a line along the railway tracks. Decades later, when its future would become threatened, people would begin to describe the elevator in romantic terms, but in the early days it was strictly a utilitarian structure whose shape and construction were determined solely by the demands of the product it was designed to store. Wheat is a heavy crop, a bushel of No. 1 Red Fife weighing over 60 pounds, so the elevator had to be strong enough to hold over a million pounds of grain. At the same time, it had to cope with harsh winter winds and cold, and the blistering prairie sun and heat. Typically, the foundation was of concrete, nearly two feet thick, while the walls were made of cribbed wood, two-by-eights at the bottom and two-by-fours at the top. The boards were dovetailed, and the whole structure clad in either wooden siding or tin sheeting. The result was a structure some 35 feet square, 70 to 80 feet high, and sturdy enough to be moved from place to place. Capacity varied—the standard medium elevator held 25,000 bushels, while the standard tall elevator could handle 40,000 bushels.

At each elevator was enacted a ritual that would become a timeless part of prairie life. Over the years the equipment may have modernized and the operation may have speeded up a good deal, but for decades its essentials didn't change much at all. To make a delivery, the farmer would pull his loaded wagon onto a platform scale, and the entire rig was weighed. Then, the grain was dumped into the pan in the bottom of the elevator and the rig weighed again, to determine the weight of the grain delivered. At the same time, the wheat's dockage—the weed seed, pebbles, and clumps of dirt in the load—was calculated as a percentage of a sample, and that percentage was deducted from the load as a whole.

The key to the entire operation was in the heart of the elevator: the endless cup-conveyor, or the leg, which used a series of cups on a rotating rubber belt to move the grain up from the pan in the floor of the elevator. At the top of the leg, the grain was funnelled into one of many bins, which stored grain either by grade or by grower. In the days before the wheat boards got into the business, the farmer then had three options. He could sell his grain outright to the elevator operator, and walk away with the cash. He could take a graded storage ticket, in which case he and the elevator agent agreed on a grade for the wheat; it was then added to that bin, and payment came later. Or, he could take a special bin ticket, in which case he essentially rented a bin from the operator and could sell his grain at a later date or ship it himself to the terminal.

When it came time to load the grain onto a rail car, the process was reversed. In turn, each bin was emptied into the pan, where the leg carried it up to the top of the elevator, out through a spout and into the car. From there, the grain travelled to the much larger cousin of the country house, the terminal elevator, located at ports such as Vancouver, Fort William, and Port Arthur (now Thunder Bay), Montreal, and Toronto, and designed to hold grain until it could be transferred to ships for onward transport.

The first shipments of grain to reach the head of Lake Superior from western Canada were simply held in sheds until they could be loaded, by handcart or wheelbarrow, onto steamer barges. But in 1884 at Port Arthur, the CPR built the first true terminal elevator, a 350,000-bushel structure known as The King, after its builder, John King. Six years later, the addition of three more elevators gave the complex a capacity of 3 million bushels. These early structures were made of wood or concrete tile, but in 1900 grain merchant Frank Peavey and engineer Charles Haglin of Minneapolis revolutionized the industry by pioneering the slipform method of pouring concrete. In this process, the concrete is poured continuously into a mould that is slowly raised upwards on hydraulic jacks as the concrete hardens. This process allowed for huge structures to be completed much more quickly than with traditional construction methods. In 1927 a farmers' cooperative built a new terminal at Port Arthur, setting a world record for construction speed in the process: in just seven months, from the first pile-driving on 31 May to the receipt of its first shipment of grain on 15 December 1927, they built the largest and most modern terminal in the world. With a capacity of 5.5 million bushels, the elevator could load 80,000 bushels of grain an hour onto a waiting freighter. The terminal elevator was an awesome sight. When the never-at-a-loss-for-words Thomas Wilby drove into Port Arthur in 1912, he was staggered by what was then the largest elevator in North America: "A sky-scraper, a François Premier Chateau and a Bastille rolled into one.... It dwarfed men to pigmies, it soared with Babylonian majesty. It breathed force and power, and it challenged the hills and the capes whose fit companion it was."

With the construction of country and terminal elevators, all controlled by elevator companies, milling companies, and the railways, the farmers, those most fiercely independent of creatures, were integrated into an increasingly complex structure for the production and shipment of grain. Whether they realized it or not, they had become cogs in a much bigger machine. And when they finally started to get a sense of the scope of that machine, they didn't like what they saw. A system that had been devised by the railway was, in the eyes of many farmers, bound to serve the railway first, the elevator operators second, and the producer a distant third. And when independent elevator companies started to pop up in the 1890s, the CPR began to flex its muscles.

In 1897, the railway began to enforce its monopoly: there would be no rail cars available for loading at farmer-built flat warehouses, so any grower who wanted to ship grain would have to use the elevators that were in the CPR's pockets. The problem for farmers was that those same elevator agents usually acted as grain dealers as well and had an interest in keeping down the prices paid to farmers. Wheat producers began to mobilize, pressuring Manitoba MP James Douglas to introduce two separate private members' bills to preserve the warehouses that were the farmers' only defence against the unholy alliance of railway and elevator company. When the clause protecting the warehouses was surreptitiously removed from one of these bills at the behest of railway lobbyists (Douglas blamed "the cold steel of Clifford Sifton," a federal cabinet minister whom many people suspected was a little too cosy with the railway interests), grain producers could barely contain their anger. They targeted the federal government, which responded with the Royal Commission on the Shipment and Transportation of Grain (1899–1900).

Headed by a judge from St. Catharines, Ontario, the commission and its three western-farmer members convened twenty-one hearings across the prairies. More than 230 farmers trooped before them to detail the abuses they encountered in the elevator system: short-weighing, either because the scales weren't inspected often enough by government agents or through outright fraud on the part of the elevator operator; over-docking, in which the agent would deduct an unfairly large percentage of the load to allow for dirt or weed seeds; and under-grading. "Your wheat sure looks like #1 Northern," the agent might tell the farmer approvingly, "but all my #1 bins are full, and #2 as well. The best I can do is put it in the #3 bin." The farmer often had no choice but to accept the lower grade and take the lower price, because other options were rarely available. Such testimony made it clear, to farmers, that all elevator operators were in cahoots; even if there were five different companies operating elevators in their town, there was little chance that the agents would let competition drive prices up. As one analyst put it, to the farmer, "the elevator owner was only one,—perhaps the most hated one,—of a long series of middlemen who stood between him and the European consumer, and took apparently an excessive toll from his product."

In the end, the commission came down squarely on the side of the producer. While admitting that elevator agents needed to act as grain dealers if they were to have any hope of turning a profit, they agreed that most of the farmers' complaints had merit. So, the report recommended that the government force the railways to provide cars, flat warehouses, and loading platforms, so that farmers had the option of loading their own wheat if they felt they were being treated unfairly by the elevator company. When the Manitoba Grain Act became law in 1900, it embodied most of the commission's recommendations.

What changed as a result? As any western wheat farmer would have told you, not much. The elevator companies simply closed ranks and found different ways to work together, to make sure that they kept the upper hand in the grain trade. Despite the commission's recommendations, few new warehouses were built, and those that remained in operation slowly declined in importance compared with the elevator. By the late 1920s, only about 5 percent of grain handled in the West went through these facilities. And while the elevator operators did try to meet another of the commission's demands, greater stability in wheat pricing, the railways were reluctant to provide cars for anything but the line elevators. It was an unlucky coincidence that the very year after the Manitoba Grain Act came into effect, a record wheat crop put an enormous strain on transportation: the CPR simply didn't have enough cars to serve all the elevators, let alone the warehouses. When agents told farmers that their wheat might not get exported that season and that they would have to pay extra storage charges, growers saw their potential profits dry up before their eyes.

Their first instinct was to accuse the railway and elevator agents of putting in place a "wheat blockade." Just as they had done in the 1890s, they vented their rage on everyone involved in the wheat economy: the banks that held the notes on their farms, the railways that transported their grain, the Grain Exchange that bought it, the terminal elevators that stored it, and the millers who milled it. But their special target was the country elevator and its agent, largely because that part of the system was most visible in farm communities. Once again, elevator operators were charged with a string of abuses, including unfair weighing, imposing excessive dockage charges, depressing prices, failing to clean grain, refusing to provide special bins so that farmers could store their grain separately, under-grading, and mixing wheat to reduce grades. The complaints prompted another government inquiry, the Royal Commission on the Grain Trade in Canada (1906), but by then most producers had had enough of royal commissions. Instead, they moved toward the kind of reform that fundamentally changed the way business was done. In each of the prairie provinces, farmers began to organize, pressuring government for real change.

The revolution came first to Manitoba, where western wheat farming was born, with the establishment of the Grain Growers Grain Company (GGGC) in 1906. Under its capable and methodical secretary, E.A. Partridge, an émigré Englishman who combined superior organizational skills with a passion for the work of socialist philosopher John Ruskin, the GGGC tackled the elevator companies head-on with the Partridge Plan, which called for the provincial government to take over the running of country elevators and the federal government to take over the terminal elevators. In February 1909, a delegation of farmers descended on the Manitoba legislature with a monster petition signed by ten thousand farmers, all demanding that the province take action. To everyone's surprise, Premier Rodmond Roblin and his cabinet agreed. Having jumped into public ownership with the creation of the Manitoba Telephone Commission, the province adopted the policy of operating country elevators as a public utility and set up the Manitoba Elevator Commission (MEC) in 1910. Although they were nervous about certain parts of the legislation—such as the fact that the commission was answerable to cabinet rather than the legislature—Manitoba farmers were ready to celebrate. At last, the wheat shipping system might work to the benefit of the whole province, not just to that of a few financiers and businessmen.

As soon as the Manitoba government started to acquire elevators, however, problems emerged. In the first place, the MEC wouldn't build or buy an elevator on a whim. Local farmers had to present a petition, signed by 60 percent of the farmers in the catchment area, asking for a government-run elevator; the government insisted on this provision because fewer than one-fifth of the province's grain producers were members of the GGGC. The petitioners also had to pledge that they would continue to use the elevator in the future, to give the MEC a guaranteed clientele. Soon it also became clear that the government had a lot to learn about building and acquiring elevators. The commission bought elevators that were in such bad repair that the elevator companies were probably delighted to get rid of them. The government inspector reported that the recently acquired elevator in Myrtle, for example, "needs repairing nearly everywhere" and probably had had only one coat of paint in its life. The MEC paid $5035 for an elevator at Nesbitt in 1910, and after pouring a further $7000 into repairing the structure, eventually sold it for $2000. The commission also bought elevators that were poorly located, such as the one in Rea, which was served by an inadequate road network and operated only intermittently—and it was gone by 1932. In places, the commission bought more elevators than needed, sometimes owning five or six in a line, where two would have been enough to handle the expected capacity.

More important, there was no money to be made in storing grain, which is why so many of the private elevator companies acted as grain merchants as well. In 1923, the average elevator cost $3900 a year to operate, but the handling and storage charges would bring in just $3100 a year. Only by acting as a buyer and seller of grain could an elevator owner hope to make a profit, but because the MEC refused to get into dealing wheat, it shut itself off from the only part of the elevator business that would have kept it in the black. Just a few years after its proud beginning, the MEC called it quits. The provincial government declared the experiment a failure and turned over its elevators to the GGGC. The entire experience ended up costing Manitoba taxpayers nearly a million dollars.

The reform of the grain handling system took on a different character in Saskatchewan and Alberta. In Saskatchewan, farmers also petitioned for government-owned elevators, and in December 1909, just days after Manitoba announced the establishment of the MEC, Saskatchewan premier Walter Scott appointed an investigative commission, chaired by Dr. Robert Magill, a professor of political economy at Dalhousie

University, and including two delegates from the Saskatchewan Grain Growers' Association (SGGA). A year later, its report validated the fear of many producers: line elevator companies and millers, because they owned most of the elevators, had a stranglehold on the grain trade. The government responded with the Saskatchewan Cooperative Elevator Act of 1911, which would create a farmer-owned elevator company. Shares in the company would be sold for $50 and farmers could petition the government for the erection of an elevator anywhere in the province, so long as the number of shares purchased roughly equalled the cost of the elevator (at current construction costs, this meant about 180 shares). Once 15 percent of the pledged cash had come in, the government would advance the rest and construction of the elevator would proceed. The Saskatchewan Cooperative Elevator Commission (SCEC) would come into being as soon as twenty-five local cooperatives had been established.

Unfortunately 1910 was a poor crop year, and few farmers could come up with the 15-percent down payment on their shares. So at the first general meeting of the SCEC, held at Moose Jaw in July 1911, the province was forced to advance enough money to get things started. The policy of the SCEC was to build new elevators rather than buy existing ones, in part because it was quicker to construct elevators than to go through the prolonged process of examining houses and negotiating purchases. The SCEC even started its own construction company so that it could deal with fewer suppliers, purchase building materials in bulk, and erect elevators that were as uniform as possible. But the other significant difference from the Saskatchewan experiment was that the SCEC dealt in wheat as well as storing it—thus, it could take advantage of the one part of the grain handling business that promised to return a profit. And profit it did. The SCEC made money in its very first year, and the profit was three times larger in its second year. The Saskatchewan experiment had succeeded where Manitoba's had failed.

Farmers in Alberta faced different and unique challenges in shipping their grain. Before the big terminals in Vancouver and Prince Rupert came into operation, Alberta wheat had much farther to travel than other western grain to reach eastern terminals and markets. This meant that rail cars took longer to get to Alberta and were often in short supply.

As a result, of all the wheat farmers in Canada, those in Alberta faced the greatest difference between the market price for their crop and the price they were actually paid at the elevator. Naturally, they laid most of the blame on the elevator companies and began to press the provincial government for action. The governing United Farmers of Alberta (UFA) struck an elevator committee and sent its delegates to Saskatchewan to investigate the cooperative elevator system there. The UFA liked what it saw but preferred to wait a couple of years to see how the new Saskatchewan system compared with the one that had been put in place in Manitoba. Finally, in early 1913, the government introduced an act to incorporate the Alberta Farmers Cooperative Elevator Company (AFCEC).

Fortune did not smile on the Alberta cooperative, however. First, it ran up against the immense economic power wielded by the elevator companies and the railway. Having prospered mightily with their patronage, the largest lumber company in the province refused to sell lumber to the cooperative to build its elevators, forcing the AFCEC to resort to smaller mills and imports from Idaho and Montana to supply its needs. At its first general meeting, in August 1913, the cooperative reported that it had bought ten elevators and started construction on forty-two more, but a year later it was running into cash-flow problems. Increasingly, the company was having to rely on financial support from the GGGC, which acted as its grain handler and loan guarantor, and by the end of its second year was in debt to the Manitoba cooperative to the tune of $90,000. Then there was an ill-advised foray into livestock handling, something that had great potential for the long term but was not the best idea for a company trying to find its financial feet.

More and more, the Albertans who ran the AFCEC began to look at a merger with the GGGC as their salvation. In 1915, at its annual meeting, the AFCEC adopted a resolution, similar to one passed by the Manitoba group months earlier, in favour of federating the three cooperative elevator companies in the West. But Saskatchewan, after mulling over the idea, declined to take part. Its farmers produced as much wheat as the other two provinces combined, demand for elevators there remained strong, its cash reserves were growing, and it had the backing of the provincial government. There seemed no reason to give up its position of strength to join with two smaller and apparently weaker organizations. Disappointed but not put off, Manitoba and Alberta decided to continue with their plans. On 1 September 1917, the United Grain Growers (UGG) officially came into existence as an amalgamation of the AFCEC and the GGGC.

The creation of the UGG was just one of the circumstances that combined to usher in the heyday of the grain elevator. Successive government commissions had recommended that there always be alternatives available to farmers, and the expansion of the railway system in the West in the early years of the twentieth century made that possible. The newcomers were two railways, the Canadian Northern and the Grand Trunk Pacific (GTP), both of which saw railway expansion and elevator construction as going hand in hand. They turned to Frank Peavey's company, which had become a major player in the American elevator business. In 1905, William Mackenzie and Donald Mann invited company officials to ride on their new Canadian Northern line to pick sites for elevators; the distance between them was to be 10 to 15 miles, so that no farmer needed more than a day to haul a wagonload of grain to the elevator. A few years later, the Peavey company struck a deal with the GTP that saw the railway construct a 2.5-million bushel terminal elevator at Fort William, in exchange for Peavey building and operating a string of elevators along the GTP line. The Canadian Northern and the Grand Trunk Pacific spread across the Prairie provinces, using rail lines to bring new agricultural regions into production. As a result, rail mileage increased dramatically; in Alberta alone it grew by 53 percent between 1906 and 1912, more than doubled over the next four years, and grew by another 50 percent by 1935. And new towns sprang up so rapidly across the West that finding names for them became a challenge. The Grand Trunk Pacific adopted the charming, or artless (depending on one's point of view), practice of naming towns alphabetically along the railway line.

Typically, elevators followed the railway. In 1882 only six existed on the prairies; by 1901 there were more than 400, and by 1910 nearly 2000. Construction soared again in the early 1920s with the continued expansion of the transcontinental railway system and the establishment of wheat pools in Alberta in 1923 and Saskatchewan and Manitoba in 1924. These farmer-owned cooperatives were founded so that producers could sell directly to wheat buyers, but they had the added effect of increasing the concentration of the elevator business in the hands of fewer companies. In 1924, the three provincial pools, the UGG, and the SCEC together controlled about half of the country elevators and one-third of the terminal elevator capacity at the head of Lake Superior. A few years later, the Saskatchewan wheat pool took control of the SCEC's elevators, becoming the Saskatchewan Pool Elevators Limited, with 575 houses, two terminals at Port Arthur, and a transfer elevator at Buffalo, New York. The Manitoba and Alberta pools both eventually created their own elevator companies to compete with the UGG. This ushered in still another era of elevator building. By 1929, the Saskatchewan wheat pool, with its aggressive construction program, controlled more than 1000 country elevators, while the Alberta pool and the UGG each had more than 400. The largest private company, the Alberta Pacific Grain Company (established in 1907 by U.S. investors and later sold to a British company—the big winner in the transaction being Alberta Pacific's principal shareholder, R.B. Bennett), boasted around 360. A decade later, in 1938, the number of elevators in Canada peaked at 5700. By that time, there were more elevators on the prairies than there were towns.

THE UBIQUITY of the grain elevator in the West made it a natural Canadian icon. The elevator was a symbol of prairie life, but it was also a symbol of Canada, one that came to be celebrated by poets and novelists, painters and composers. No other utilitarian structure—not the milk shed, the garage, the outhouse, or even the barn—has been the subject of so many books, and none has graced so many postage stamps, coins, and banknotes. Sculptor Elizabeth Wyn Wood proposed a design for the Centennial coin series in 1967 that included a grain elevator, but officials in Ottawa decided to go with animals instead, so the elevator had to wait until the provincial coin series issued for Canada's 125th birthday in 2002 to make it onto a quarter honouring Saskatchewan. By that time, the elevator had already spent decades on the back of the dollar bill and had been featured on a handful of postage stamps since the 1940s. Like the Mountie, the beaver, and the maple leaf, it has also become a highly marketable symbol. One prairie artist couldn't generate much interest with her batik wall-hangings of abstracts and wildflower scenes, but had trouble keeping up with the demand when she switched to creating batiks of grain elevators.

What did grain elevators mean to the towns that had them? One observer has used an analogy that Walter Herbert would have appreciated. In the towns of medieval Europe, the tallest structure was almost always the church spire. A mark of reverence, yes, but also an object of pride and prestige; a fine spire meant that a town mattered. The same was true of the grain elevator. If towns followed the railway, they also followed the elevators—often the first structures erected in any community, and also invariably the tallest. Almost from the time that they began to appear on the prairies, the country house was touted as a town's best drawing card. In the countless books, pamphlets, and newspapers articles that tried to draw settlers to the West, singing the praises of this or that town always involved mentioning the number of grain elevators there. The main attractions of Brandon, according to one 1897 publication, were the well-made streets, the many substantial buildings, and the eight grain elevators. The Manitoba government's immigration agent in Toronto even issued a special map that showed, along with the towns, railways, roads, and post offices, the grain elevators that were ready to accept the crops of new farmers. In short, an elevator meant success—the more elevators, the more prosperity. A line of elevators became a symbol of civic accomplishment; it proved that a town had arrived.

For people whose entire lives were spent in its shadow, the grain elevator was more than just a symbol of economic prosperity or civic achievement; it was a living, breathing part of their lives. To imagine a village without an elevator was to imagine a village without streets, or houses, or even people. "They were just there, they were just life," reflected author Sharon Batula, who was born on the prairies when the elevator was in its heyday. "I know that by the time I was an adult I had long since stopped seeing them, even when I was staring right at them." They offered a sense of comfort, a sense of security, and a feeling that all was right with the world. "I always feel I'm home when I can see the elevators on the horizon, especially in the early morning," recalled farmer Lloyd Nowlin of Porcupine Hills, Alberta. "I've been a few different places where I couldn't see the elevators and I always felt homesick when I couldn't."

The presence of the grain elevator also gave people a welcome sense of familiarity when they visited prairie towns. Coupled with the fact that the bank branches and post offices tended to be built to standard patterns, the existence of grain elevators of identical design across the West filled small towns with repetitive features. Cynics might say that this made one prairie village look pretty much like the next; others would argue that someone from one town could easily feel at home in any other. The elevators also added splashes of colour, thanks to the tendency of different companies to "brand" their elevators with recognizable paint schemes and logos— the circled triangle of Federal Grain Limited (which by 1940 had become the largest private elevator company), the yellow and red hexagon of the Saskatchewan pool, the blue banner of the United Grain Growers, the grey-green of the Alberta pool. The distinctive orange and yellow livery of the Pioneer Grain Company, once the second-largest private elevator company and controlled by the same family that had founded Western Canada Airways, came from Pat Cruickshank, an architect whose husband was an engineer with the company. For many people, this mix of colours made for the quintessential prairie scene: a shimmering golden field, a clear blue sky, and a brightly coloured grain elevator.

NEVERTHELESS, the glory days of the grain elevator were about to come to an end. Just as technological change had brought them to the prairies in the first place, technological change would slowly strip them from the landscape. The move started after the Second World War, as more and more farms mechanized, roads were improved across the West, and cheaper and more reliable trucks came on the market. All of these made it easier for the farmer to haul his grain, and he was no longer limited to the nearest elevator. With a good half-ton truck, he could now haul grain three times as far in a day as he could with the old horse-drawn rig. As a result, elevators now had to vie for the farmers' business and many of them, particularly older ones, found their business dropping off dramatically when they couldn't compete with more distant houses that offered farmers a better deal.

Even with mail delivery, telephones, and hydro, rural depopulation continued. As family farms were replaced by agribusinesses, the local elevator became less important. The farmer's personal relationship with the elevator agent was replaced by a corporate agreement between an agribusiness and an elevator company. More and more, these companies realized it was good business to close some of their elevators. Why pay property taxes in a dozen small towns when operations could be consolidated at three or four sites? Furthermore, there seemed to be no point in operating dozens of older, smaller capacity elevators (buildings that were starting to need major repairs) when they could be replaced by a few much larger facilities made of more durable and lower-maintenance concrete. The older elevators had been constructed to handle about twenty rail cars' worth of grain; the railways, however, were now routinely using trains a hundred cars long and needed grain storage facilities able to carry that amount of wheat.

At the same time, the railways were becoming aware that the orgy of track-laying in the early part of the century no longer made good business sense. They came up with a break-even point—any branch line that couldn't ship 30,000 bushels of wheat per track mile wasn't worth keeping open. The federal government went along with this, the 1961 MacPherson Royal Commission on Transportation recommending that railways not be forced to maintain unprofitable branch lines—of which the commission said there were 8600 miles—unless governments were willing to provide subsidies. In most cases, they weren't. In 1974, a government report advised that 525 miles of railway be abandoned, and three years later the Royal Commission on Grain Handling and Transportation advised the abandonment of another 2100 miles of line. As rail companies closed branch lines, they left many small towns stranded, their elevators, even if they had been competitive and profitable, no longer fulfilling any useful purpose.

Corporate concentration in the elevator business was another factor. There had been three hundred companies in 1916, but in 1970, when there were still some 5000 elevators in 1,900 towns, the president of one private company urged that these numbers be slashed to 1000 large modern elevators in 266 primary marketing towns. Between 1971 and 1975, four elevator companies ceased to exist, including two of the biggest: Federal Grain Limited (whose houses were divided up among the provincial wheat pools) and National Grain Limited (whose assets were taken over by Cargill). With these acquisitions and the resultant need to avoid duplication of services, nearly seven hundred elevators were taken out of service. By 1986 only six major elevator companies were operating in the West.

An even bigger change came in 1984, when the federal government finally cancelled the Crow Rate. Enshrined in federal statute in 1925, the rate had been intended to keep down rail transportation costs between the head of Lake Superior and the West. It had been the cornerstone of the grain transportation system for decades, but that system was becoming increasingly outmoded. Unable to increase freight rates, the rail companies refused to buy new cars because they believed that under the current system they could never recoup their expenses. At the same time, the survival of thousands of elevators across the prairies had been guaranteed by a marketing system that encouraged the storage of grain as a way to stabilize prices; elevator companies were paid by the federal government for storing grain, so they had every reason to retain as many elevators as possible to keep their storage capacity high. Neither the railways nor the grain companies had any incentive to change practices that had been in place since the early twentieth century.

When the Crow Rate was abolished, however, the system started to change quickly: more rail lines were abandoned, more elevators were taken out of operation, more grain companies were amalgamated, and there was a move toward consolidating grain-buying services into newer, larger structures. As a replacement for the old, wooden elevators, companies started to build huge, concrete superelevators, also known as high-throughput elevators. Located outside of towns (where there were no municipal property taxes), they looked, according to one writer, like "a cross between a drive-in movie screen and the world's largest slope-roof tool shed." One of the first was the Buffalo Sloping Bin at Magrath, Alberta, built in 1980 at a cost of $800,000. Eighteen years later, in September 1998, the Saskatchewan Wheat Pool announced that it would close 235 elevators at 170 points and replace them with twenty-two high-throughput elevators, immense facilities like the Carseland Inland Terminal, just east of Calgary, which the UGG opened just a few weeks after the Saskatchewan Pool's announcement. With a capacity of more than 1.3 million bushels, the terminal can load 112 rail cars at once. The new facilities come with a cost to the producer—designed to serve a 50-mile radius, they result in higher transportation costs for farmers who deliver their grain to them—and they also score poorly on aesthetic grounds. Their grey concrete contrasts starkly with the bright yellows, reds, and greens of the old wooden elevators, leading some people to lament the impact of these new industrial behemoths on the landscape: "They seem out of context with the surrounding golden wheat fields," wrote R.F.M. McInnis. "They are not part of their locations, unlike the earlier elevators that seemed to form an aesthetic and harmonious centre for the town."

As the superelevators go up, the old sentinels of the plains come down. From the 1938 high of 5700, the number had dropped to 3324 by 1981, 1578 a decade later, and just 627 by 2001. In 1997, a survey by the Alberta government revealed that there were only 327 licensed elevators still standing in the province; by August 2000, that number was down to 209, and dropping every month. In a seven-week period over the winter of 2001–2, eight elevators were demolished in Lacombe, Ponoka, Delia, and Eckville, Alberta. The following year Dave Cuthbert, who had been instrumental in helping to save an elevator in Andrew, Alberta, predicted that of the hundreds of houses that once stood in the province, perhaps ten, if they were lucky, could be preserved.

There have been some conservation success stories. Nanton, Alberta, had three remaining elevators in 2001 and when news got out that they were to be demolished, a local group called Save One began to raise money and lobby Pioneer Grain to preserve at least one of the houses. Pioneer told the group that it would first have to purchase from the railway the land upon which the elevators sat, so Save One opened nego-tiations, and in late 2003 concluded a deal to buy the land for $10,000. But when it came time to sign the papers, some of the group balked. Their group, which had begun in 2001 with fifty enthusiastic members, had dwindled to fewer than a dozen, and some of them wondered why they were bothering, when so little local interest was evident among the prag-matic farmers, who couldn't see the point in saving a non-functional building. "Are we right in forcing these elevators on this town?" wondered president Nancy Parsloe. "Maybe their silence has been an answer." Eventually, the group had to make a decision: buy the railway land, negotiate for the elevators, and hope to cover the substantial upkeep costs (for example, the elevators needed to be professionally cleaned at a cost of $16,000 each), or give up the fight and let them be demolished. In the end, they were swayed by their feelings on seeing the demolition of elevators all around them. In March 2004, Save One finally closed the deal, acquiring the elevators from Pioneer for $1. As of June 2004, the plan was to turn the orange single elevator into an art gallery, and the grey twin elevator into an interactive museum. The group hoped that the revenues from the gallery could help fund the museum and would also continue with fundraising efforts such as the August 2004 Still Standing Festival.

One of the most interesting conversions was not of a country elevator at all, but Silo No. 5 in the Port of Montreal. A 656-foot-long, 52-feet-wide, 148-feet-high mass of reinforced concrete, it had been built in four stages between 1906 and 1958. But as port usage changed in the 1960s, many of the elevators around the silo were demolished, leaving No. 5 standing alone. Yet the building that the legendary architect Le Corbusier had once called "near perfect in its concrete symmetry" was not destined for the wrecking ball, at least not yet. In 2000, the team of composer Emmanual Madan and architect Thomas McIntosh temporarily turned it into the Silophone, its 115 vertical chambers acting like huge organ pipes to "transform, reverberate and colour" sound to create a new sonic art form. With support for its first year from Bell Canada and Radio-Canada, the Silophone attracted sound artists from around the world and is now operated by an independent, non-profit organization.

Perhaps the biggest success story of all took place in Inglis, Manitoba. When the province inventoried remaining elevators in 1992, the five-in-a-line at Inglis were at the top of its list for protection, and so a campaign to save them got underway. When the harvest season closed in 1995, Inglis's five elevators were taken out of service, along with the Russell–Inglis rail line that served the town. In February 1996, the elevators were designated a National Historic Site (provincial heritage designation followed in 1999). Members of the Inglis Area Heritage Committee were stunned when an engineering assessment revealed that as much as $2 million was needed to restore the houses, but raising money turned out to be less of a problem than they had imagined. The Department of Canadian Heritage came up with a cost-sharing agreement for $1 million, the province contributed another $370,000, private foundations and individuals have contributed generously, and the companies that owned the elevators, in addition to donating the buildings, gave a sum equal to the demolition costs. The first completely restored elevator was opened in time for the summer 2002 tourist season, and others followed. After the first year, the elevators as tourist attractions were already providing more local jobs than they had as grain-buying facilities.

Sadly, such campaigns did not always have happy endings. When Agricore (created by the merger of the Alberta and Manitoba Pools and the UGG) finished building its terminal elevator in Viking, Alberta, it decided to demolish the last remaining house in Irma, 100 miles southeast of Edmonton, a community of five hundred that had once handled 1 million bushels of grain a year. But local farmer Harold Gulbraa, whose family had farmed in the area for nearly a century, pestered Agricore to sell it to him instead of tearing it down. Gulbraa hoped to see it continue as a working elevator, but was willing to have it used as a museum— anything was better than the disappearance of the landmark that had dominated the town's skyline for Gulbraa's entire life. But in October 2000, he lost the battle. Agricore refused to sell, and the elevator was demolished. "Within five days," Gulbraa said bitterly, "there wasn't a chunk of wood the size of your thumb left."

Even heritage designation has proven to be of little help to elevator supporters. Since 1992, only four elevators have been preserved using heritage designation from the Alberta government—two in St. Albert and one each in Scandia and Paradise Valley. More recently, on 15 May 2003, Alberta's premier, Ralph Klein, proclaimed the elevator in Leduc a provincial historic resource, noting that "Grain elevators didn't only serve an economic role; they also served a far greater purpose by uniting communities." Elevator groups urged the federal government to come up with something like the 1990 Heritage Railway Stations Act, designed to stem the destruction of those buildings, but no similar legislation has been enacted.

Part of the problem is lack of agreement on the desirability of saving any given elevator. As the Inglis committee discovered, to many farmers "the elevators were not shrines to commercial progress, but rather places that frustrated their efforts to reap the economic benefits of their labour ... many agriculturalists in the Inglis area, when apprised of the project to save the elevators, advocated tearing them down." Not even the heritage community can agree on a position. Jane Ross, the curator of western Canadian history at the Provincial Museum of Alberta, wondered how many old elevators can reasonably be operated as tourist and educational attractions. After all, she noted, there is only so much demand for that sort of thing. Edmonton-born architect Trevor Boddy cautioned against the temptation to idealize the grain elevator, which was in truth a noisy and unhealthy workplace that may have created economically unsustainable communities and enriched only the rail barons. His preference is to leave the elevators in place but to allow them to decay like the ruined castles of Europe.

And who is to blame for the disappearance of the prairie sentinels? The grain companies and railways are both concerned about insurance liability: as long as a company's elevator is standing on railway land, there is the potential for an accident that could land both parties in court. Railways blame the grain companies for building too many elevators in the first place, while the companies blame the railways for abandoning branch lines and leaving elevators stranded. In some cases, the towns themselves should bear some responsibility. The vice-president of the Saskatchewan Pool accused some communities of driving elevators out by looking at them as bottomless pits of property tax revenue. The pool's property tax bill for Saskatchewan in 1997 was $7 million, and in some areas the charge had tripled from one year to the next. "One community on a line scheduled for closure upped our bill from $30,000 to $100,000," he observed. "Those towns are hurting their own cause."

If responsibility for the disappearance of country houses is hard to pin on any one group, the consequences are crystal clear. For the affected towns, losing an elevator was more than just losing a building; in many cases, it was as good as a death sentence. The town of Torrington, Alberta, had two elevators, but in 1996 the CPR decided to close the

Acme–Wimborne branch line that served Torrington. When the elevators were taken down, the town instantly lost one-third of its tax base. The local restaurant's business dropped by one-third, and the school's enrolment fell so low that after it closed for the Christmas holidays in 1997, it didn't reopen the following January. Unable to cope with a projected 50-percent tax hike, residents voted to be absorbed into the Municipal District of Kneehill. Torrington had prospered for decades thanks to its grain elevators; when they disappeared, they took the town with them. The same thing happened in Whitford, Alberta, which once had five elevators, a post office, a gas station, and a handful of stores. On 11 April 1975, its last two elevators were sold to farmer George Kapitski, who bought them for $100 each and moved one to his family farm to store his grain. Now Whitford, the home of painter William Kurelek and the town that had inspired so many of his paintings of prairie life, no longer exists. Situations like this convinced the mayor of Stenen, Saskatchewan, Merv Secundiak, to refuse to sign a permit allowing the demolition of his town's last elevator. With the school and the bank already lost, he knew the razing of the elevator would be the last straw.

In the battle between corporate efficiency and the small-town way of life, the grain elevator has become an unlikely symbol. In the eyes of supporters, it is more than simply a building. "Every culture needs its magic, its symbols, to represent where we have been and where we can go," said a supporter of the Nanton elevator project. "Are our elevators any different than Holland's windmills or Egypt's pyramids?" Detractors would find it easy to argue with the analogy, but not so easy to dismiss the notion that grain elevators are more than just old buildings. They are testaments to the people whose hard work produced the staple resource that helped build the country. From the smallest elevator in the remotest corner of the rural West, to the mighty terminals in Thunder Bay, Toronto, and Montreal, they are all part of the infrastructure on which Canada evolved. A century ago, the Canadian nation was being built on wheat, the railways, and western settlement. All of those factors, and ultimately Canada itself, came together in one structure, the lowly—and yet inspiring—grain elevator.

TOWERS OF POWER

E recting great towers to commemorate a leader's deeds, to symbolize strength, or to mark territorial claims is a tradition stretching back centuries. None of these tendencies seems particularly Canadian—we're not inclined to put our leaders on pedestals, and we've convinced ourselves that we're too self-effacing to trumpet our influence or mark our turf. But Canada has its fair share of towers and, if they're not exactly part of our infrastructure in a conventional sense, they have all stood as icons to symbolize the nation's sense of itself. At first glance, there doesn't seem much to connect nineteenth-century towers built to honour military leaders with their twentieth-century counterparts that celebrate economic success. Yet in their own time, the six towers discussed here were icons that became part of our emotional infrastructure as Canadians: the column to Isaac Brock was always about much more than one dead general, just as the CN Tower was much more than a monument to the corporation whose name it bears. People of different eras value different things: these towers help us to understand what was important to particular generations of Canadians, and what they believed was most worthy of commemoration.

A legend surrounding the erection of Nelson's Monument in Montreal tells of a grand society ball in December 1805 that was rudely interrupted by a messenger. After downing a mug of punch to steady his nerves, he relayed the news of the Battle of Trafalgar, how the Royal Navy had bested the French fleet, and how Admiral Lord Horatio Nelson, the great British naval hero who had beaten the French at Aboukir and vanquished the Danes at Copenhagen, had been mortally wounded. Surrounded by his loyal men, Nelson breathed his last, the very embodiment of the words he had signalled to his fleet at the start of the battle—"England expects every man to do his duty." The tale left scarcely a dry eye in the ballroom, so Samuel Gerrard, the president of the ball and one of the city's leading fur merchants, came forward with a proposition. The city of Montreal should erect a memorial to the great hero, and he was prepared to pledge £20 on the spot. Not to be outdone, other guests piped in—even the fathers of the Seminary of Saint-Sulpice—and before the evening was out, they had sufficient money. Montreal would do its duty to the empire's hero. The monument would go forward.

Sadly, the story sounds more like the history Montreal wanted than the history it had. While the bare bones may well be accurate, the reality was a little less inspiring. Not even a hero as great as Nelson could have convinced Montrealers to part with their money so readily, and in January 1806 the *Gazette* was still soliciting contributions, even offering a selection of needlework for sale to raise funds. With these delays, Montreal suffered the indignity of being beaten to the chase. While the *Gazette* peddled patriotic embroidery, the city of Glasgow raised the first memorial in the British Empire to the great admiral.

No matter—Montreal would press ahead. After all, not only was the admiral an imperial hero, but he also had some slight connection to the area. While Nelson had never actually been to Montreal, he was at Quebec in the autumn of 1782, as captain of HMS *Albemarle*. He liked the city. "Health, that greatest of blessings, is what I never truly enjoyed till I saw Fair Canada," he wrote to his father, and that was before he met Mary

Simpson. Sixteen years old and the daughter of the Provost-Marshal of the British garrison, Mary captivated Nelson, who was eight years her senior, with her charms. But the budding romance came to nothing. Ordered to New York, he took the advice of a friend that remaining in Quebec to court Mary would do irreparable damage to his naval career. Duty (and the fact that Mary wasn't as enthusiastic about the relationship as Nelson) won out over infatuation, and Nelson left Canada for good.

The elite of Montreal were determined, however, that he would return in stone and struck a committee to consider proposals for a design. They eventually chose a London architect, Robert Mitchell, whose pragmatism appealed to the wealthy but eminently practical fur barons: his 8-foot-tall stone statue of Nelson (to be mounted upon a column) would be impervious to any climatic conditions, he promised. The monument eventually arrived in seventeen pieces in April 1808, and the committee engaged a local stonemason, William Gilmore, to prepare the column, base, and capital from local stone and to assemble the entire structure. But Gilmore seems to have won the contract more on the strength of his early donation to the project than on his professional efficiency, and it was eighteen months later, in August 1809, before he got around to laying the first stone. Unfortunately, the English artisan who carved the inscription had expected prompter action; his panel declared that the memorial had been erected in 1808.

Then in 1815 Thomas Talbot, who was passing through the city on a tour of Canada, asked a rather pointed question: why was Nelson facing away from the St. Lawrence River? "The water was the theatre of all his actions, – the element on which he acquired his glory, fought all his battles, and at length triumphantly ended his mortal career…. Why then should even the unconscious statue of such a great man be deprived of the pleasure, so to speak, of contemplating a portion of that element which gave immortality to its prototype?" In fact, local lore has long held that the positioning was an act of posthumous kindness. Throughout his life, Nelson was plagued by seasickness—his customary advice to fellow sufferers was that the best cure for the malady was to sit under a tree. Perhaps it seemed generous that his image not be forced to face the water for eternity.

Regardless of its orientation, Nelson's Monument soon became a favourite subject for passing artists and a compulsory stop on any grand tour. In 1812, Josiah Snelling, a Boston-born soldier captured at the surrender of Detroit, was brought to Montreal as a prisoner. When the party reached Nelson's Monument, a British officer ordered Snelling to remove his hat in deference to the great admiral. As Snelling held his hat firmly on his head, two soldiers struggled to remove it; further violence was only averted by the appearance on the scene of a senior general, who called the soldiers off in order to respect Snelling's scruples. Decades later, another American had a different reaction to the column. Mark Twain, on a publicity jaunt through Canada in 1881, wrote a series of dispatches for the *New York Times,* one of which covered his visit to Montreal. After describing the many delights in the city, Twain recalled wryly that "I have looked with emotion, here in your city, upon the monument which makes forever memorable the spot where Horatio Nelson did not stand when he fell."

By that time, Mitchell's climate-proof monument was beginning to show the effects of time, and the Montreal *Herald* inaugurated a fund-raising campaign to renovate the column. On 20 October 1900, Lord Strathcona, who went down in history for driving the last spike to complete the Canadian Pacific Railway, presided over a ceremony to re-dedicate the rebuilt monument. It was then the height of the war in South Africa, and it was perhaps inevitable that Nelson would be conscripted to serve contemporary politics. The decision to send Canadian troops to South Africa had been politically divisive, but speaker after speaker used the monument to heal those divisions by celebrating the values it enshrined: a spirit of loyalty, the importance of duty, the patriotism of the past and its relevance to the present. Louis-François-Georges Baby, a retired judge and passionate historian, emphasized ethnic harmony, recalling the legend of the monument's genesis to affirm that French and English Canadians had all donated to the cause. Henri Cesaire St-Pierre, a criminal lawyer and veteran of the American Civil War, even suggested that the original idea had come from the French-Canadian Samuel Girard. Samuel Gerrard was entirely Irish without a drop of French blood, but St-Pierre's version of history made for a more stirring speech. It also allowed the admiral to be conscripted as a foot soldier in the war to forge a Canadian nationalism.

Thirty years later, Nelson's Monument became a political symbol of another sort, when a statue was erected on the other side of the square to Jean Vauquelin, who may have been the last naval defender of New France when his ships engaged British vessels in the St. Lawrence in the spring of 1760. The Montreal *Gazette* noted the irony of the two stone admirals facing one another—"[F]rom his perch atop the column the old English admiral bent a quizzically attentive gaze on those who had come to do honor to a representative of that race of French 'seadogs' against whom he himself had fought so valiantly"—while Nelson would have been outraged to hear Montreal mayor Camillien Houde, in his dedication speech, constantly refer to Britain as the enemy. For French-Canadian nationalists, the imperial hero's presence in Montreal was becoming an embarrassment.

Indeed, in 1996 Vauquelin almost won the staring match when Montreal officials quietly investigated moving Nelson out of the downtown core and to the more appropriately named (but also less conspicuous) Trafalgar Road, in the predominantly anglophone district of Côte-des-Neiges. Radio host Gilles Proulx derided the column as a symbol of Britain's former domination of Quebec, while Councillor Jeremy Searle called the planned move "a Stalinist attempt to rewrite history." Facing growing outrage, the administration of Mayor Pierre Bourque quickly backtracked—the statue would stay where it was. But the elements almost achieved what Quebec *nationalistes* couldn't. In 1997, the badly deteriorated figure was removed from the column for inspection, and experts concluded that it couldn't be saved. The city and province had budgeted $250,000 to repair the monument, but engineers expected that the restoration of the column alone would eat up most of that money. The city eventually decided to commission a new statue, to be sculpted by Lawrence Voaides-Cajban and carved by the Toronto firm Traditional Cut Stone. And so, on the 9th of November 1999, the great admiral was once again hoisted to the top of his column and placed above downtown Montreal, a city he had never seen but one that, once upon a time, had valued him above all others.

The Battle of Trafalgar's impact in Canada was emotional; the Battle of the Plains of Abraham, on the other hand, changed the destiny of British North America. The protagonists, James Wolfe and Louis-Joseph de Montcalm, were career soldiers for whom North America was another in a long string of overseas campaigns. Wolfe was thirty-two, Montcalm fifteen years older, when they faced off at Quebec in September 1759 in a battle that, at a half-dozen different points in the fighting, could have gone either way. Had Wolfe not been shown a path up the heights from the river, had the small French detachment guarding the track offered stiffer resistance, had Montcalm waited for the reinforcements that he knew were coming, had the British line broken at the approach of the French force—any of these might have altered the outcome of events. But the path leading directly to the plains was surrendered with scarcely a shot being fired, Montcalm advanced prematurely on the British lines, and Wolfe's riflemen calmly shredded the French soldiers with volleys of fire. Everything went well for Wolfe—until he was leading his troops against the retreating French and took two bullets in the chest. He died quickly, but so too did Montcalm, felled by a musket ball while trying to bring his men back inside the walls of Quebec.

The campaign in New France continued for another year, but the death of both generals at Quebec has given the battle more significance in the grand scheme of Canadian history than it may deserve. Indeed, the wonderful symbolism of two generals dying in a single engagement motivated the construction of a tower to honour the adversaries. It all began with the Earl of Dalhousie, a Scottish nobleman (and founder of the university in Halifax that bears his name) who became governor-in-chief of British North America in 1820. Upon arriving in Quebec, Dalhousie immediately decided that his mission should be to reconcile French and English. He tried to accomplish this through political means, with indifferent results, but he knew that symbolism could also help the cause. In 1827, he began to take an interest in erecting a memorial to Wolfe and Montcalm. Each had been commemorated individually, but Dalhousie felt that, in the interests of racial harmony, a combined monument would not go amiss. He struck a committee of local politicians and military officers, and commanded them to produce designs for the memorial. For the inscription, Dalhousie decided to open a competition, the winning entrant to receive a handsome gold medal.

On 1 November 1827, Dalhousie summoned a general meeting of subscribers to find out whether there was sufficient interest in the project—"to advance to the work or to abandon it at once," as he put it. At that meeting, the committee got its first look at a memorial design by Captain John Young of the 79th Regiment, an Egyptian-style obelisk that towered 50 feet over a cenotaph. Constructed from limestone quarried near Montreal, it would be decorated by inscribed plaques of white marble. Much was made of the fact that the monument would be paid for by public donation; in fact, Dalhousie eventually had to contribute a good deal of his own money to make up for what he decided was the indifference of *les Canadiens* to their great general's memory.

If the monument itself was rather plain, at least the competition to produce the inscription yielded an inspired response from John Charlton Fisher, the editor of the *Gazette du Québec*. It neatly skirted the language issue by using Latin: *Mortem virtus communem / Famem historia / Monumentum posteritas dedit* (Military virtue gave them a common death / History a common fame / Posterity a common monument). Simple yet powerful, the inscription was even praised highly by the great Henry David Thoreau. It was probably the best thing about the monument.

The ceremony to lay the cornerstone was arranged for 15 November 1827. On that morning, the garden between rue des Carrières and rue Mont-Carmel was a bustle of activity. The Montreal garrison marched from its barracks and formed a line in the street, then opened ranks so that the parade could pass through: the band of the 66th Regiment, the Grand Lodge of Masons, the Sussex and St. Andrew's Lodges, and the Marchands et Frères du Canada. Entering the garden, they were joined by Montreal glitterati, including the Countess of Dalhousie "and a large party of fashionables," the Lord Bishop of Quebec, Captain Young, "the officer whose pencil produced the chaste and appropriate design," and the governor himself. Dalhousie couldn't have been in the best of humour that morning. The following week, his frustration at the political situation would finally boil over and he would dissolve the legislature when reformer Louis-Joseph Papineau, whom he regarded as a seditious troublemaker, was elected speaker. He was about to lay the cornerstone to a monument that would symbolize the reconciliation of English and French in Canada, but again and again, as he confided to his diary, his attempts to foster unity had failed: "[A] Canadian hates his British neighbour, as a Briton hates a Frenchman, by an inborn impulse," he wrote bitterly.

Still, Dalhousie knew his duty, so he put on his best face and said the appropriate words: "We are met today to lay the foundation of a Column in honour of two illustrious men, whose deeds and whose fall have immortalized their own names, and placed Québec in the rank of Cities famous in the history of the world." He led the dignitaries in prayer, and then invited the Masons to assist in lowering the cornerstone. The celebrity that morning was ninety-five-year-old James Thompson, perhaps the only survivor of the two armies commanded by Wolfe and Montcalm. Thompson was a tough old coot who was just about to retire after sixty-four years in public service, not because age had diminished his faculties but because a battle wound suffered in the siege of Montreal in 1775 had flared up. At Dalhousie's invitation, the old soldier came forward and "gave the Three Mystic Strokes with the Mallet on the Stone" as it was being lowered into place. On the stone was another plate whose inscription contrasted strongly with Fisher's distinguished prose. Composed by Dr. Joseph Langley Mills, the chaplain to the garrison, it said more about Dalhousie than about the two generals, noting that the monument was "a work neglected for many years" and one that only came about because of the Earl's dedication: "[H]e promoted by his influence, encouraged by his example, and favored by his munificence."

Within a year, the monument was completed and the unveiling set for 8 September 1828. By that time, Dalhousie had already been named Commander-in-Chief in India, so the ceremony would be his final official duty in Canada. The last few months of his appointment had done nothing to change his views on French–English reconciliation (he continued to suspect that the French had undermined his administration and resented the fact that "the Canadians alone appear stupidly indifferent" to his monument), and he insisted on referring to the column as Wolfe's monument. The day after the unveiling, he turned everything over to his successor and left Canada, never to return.

Most observers saw in the monument precisely the meaning that, in his earlier, more tolerant days, Dalhousie had intended. Catherine Parr Traill remarked that it evoked a "liberality of feeling that cannot but prove gratifying to the Canadian French, while it robs the British warrior of none of his glory." The passage of time, however, would soon compromise the monument's symbolism. In the 1860s, a large vertical crack started to appear in the column and widened to the point where engineers decided that it was in danger of splitting in half, a fate that would have been the irony of ironies. Under the direction of stonemason Henri Hatch and architect J.F. Rickson, the monument was demolished and completely rebuilt, and went on to become a favourite symbol of unity for generations of politicians. In 1927 Prime Minister Mackenzie King echoed his mentor, Sir Wilfrid Laurier, in calling the monument "a fitting symbol of the spirit which has made our nation; a spirit which, in preserving the heroisms, has buried the animosities of the races which have shaped its destiny." Wolfe and Montcalm might have been mystified at being held up as symbols of something they never could have imagined— a nation that stretched from sea to sea—but Dalhousie would have been satisfied.

Nelson could claim only a few months' contact with Canada. Wolfe and Montcalm were leading actors in a campaign that changed the course of Canadian history, but neither spent more than a few years in North America before falling in battle. Isaac Brock, on the other hand, spent more than a decade in Canada before his death, and can more easily be constructed as a true Canadian hero. A soldier since the age of fifteen, Brock arrived in Quebec in 1802, gradually rising through the ranks until 1811, when he took command of both the military and the government in Upper Canada. A competent administrator with little battle experience, Brock got the chance to prove himself with the War of 1812. He didn't waste the opportunity. In August 1812, a bold move against Detroit frightened the American commander into surrendering the city and its garrison to the British. Moving quickly to Niagara to deal with another threat there, on 13 October he was riding hard for Queenston, where an American force had landed. Brock's troops were pushing the invaders back, when a single bullet pierced his chest; he was killed. Rattled by the death of their commander, Brock's men wavered and the battle hung in the balance, until Major-General Roger Sheaffe led a bold attack that routed the invaders and saved the day.

Sheaffe may have won the battle but it was Brock whose blood was spilled on the battlefield and it was Brock who emerged as the hero of Queenston. Thus it was Brock who the Upper Canadian legislature decided to honour in March 1814 when it accepted Robert Nichol's proposal and voted £500 to start a fund to commemorate the general with a monument near where he fell. Nichol, described by a contemporary as a "mean looking little Scotchman, who squinted very much," had been a friend of Brock's before the war, so it seemed natural that he should take charge of a committee. He promptly appointed two friends: local politician Thomas Dickson and wealthy Niagara merchant Thomas Clark, both veterans of the war.

Their first task was to consult the Brock family in England, to determine what kind of memorial they deemed suitable; unwisely, Nichol promised airily that money would be no object. Months passed with no word from the family, and then in August 1817, John Brock, Isaac's younger brother, appeared at Dickson's door. He carried plans by Richard Westmacott, one of Britain's most sought-after sculptors and the very man who had created a memorial to the general in Westminster Abbey, for an 8-foot statue on a 10-foot pedestal, with reliefs illustrating the battles at Detroit and Queenston. The cost? A mere £2500, including shipping from England. After all, hadn't the Canadians said that money was no object?

In fact, money was very much an object, and the committee sat uncomfortably on the proposal for two years. When they finally brought Westmacott's ambitious design before the legislature, they heard the disappointing truth: the expected flood of donations had never come, and the fund now stood at only £1500, most of the increase coming from interest on sound investments. There was talk of erecting a much more modest (and cheaper) memorial, but the committee held firm. Brock deserved an "appropriate testimonial of the Strong feeling of veneration of public."

It was one thing to venerate, quite another to donate. By January 1824, the fund still stood at under £2000, so the call went out for designs for a simple tower at least 50 feet high, 16 feet wide, and with an internal staircase leading to an observation platform. In the end, the committee selected a column designed by engineer Francis Hall. At £2200, it wasn't much cheaper than Westmacott's, but at least the money would go to local labourers and suppliers. In any case, the wise investment of the original grant continued to pay handsome dividends, and the committee had every confidence that the required amount would soon be reached.

In June 1824, the cornerstone was laid, an occasion enlivened by soon-to-be-rebel William Lyon Mackenzie, who slipped under the stone a bottle containing some coins and a copy of his radical newspaper *The Colonial Advocate*. This threw the organizers into a flurry of activity, as one contemporary observed: "When the fact became known to the authorities, the foundation was ordered to be torn up and the obnoxious paper taken out, that the ghost of the immortal warrior might not be disturbed by its presence, and the structure not be rendered insecure." On 13 October 1824, some six thousand people travelled to Queenston for the ceremony to inter the remains of Brock and Lieutenant-Colonel John Macdonell, Brock's aide-de-camp who died on the battlefield shortly after his commander. It would be the second burial for both, and the *Globe* remarked rather ghoulishly that "the body of the General had undergone little change, his features being nearly perfect and easily recognised, while that of Lieutenant-Colonel McDonell [*sic*] was a mass of decomposition."

Three years passed, and work on the monument continued. Both Nichol and Dickson died (Nichol and his buggy plunged over the cliff near the monument site late one night in 1824), leaving Clark in charge. By 1827, the tower had reached its intended height of 135 feet, but there was no inscription at the base, the railing around the observation deck had not been installed, and there was no sign of the promised statue of Brock. Three more years went by, Clark too died, and the government had to strike a new committee to find out what was going on with the memorial. The short answer was nothing—so the legislature ordered a simple ornament to be placed where the statue should have gone, and Brock's Monument was declared complete.

Then on 17 April 1840, just before dawn, a powerful explosion shook Queenston Heights. A bomb exploded inside the column, leaving the wooden staircase completely destroyed, the shaft itself badly cracked, and a section of the top blown off; if the door at the bottom hadn't been opened, allowing some of the force of the blast to escape, the whole tower likely would have come down.

When news of the bombing spread through Upper Canada, the people were gripped, as a contemporary put it, by "one universal feeling of disgust and abhorrence." The lieutenant-governor, Sir George Arthur, offered a reward of £1000 for the apprehension of the culprits, and suspicion immediately fell on Benjamin Lett, an Irish immigrant who was accused of a string of crimes along the Upper Canadian border. Lett already had a price on his head for a murder in Cobourg in 1839, and the *Globe* expressed the general sentiment that he had bombed Brock's Monument "to gratify his malicious and vindictive spirit, and at the same time wound and insult the people of Canada." Lett was soon in custody in New York State, charged with planting a bomb on the steamer *Great Britain* at Oswego. But he would never face trial in Canada. After being convicted of the Oswego bombing, he escaped from the train that was taking him to jail. He eventually did spend four years behind bars, then headed west and died in Milwaukee in 1858.

Whether or not Lett actually committed the crime against the people of Upper Canada, Hall's column had been turned into what Susannah Moodie called "a melancholy looking ruin … resembling some tall chimney that has been left standing after the house to which it belonged had been burnt down." Clearly, it couldn't be left in that state, either for symbolic or safety reasons. Hall ventured that the tower could be repaired for £370, but others said that it should be pulled down and replaced with a grander one to reflect the community's veneration of Brock and its anger at the vandalism. There was nothing to do but call a public assembly to decide on a course of action. It would go down in local history as the Indignation Meeting.

The great day was 30 July 1840. A public holiday had been declared in Toronto, Niagara, Queenston, and St. Catharines, and nine lake steamers festooned with patriotic banners and packed with cheering crowds sailed toward Queenston from Toronto, Cobourg, Kingston, and Hamilton. They had all been timed to arrive at ten o'clock in the morning, when they formed up and ascended the river in a line abreast, led by HMS *Traveller* with the lieutenant-governor aboard. As well as the eight thousand people on the steamers, thousands more came by cart, horseback, or on foot, and they clustered around a platform at the base of the ruined monument.

Organizers had decided that the British flag must fly over the ruined column, but the only steeplejack willing to take on the job was a fellow from Buffalo. This was too much for Matthew Murphy, a roisterer from Ottawa who happened to be passing through the area. When he heard of the plans, he immediately volunteered to do the job himself. "I'll put the British flag on top, or die in the attempt, before any foreigner will do it," he announced. And to the delight of the crowds, he did. By climbing the iron lightning rod that ran up the side of the column, he eventually reached the observation deck and unfurled the flag. Murphy's climb was the most exciting part of a day that degenerated into a marathon of speech-making. Sir George Arthur started things off and was followed by twenty-four other speakers, all of whom said essentially the same things— Brock was still revered, the vandalism was an act of pure malice, a new memorial should be erected as soon as possible, and a committee should be formed to that end. Exhausted by the speechifying, Arthur and six hundred of the chosen retired to a huge marquee for the official banquet.

The new committee immediately decided that no money would be sought from the legislature; the entire monument would be funded through private donations. But for over a decade they dithered—over the plans, the cost, the location—and it wasn't until 1852 that a mutually satisfactory design was selected. The winner was Toronto architect William Thomas, whose tower was judged "very bold and effective," particularly in that its height would make it visible from a great distance. (Were they thinking of New York State?) At the base, a mausoleum would hold the mortal remains of Brock and Macdonell, but the main attraction was the column rising 185 feet; at the top, each of the four faces of the capital featured a winged figure of victory, all surmounted by a 16-foot figure of Brock, with one arm pointing toward Toronto. It would be the second highest structure of its kind in the world, after Christopher Wren's column in London commemorating the 1666 fire.

With the design agreed upon, in July 1853 the committee entered into a contract, valued at £5,350, with Thomas and builder John Worthington. It arranged for the demolition of the original monument, and then the remains of Brock (who surely no longer looked "nearly perfect and easily recognised") and Macdonell were unceremoniously shovelled into a couple of pine boxes for temporary burial at a nearby estate. On 13 October 1853, the mausoleum was ready for the fourth interment of the two heroes' remains, though this ceremony was rather less impressive. There were complaints that Brock and Macdonell should have been placed in full-size coffins instead of miniature ones, which were all they needed given what was left of them. Furthermore, the keynote speaker, the canal-builder and entrepreneur William Hamilton Merritt who had fought at Queenston Heights that fateful day, seemed embarrassed and uncomfortable; it didn't help that he was constantly interrupted by other veterans of the battle, who sat in the front row and loudly contradicted Merritt's version of the events.

The dismal ceremony may have been something of an omen, for by the spring of 1854 it was clear that Thomas was running into trouble, thanks to problems with the stone, unusually wet weather, and a late decision to move the monument to higher ground. The building committee suggested hiring other contractors to speed up the work, but Thomas held firm, staking his reputation on John Worthington. And when the promised deadline passed, Thomas personally accepted the blame. He implored the committee not to bring in someone else to finish the work or levy a penalty on Worthington, for he knew that the luckless contractor was already working only for pride; far from making a profit, the entire job eventually cost Worthington £500 out of his own pocket.

Even with Thomas's apologies, the legislature was not happy about the delays, or the spiralling costs. Thanks to wise investments, the original fund had ballooned to £6990, but labour and material costs were so high that Worthington had already spent £1071 more than his original estimate. At current costs, by the time the monument was completed, another £2262 would be owing, not including the expenses of developing the adjoining land, building the caretaker's lodge, fencing the area, and landscaping the approaches; the total cost for the project would exceed £12,000. Still, legislators had no doubt that it would be money well spent: "This Monument is the only National Structure which commemorates the gallant defence of *Canada* and should, in the opinion of Your Committee, be completed in a style worthy of the heroic deeds." Like Nelson, Wolfe, and Montcalm, Brock was becoming a national hero before the nation even existed.

Thomas managed to finish in time for the unveiling on 13 October 1859, the anniversary of Brock's death. The best account of the occasion was published in the *Globe,* which dispatched an anonymous correspondent with an endearing eye for the absurd. He left Toronto on the steamer *Zimmerman,* accompanied by soldiers of the city's garrison and about 150 spectators. Leaving the safety of the harbour, they soon encountered rough waters, making the journey a misery for those on board: "[A]s a natural consequence many a gallant volunteer was soon in a state of commotion … [and] had to bend before the remorseless persecutor of 'land lubbers.' Men whose backs no enemy will ever see, were obliged to turn their backs upon the ladies who had come to see them, and seek refuge on the pillows below." But their discomfort was short-lived, and soon the steamer drew into the Niagara River to berth at Queenston. There, the Toronto troops began to scale the Heights four abreast, but still nature refused to cooperate and gusts of wind blew "dust into the eyes of all, and soon sobered down the gaudiest uniforms into an almost Quaker drab." Meanwhile, the civilians from the *Zimmerman* were poking around a large tent filled with refreshments for the post-unveiling banquet—cider, ginger cakes, sugar sticks, pots of ale. Not everyone was pleased by the sight of so much food, observed the reporter ("Especially distressed were some of those whose morning meal had been rendered up as an offering to offended Ontario"), but for those with strong stomachs, the sight of the feast "excited disagreeable recollections that six hours had been spent in the fresh air without breaking fast." An outright assault on the tent was averted only by the arrival of the steamer *Peerless* from Hamilton, bringing that city's garrison and more spectators. Anyone with a shilling to spare could climb the monument, although the *Globe* reporter noted sourly that many of them were defeated by the stairs and only got three-quarters of the way up.

The featured speaker for the day was the entrepreneur and railway promoter Sir Allan MacNab, who had served in the War of 1812 as a teenager and later led the militia against William Lyon Mackenzie's rebels in 1837. By 1859, his best days were behind him, his once-great fortune dwindled to nothing and his body racked by the agonies of gout. Still, he used the occasion to revisit the glory days of the past. Mindful of the fact that it was also the centenary of the Battle of the Plains of Abraham, he compared Brock to the other great military heroes of Canada's past, Wolfe and Montcalm. He couldn't resist making reference to the "wanton and malicious spoliation" of the first column, but asked the crowd to reflect instead on Brock's heroism and the example he set for future generations. A succession of retired colonels and generals followed MacNab to the podium, but by now the reporter noticed that the spectators were getting restive. Finally, a voice called out, "What is the next item in the programme, Sir Allan?" MacNab, still the canny politician, didn't miss a beat. "Go to dinner!" he bellowed.

With that, Brock's Monument became a fixture on the Niagara skyline. There were no more bombings (although a lightning strike in April 1929 snapped off Brock's right arm and sent it crashing to the ground; the half-ton limb was eventually replaced) and, according to countless post-Confederation textbooks, travel guides, and popular histories, the tower became a national icon for the new Dominion of Canada. It was also an obligatory stop on the tourist route through the Niagara Peninsula. One traveller was the poet Charles Sangster, whose visit inspired the poem *From Queenston Heights*. After waxing rhapsodically about Brock's column, he concluded with a description of the bridge across the Niagara River, a sight that contrasted strongly with the monument and reminded him that "[T]he wondrous skill / Of the mechanic, with this iron web / Has spanned the chasm." As Sangster realized, the times were changing. The courage and gallantry of the great soldiers, whose deeds built nations, were being joined by the skill and vision of the great engineers, who would also build nations. He could not have imagined it, but the tower that inspired his verse, as well as the columns to Nelson, Wolfe, and Montcalm, would have their twentieth-century counterparts—towers erected not as monuments to a nation built on the battlefield, but as monuments to one built on commerce.

MAYBE IT WAS Brock's Monument in nearby Queenston that convinced Niagara Falls hoteliers George Sainovich and his son-in-law John Gruyich that their city needed a tower of its own. After all, there was nothing particular to see from the top of Brock's Monument, but a tower in Niagara Falls would provide views of one of the world's most popular

tourist attractions. So, in December 1960, they announced plans for a
480-foot-tall tower with a revolving restaurant and lounge at the top and
a convention centre at the base. It would be built on land purchased from
the family of the fabulously wealthy gold baron Sir Harry Oakes, a leading
benefactor of the city and a man whose brutal murder in the Bahamas in
1943 had overshadowed much of what he had done in his life. But the
price tag was big—from $2 million to as much as $5 million, depending
on the variables. So, the pair went back to rethink their plans. By 1964,
they had put together a consortium of investors who saw the same potential in the project that they did: William Young of the Hamilton Cotton
Company (the grandfather of Bob Young, co-founder and former chairman of Red Hat Software, the creator of the Linux computer operating
system); Edward Buell Senior and Junior of the Niagara Wire and
Weaving Company; William Pigott of Pigott Construction, the company
that had built the Fathers of Confederation Memorial Building in
Charlottetown; and candy-maker Richard Reese, whose family name
would later grace the peanut-butter cup. They announced that their
project would be known as the Skylon, a term first used for a suspended
steel column displayed at the Festival of Britain in 1951. It wasn't really
a word yet—Edward Buell, Jr., said that it meant a space-age version of a
skyscraper—so they went ahead and copyrighted it, just to make sure that
no one else used it again before they did.

Soon they had a property—the Oakes land and an adjacent parcel as a
right-of-way—and an architect, the firm of Bregman + Hamann of
Toronto. Their design was just what Sainovich and Gruyich had envisioned four years earlier: a 520-foot tower topped by a three-storey dome
(representing, according to the designers, the northern hemisphere) that
held an indoor/outdoor observation deck; a dining room that would
revolve once every hour, all on the strength of a three-horsepower motor;
and a stationary buffet restaurant and lounge. At the base of the tower, a
three-storey exhibition area would contain shops, lounges, restaurants,
and convention halls to be used for everything from trade shows to art
exhibitions. Inspired by the Space Needle in Seattle, the design won the
Ontario Association of Architects First Award for Design, and was a finalist for the Massey Medal for Architecture that same year.

Designing the tower was one thing—making it happen was quite another. William Pigott's company handled the construction, and the engineering challenges were significant. It had to be wind resistant (the average wind speed in Niagara Falls is only about 14 miles per hour, but the tower was engineered to withstand gusts of up to 110 miles per hour—the maximum gust ever recorded at the top of the tower is 91 miles per hour) and was also built to withstand earthquakes. When Pigott started excavating in May 1964, the foundation was sunk to a depth of 35 feet; at that point, it was 94 feet in diameter, but the foundation widens out to 160 feet just below ground level. The foundation alone took 6000 tons of concrete and 300 tons of reinforced steel.

The big innovation came in the method of construction, the slipform technique that Frank Peavey had pioneered the previous century to build grain elevators. Those structures were relatively simple because they were columns; the Skylon tapered, from about 72 feet in diameter at the bottom to about 33 feet at the base of the dome, which meant that the slipform had to shrink as it moved upwards. The concrete pouring began on 23 September 1964 and continued, twenty-four hours a day, for thirty-eight days. The 40-inch-high form was moved upwards by fifteen hydraulic jacks, each weighing 2 tons, at a rate of one inch every ten minutes, or 12 feet per day. When finished, the shaft had used 12,000 tons of concrete and 800 tons of steel.

The dome was next, and things didn't get any easier. The concrete form for the base of the dome had to be constructed on the ground, around the base of the tower, and then raised by hydraulic jacks to the correct height, 380 feet, a process that took eight days. It was then secured in place with thirty-six massive steel bolts 25 feet long and 2.5 inches in diameter. Once it was in place, the next pour began, using 800 yards of concrete and 125 tons of steel to reinforce the base of the dome. When the dome was completed the following summer, the form started its slow journey back down the column, this time carrying a work crew who painted the shaft as the form descended.

When complete, the Skylon was rightly viewed as an engineering marvel. Standing 520 feet tall (including the 43-foot-tall top mast), it rose 775 feet above the base of Niagara Falls, making it the tallest structure of its kind in the world. To get to the dome, visitors could use one of the three Yellow Bugs, the high-speed elevators (the first external building elevators in Canada) that whisked people up at 500 feet per minute, or one of the two 662-step staircases that ran up the middle of the shaft. The tower certainly did look space age, just as Buell had suggested, and the $12 million price tag seemed a small price to pay for such a wonder.

Ontario premier John Robarts and Nelson Rockefeller, the governor of New York State, shared a pair of golden scissors to cut the ceremonial ribbon and officially open the Skylon on 6 October 1965. Outside the observation deck, rockets fired small parachutes carrying the Canadian, British, and American flags, which floated gently to the ground. Despite the fact that one newspaper advised tourists to avoid the tower until everything was finished—the cavernous exhibition halls remained empty, and the manager blasted the federal and provincial governments for not renting display space in what he said would become a tourist mecca—there were still more than enough people willing to pay the dollar to ride a Yellow Bug to the observation deck.

The tower immediately became a magnet for the millions of tourists who already flocked to the falls each year, as journalist Scott Young wrote in an irreverent article about the sexualization of the Honeymoon Capital of the World: the waitresses in restaurants and taverns were wearing less and less clothing, the advertisements were getting more and more racy, and now the city was filling up with huge, phallic observation towers. Never mind, he concluded, it was all about meeting the challenge of the changing times. It was also about generating tower envy among other civic leaders. In January 1966, Montreal mayor Jean Drapeau, then deeply immersed in the construction of Expo '67, visited Skylon as part of his campaign to get a similar observation tower built at the Expo site. He returned to Quebec mightily impressed by the number and size of towers in Niagara Falls.

The Skylon has passed through a number of owners over the years, including the CP Hotel chain, and has also seen its share of oddities. In 1975, European stuntman Henry Rechatin balanced on two chairs at the top of the tower, in an effort to draw attention to his bid to get Niagara Falls officials to let him walk a tightrope across the falls. In June 1985, the first parachutist jumped from the tower's observation deck; at least a dozen other base jumpers followed him in later years, and there have been no casualties. There have, however, been suicides, the first in June 1972, when a twenty-one-year-old jobless man from Flint, Michigan, clambered over the 7-foot guard fence on the observation deck and, to the horror of security guards desperately trying to talk him back, plunged to his death. The true mark of the tower's success, though, beyond its promotion to one of the most recognizable symbols of Niagara Falls as a magnet for tourists, is surely the fact that it was followed by so many imitators—Jean Drapeau didn't get his tower for Expo '67 (although the city did get one in 1987, when the 574-foot tower leaning over Olympic Stadium was completed), but other municipal politicians were luckier.

If Niagara Falls could have a world-class observation tower, why not Calgary? When oil was discovered in Turner Valley in 1947, it was natural that Calgary, just 175 miles away, should become the administrative centre of the province's oil and gas industry; by the late 1960s, some four hundred energy-related companies had their head offices there. And the city boomed along with the oil and gas industry. Between 1947 and 1972, Calgary's population quadrupled, housing developments began to spread out into the south Alberta plain, and tall buildings were crowding the skyline. The city needed something big to symbolize its new status. The downtown core could use some revitalization—wealthy Calgarians had deserted the city centre for the new, affluent suburbs—and what better way to do that than with a massive building project that would put Calgary on the map? As usual, the railways were involved. The CPR had spun off Marathon Realty to manage its real estate holdings, particularly the urban land it owned, and in Calgary, Marathon had to find something to do with a downtown site that used to house the passenger depot and train sheds. The solution was to partner with Husky Oil, a local company looking for head office space, to erect a complex on the site. The centrepiece would be a huge observation tower like the Skylon, something that would dominate the city's skyline and act as a symbol, both of corporate strength and of the nation's one hundredth birthday, which was fast approaching.

At first city councillors shook their heads in disbelief when the idea for a tower like the Skylon came before them. "They thought it would be too tall. They thought it would fall over," recalled Rod Sykes, who would later become manager for the construction project and would parlay that success into a term as the city's mayor. But Sykes was determined to change their minds and brought in technical experts and engineers from around the world to convince them the idea would work.

In time, everyone was brought onside and construction began on 19 February 1967. In many respects, the new tower replicated the Skylon. The slipform method was the same (continuous pouring began on 15 May 1967 and finished twenty-four days later, with a record one-day pour of 39 feet), and, although Calgary is not in an earthquake zone, the tower was also engineered to withstand quakes, the first building on the prairies to be so designed. Wind was also a concern, more so on the prairies than in Niagara Falls, so the tower was built to take winds of up to 100 miles per hour; on a windy day, the top will sway up to 7.5 inches. The tower also had the same high-speed elevators as the Skylon (a sixty-two-second ride would get you to the top).

Just how high was the top? The magic number was kept under wraps until the last minute. Officially, it was to be 613 feet tall, but the day before the official opening, the engineers let slip their secret. They had feared being beaten by a late competitor, and, sure enough, in the spring of 1968, the city of San Antonio, Texas, announced that its new Tower of the Americas was 622 feet tall, making it the tallest in North America. Only then did the Calgary builders show their hand. The Husky Tower actually stretched up to 626 feet—San Antonio had been tricked. Calgary's engineers even admitted that they still had some capacity left if the Texans tried to add a few feet to their tower and reclaim the title.

In June 1968, the Husky Tower was given three separate opening cere-monies: the North American opening on the 28th, the Alberta opening on the 29th, and the public opening on the 30th. That was the only way they could do it—there were simply too many dignitaries involved to fit on the observation deck at once. But that didn't bother Calgarians, who started showing up at the tower at four o'clock in the morning on opening day to be the first up, or the journalists who were given a tour by property managers. Lawrie Joslin of the Calgary *Herald,* after admitting that the view from 600 feet gave him new insights into the city—too much smog, too many parking lots, not enough green space—was nevertheless enthusiastic: it was "sure to give Calgarians a new vantage point for reinforcing their pride and appreciation of the city." Grant MacEwan agreed that the tower would give citizens a new perspective on their city as a linchpin linking the prairie wheat fields with the markets beyond the Rockies; it was "symbolic of achievement, also a symbol of faith in the city's future."

Almost from the beginning, Calgary marketed its tower aggressively, particularly to businesspeople from eastern Canada. The revolving restaurant was a top draw—chef Donald Cutler was named Canadian Chef of the Year in 1969, even though he admitted a preference for peanut butter sandwiches and his wife's soup—and advertisements warned of the consequences for the corporate executive who went back to Bay Street without having eaten in the tower's restaurant: "Don't take chances on being embarrassed, make sure you dine in the sky at least once."

On 1 November 1971, the structure became the Calgary Tower (airlines still use the old name because the control tower at the city's airport is called Calgary Tower) when Husky Oil sold its share to Marathon Realty, the first in a series of changes for the structure. It was thirteen years later, in 1984, that Calgary Tower suffered its first indignity: with the completion of PetroCanada's West Tower, Calgary's former record-breaker became only the second-tallest building in the city. The tower had another moment in the sun in 1988, when Calgary hosted the Winter Olympics. On 13 February 1988, the Olympic flame was lit atop it in a specially installed natural gas cauldron. Visible from just over 9 miles away, it would burn for sixteen days, using more than 30,000 cubic feet of good Alberta natural gas every hour, before being extinguished as part of the Games' closing ceremonies on 29 February. The torch is still used on special occasions. In fact, just two weeks after the Olympics ended, it was relit as part of a satellite television link-up between Calgary and the Namsan Tower in Seoul, to commemorate the Olympic movement and, not incidentally, to use the spirit of the Games to capitalize on boosting trade with Asia. But in 1990, when Bankers Halls was built, the Calgary Tower slipped to third place in the height competition. Every once in a while, Calgarians speculate that the owners might want to add to the top of the tower, to restore its status as the city's tallest structure, but developers and engineers have always derided the idea. As Rod Sykes said of such dreamers, "If they tell people that it can be added to, then they're out to lunch. Anybody who looks at it seriously will know it's ridiculous."

Just six years later, as part of its overall campaign to shed debt, Marathon put the Calgary Tower up for sale as part of a bundle of downtown properties that included office towers, a gas station, a power plant, and 1200 parking spots. It was priced at $50 million, and a commercial realtor was sent on a whirlwind tour of Canada, the United States, and Asia to beat the bushes for potential buyers. And then came the ultimate insult—the pride of Calgary was sold to the Toronto-based Oxford Property Group, which was becoming one of largest office landlords in the city. Relations between the two cities had never been warm—when Calgarians called the new Toronto City Hall a giant clamshell, *Globe and Mail* columnist Orlando French compared the Calgary Tower to a fire hydrant in Tuktoyaktuk— and the prospect of one of the city's architectural showpieces falling into the hands of Easterners was too much for some people to bear.

Yet in some ways things are looking up for the Calgary Tower. From 1987 to 2003, a series of renovation projects refurbished most of the interior, providing more usable space and modernizing the facilities. By 1999, *Globe and Mail* writer Peter Menzies had to admit that the tower was once again becoming a symbol for Calgary's economic vitality, although he, like Scott Young two decades earlier, couldn't resist remarking on the sexual overtones: "The city, with its all-too-obvious phallic land-mark, the Calgary Tower—the inspiration for Toronto's look-alike—surges with an economic virility." Unfortunately for Calgarians, the look-alike had long since eclipsed its inspiration.

It is ironic that Canada's greatest tower, the CN Tower in Toronto, is the best known of the three, despite the fact that it is really just a larger copy of the towers in Niagara Falls and Calgary. But at least when you're talking about towers, as Young and Menzies realized, size does matter, especially when one of the considerations going into designing the build-ing is the expected quality of television signals.

The Toronto skyscraper-building spree of the 1960s and early 1970s had been a boon for developers and real estate firms, but a disaster for anyone in the city who wanted to watch television. As the skyline became more and more crowded with tall buildings, television and radio signals had an increasingly difficult time navigating their way from antennas to TV sets. They bounced off buildings at odd angles, creating a phenomenon known as ghosting: when a weaker signal competes with a stronger one, both can occupy your screen at the same time, forcing you to watch two programs simultaneously. One Torontonian recalled that the only station that reached his set clearly was from Buffalo, New York—not even the local television stations came in clearly. The sound was perfect, but the image was repeated four or five times on the screen, producing a "psychedelic colour combination that could cause migraine in a rock."

One way to solve this was to build a much bigger antenna, and, luckily for Torontonians, two of the nation's biggest and most historic corporations, Canadian National Railways and the Canadian Pacific Railway (through Marathon Realty), were thinking in the same direction. They came up with the Metro Centre Project, a $1-billion plan to develop 190 acres along Toronto's waterfront into a new downtown of residential and commercial buildings. The plan didn't have much to do with railways, but CN's executive vice-president, Norman MacMillan, believed in diversity in operations and threw his support behind the project. City council approved the scheme in 1972, but then it ran head-first into local anti-development sentiment. Having watched helplessly as architectural gems fell to the wrecker's ball in the 1960s, citizens were in no mood to see the historic Union Station reduced to rubble, as the project envisioned, so at the earliest opportunity they elected a reformist city council and got the project approval overturned. With that, Marathon, which was to share the costs of the project on a fifty-fifty basis, pulled out, leaving CN to do what it could to salvage the plan. One project they decided to go ahead with was a communications tower, to deal with Toronto's television signal problem, but it soon became much more than a tall antenna. The corporation sensed an opportunity to showcase the strength of Canadian industry by building the highest tower in the world. The practical and the symbolic came together—CN was going to reach for the clouds.

CN Tower lore has Bud Andrews, a development consultant for the railways, sketching out a rough design on a napkin, and then passing it on to the architects and engineers. Just who was responsible for the final design is a matter of some debate—"No one ever sees a CN Tower on resumés," observed one engineer—but we do know that an early design envisioned three separate tubular towers, linked by structural bridges every 150 feet. Testing revealed that such a structure would be almost unbuildable, so the design was refined into a single tower standing on three legs, built in the shape of a symmetrical Y. In 1972, after final testing on a scale model at a wind-tunnel facility at The University of Western Ontario, the CN board gave the go-ahead.

Built at a time when the disaster film was Hollywood's big-money genre (the Steve McQueen epic *The Towering Inferno,* about a fire in a huge office building, was released while the CN Tower was under construction), the new structure incorporated every conceivable safety feature. It claimed to be able to withstand gusts of up to 260 miles per hour, and was said to be impervious to an impact by a fully loaded Boeing 747. Engineers designed a complex system for electrical grounding (the tower could expect some two hundred lightning strikes a year), and electric heaters were strategically placed around the dome, to prevent the accumulation of ice (one of the problems that plagued the Ostankino Tower in Moscow was immense chunks of ice, some weighing as much as 275 pounds, that fell from the tower and landed up to a third of a mile away). Even the elevators were the subject of intensive testing. Built by Otis, which had created the Skylon's Yellow Bugs, the CN's would rise higher than anything the company had yet produced, including the elevators built for the Churchill Falls hydroelectric project in Labrador, which reached a height of 1000 feet. The elevators would travel at a speed of 1200 feet per minute, and CN hired specialists to determine whether the rapid ascent in such a small elevator would cause eye problems or trigger claustrophobia. There was little they could do to help claustrophobic visitors, but consultants advised painting horizontal black lines on the elevator shaft to prevent eye-fixation problems. Every visitor to the tower will be grateful that the other suggestion, piped-in music, was rejected.

On 6 February 1973, the excavation work began. A structure of that size required an enormous foundation, so the engineers had to drill test holes 118 feet deep, before calculating how deep the foundation should be. They decided to dig down 49 feet, removing 62,000 tons of fill, and then groom a flat, smooth base of shale, which was subsequently covered with wet burlap to prevent the shale from deteriorating while the concrete was prepared. Onto that base, crews poured a 12-inch-thick pad, and then a 23-foot-thick foundation of concrete and steel, for a total of 9200 yards of cement, 500 tons of reinforcing steel, and 40 tons of tensioning cables. Four months were needed to prepare the foundation, to make it ready for each leg of the Y to support a share of the tower's total weight of 130,000 tons.

The construction of the shaft itself used the slipform method, with the six-piece form being raised in unison by forty-five hydraulic jacks; concrete was poured twenty-four hours a day, seven days a week, with the tower rising about 16 feet each day. By the fall of 1973, the shaft was the tallest structure in Toronto; on 22 February 1974, when the top of the tower segment was reached and the pod could be constructed, it became the tallest in Canada. At that point, twelve massive brackets, each weighing 313 long tons, were inched up the tower using the same process as the slipform. When they were anchored in place in August 1974, the concrete floor and walls of the seven-storey pod could be poured. At this level, 1109 feet above the ground, workers installed the first of the telecommunications equipment, to accept UHF and VHF television signals and feed them to antennas for broadcasting. Protecting the equipment from the elements was a radome, an inflated bubble of Teflon-coated, fibreglass-rayon fabric.

When the pod was completed, all that remained was to install the antenna. But first, the crane that had sat atop the dome to bring up construction material had to be removed. It was then that the construction ran into one of its only close calls. A helicopter was hooked up to the crane, but as the retaining bolts were removed, the crane lurched sideways, twisting the base and making it impossible to remove the rest of the bolts. The helicopter couldn't pull away, and had only fifty minutes of fuel in its tanks. It was a Hollywood disaster-movie scenario, but in the end an emergency crew saved the day: they managed to cut away the last of the bolts, and the helicopter lifted the crane down to safety.

In March 1975, a heavy-duty Russian helicopter nicknamed Olga (she became an attraction in her own right, her schedule appearing in local newspapers so people could watch her at work) began to lift the forty-four pieces of the 335-foot antenna mast to the top of the tower. On 2 April 1975, as traffic on the nearby Gardiner Expressway ground to a halt and people lined the windows of downtown office buildings to watch, the final section was lowered into place and the last of the 40,000 bolts holding the mast together was reefed home. Doing the honours was ironworker foreman Paul Mitchell, who then danced a jig at the top of the tower to celebrate its completion.

By any measure, the building of the CN Tower was a remarkable achievement. It's easy to get caught up in the statistics on height (the official figure is 1815 feet, 5 inches), yards of concrete, or tons of steel cable, but the real strength behind the project was in the 1567 men and women who built it. There were no labour disputes (if we don't count the worker who was fired for parachuting off the crane at the 1526-foot-level), and only one worker died on the jobsite, project inspector John Ashton, who, ironically, lost his life while working at ground level.

The official opening was set for midnight on 25 June 1976, but long before then the lines had started to form. The first people were two young men from Toronto whose previous claim to fame had been an attempt to break the world record for continuous card-playing—they had spent days camped out at the foot of the tower and were rewarded with free passes for their perseverance. To honour the structure properly, CN had invited all the tall people it could find, including the tallest member of the federal cabinet, Donald Macdonald, at 6 feet 5 inches. Helping him switch on the lights to open the tower were Roger Tickner, a 7-foot-tall Downsview man, and Paula Lishman from Blackstock, Ontario, who stood a shade over 6 foot 3. The Toronto *Star* got into the act by dispatching staff writer Joe Hall, who at 6 foot 4 claimed to be the world's tallest free-standing reporter. There was champagne and fireworks, clowns and jugglers—in short, a great party.

And it wasn't long before the CN Tower proved itself. It quickly became one of the city's major tourist draws—a million visitors came through the doors in the first six months of operation alone—and profits from the tower consistently offset CN's operating losses on the rail side. The tower immediately claimed a number of superlatives. Ross McWhirter of *The*

Guinness Book of World Records was on hand at the official opening to certify it as the world's tallest free-standing structure, and it also holds the titles for the world's longest metal staircase and the world's highest wine cellar. In 1995 the American Society of Civil Engineers ranked it as one of the Seven Wonders of the Modern World (with the Itaipu Dam on the Brazil/Paraguay border, the Golden Gate Bridge in San Francisco, the Panama Canal, the Chunnel, the North Sea protection works off the European coast, and the Empire State Building). But like the Skylon and the Calgary Tower, the CN Tower has never been able to shake the sexual metaphor. Actor Don Harron once commented that it was built to teach Canadian men humility, and Will Ferguson called it an ode to virility. Journalist Lisa Rochon denied that the tower has ever been characterized as "oppressively masculine," but as it celebrated its twenty-fifth birthday in June 2001, she couldn't resist sexualizing it as "an elegant body in a permanent state of undress ... [that is] as smooth as young flesh." One wonders how Brock or Nelson would have reacted to hear their towers described in such terms.

GREAT TOWERS have been built around the world, of course, but perhaps they mean a little more in Canada than elsewhere. In a country of huge spaces, people have always looked for ways to make a mark on their surroundings and have used buildings as a sign of their domination of the landscape. The provincial legislatures and the railway hotels were certainly designed with that in mind—to awe the visitor even while they staked claim on the territory they overlooked.

The great towers of the nineteenth and twentieth centuries come from the same tradition. For the men who sponsored the monuments to Nelson, Wolfe, Montcalm, and Brock, the monuments' size was important because they were impossible to ignore. They loomed over their surroundings, a constant reminder of the values—duty, honour, courage, patriotism—that they symbolized. And if they have lost much of the symbolic impact that they once had, the recent battle over Nelson's Monument reminds us never to underestimate the enduring power of old icons.

The builders of the Skylon, the Husky Tower, and the CN Tower also wanted to make them impossible to ignore, although the values they symbolized—economic might, commercial success, civic pride—were a little different. As well, though, the new towers were for seeing as much as being seen. Brock's Monument had an observation deck, but that function was purely secondary to the commemorative use of the memorial. With the twentieth-century towers, the erection of a vantage point in the clouds has more symbolic meaning than might at first be apparent. Certainly they are great tourist draws, but they also say a lot about how we as Canadians view our land. Will Ferguson's comments on the CN Tower might apply to any of these structures: "You feel as though, if the light were right and you squint your eyes just so, you might even see the Rocky Mountains. Perhaps that is why the CN Tower is such a Canadian icon: in a country as big as ours, it takes a tower this tall just to get a decent view."

CARVED IN IMPERISHABLE GRANITE

We probably don't realize it, but we all carry some of Emanuel Hahn's work around with us. The *Bluenose* sailing majestically across the Canadian dime? That's his design. So is the caribou that graces our quarter, and the *voyageur* scene on the old silver dollar. In the 1950s, Canadians saw his creations every day on their postage stamps, and his work still gets a showing every year when the Lou Marsh Trophy he designed is awarded to the year's outstanding Canadian athlete. From the late 1930s until his death in 1957, the German-born, Toronto-based Hahn built a reputation as one of Canada's foremost designers of coins, postage stamps, medals, and trophies. If you look closely, you can see his initials on his coins, but he was the kind of artist whose creations were much better known than his name—few people have heard of Emanuel Hahn, but almost everyone is familiar with his work.

Earlier in his career, though, Hahn had worked on a much larger scale, creating some of the most impressive monuments to grace the Canadian landscape. The highs and lows of his career were embodied in two designs for war memorials. One, for the city of Winnipeg, was never even executed, yet it brought Hahn the kind of notoriety that he could have done without. The other, a young soldier standing solemnly over a battlefield cross, doesn't even bear his name and has brought him few accolades. Yet it was purchased by towns across Canada, the iconic figure providing a link between distant communities and becoming a symbol of the young nation's sacrifice in war.

How fitting that a sculptor whose work became a visual symbol of Canada's collective effort in wartime owed his presence here directly to the nation-building plans of the federal government. Sir John A. Macdonald's vision was about transforming Canada from a scattered collection of provinces into a unified nation stretching from sea to sea. To achieve that, Macdonald laid down three major planks in the raucous federal election campaign of 1878: the transcontinental railway, a ribbon of steel to draw the ends of the country together; a protective tariff to give Canadian manufacturers a chance to grow in a sheltered marketplace; and immigration, to fill Canada's vast western plains with farmers who could bring the region into agricultural production. The first two obviously demanded action on the part of the federal government, but so too did the third. In the past, immigrants had come to Canada willy-nilly—the authorities were happy to welcome them when they reached Halifax or Montreal but did little to encourage them to come here in the first place. No more. To draw the number of immigrants that the West could support, the government had to get out there and sell Canada as a land that was open for settlement. Ottawa had to search out potential immigrants, inundate them with publicity material, and encourage them to choose Canada over the United States. The trick was to avoid getting too many of the urban working class—what the government really wanted were sturdy European farmers ("stalwart peasants in sheep-skin coats," as the minister of the Interior, Sir Clifford Sifton, called them) who had the skills and experience to take up homesteads in the West and quickly bring farms into production. To help locate suitable settlers, Ottawa employed dozens of agents in Europe.

One man with aspirations in that direction was Dr. Otto Hahn, a lawyer-turned-natural-scientist who visited Canada in 1878. He made a second trip to Canada in 1881 and, with hopes of securing a commission from the federal government, immigrated to Toronto in 1888 with his wife and their ten children. Unfortunately the anticipated appointment never materialized and Dr. Hahn found himself in an alien city with a large family to feed. Unable to practise law in Canada and without a strong command of the English language, he had to rely on his five sons to help support the family in a kind of genteel poverty. Paul got a job with a piano manufacturer, Walter and Fritz earned steady incomes as concert violinists, and Gustav quickly became a successful artist. That left the youngest, Emanuel. Dr. Hahn had never expressed much confidence in his youngest son's intellectual potential, and when Emanuel finished grade eight he was sent out to work, soon finding a job as an office boy.

When the Hahn family first arrived in Toronto, Emanuel was seven, an impressionable child deeply in awe of his eldest brother Gustav, twenty-one years his senior, who had trained as an artist in Germany and who joined the Ontario Society of Artists just two years after arriving in Canada. Gustav had done well, one of his most important early commissions being the ceiling murals in the Ontario legislature, and it seemed a foregone conclusion that the younger brother would follow in the footsteps of the older. Emanuel enrolled at the Toronto Technical School in 1899, the Central Ontario School of Art and Design the following year, and in 1901 was hired as a sculptural designer and draughtsman at Toronto's McIntosh Granite and Marble Company. The position offered fine experience (as did a job with the Canada Foundry Company, where he learned all about casting metal), but Hahn nevertheless felt the need to broaden his artistic horizons. In 1903, when he was twenty-two, he returned to Europe with his father and enrolled in the School of Arts and Crafts in Stuttgart.

For the next three years, Emanuel studied art and travelled throughout Europe, soaking up as much about art as he could. By the time he returned to Toronto in 1906, he had matured into a young man steeped in Old World culture, cosmopolitan yet naively idealistic about art and humanity, and he sufficiently impressed the administrators of Toronto's

Central Technical School that they hired him as an instructor of design and drawing. He began to attract the attention of people who mattered in the business, working as studio assistant to the doyen of Canadian sculptors, Walter Allward, from 1907 to 1912 and doing occasional contract work for the Thomson Monument Company, on everything from blueprints to bases to materials to casting. In 1913 he was appointed head of the sculpture department at the new Ontario College of Art (formerly the Central Technical School) and also got his first official recognition as an artist, when the National Gallery of Canada ordered a bronze casting of his bust of the native scout Thunder Cloud. But Hahn was destined, at least for a time, to work on a larger scale.

In 1916, Thomson asked him to create a memorial in Toronto's Mount Pleasant Cemetery to the 167 members of the Salvation Army who died when the steamship *Empress of Ireland* sank in May 1914 after striking a freighter in the mouth of the St. Lawrence River. Hahn worked from a design presented to him by Salvation Army Major Gideon Miller, but the assignment whetted his appetite for transforming his own visions into monumental sculpture. By the mid-1920s, Hahn was doing just that, making a name for himself as a sculptor of major public memorials. In 1926, he won the contract for a monument on Toronto Island to the great Canadian rowing hero Ned Hanlan, and the following year was commissioned to erect a statue of Sir Adam Beck, the founder of the public hydro movement in Ontario and a champion of rural electrification, to be situated on Toronto's University Avenue. At the same time, his stature among peers was growing. In 1928 he was one of the founders of the Sculptors Society of Canada, serving as its president until 1935, and in 1941 was elected secretary-treasurer of the Royal Canadian Academy.

By then, Hahn had already moved away from monumental sculpture and was working on the smallest scale yet, pouring his creativity into coins, medals, and trophies. In 1935, the Royal Canadian Mint issued the first of the new Canadian silver dollars, for which Hahn's design had won him the commission in 1933. The *voyageur* scene drew rave reviews, and Hahn was asked to work on the new quarter and dime as well. He created the Lou Marsh Trophy in 1936 and later turned his hand to postage stamps, bringing his usual meticulous approach to bear. His first stamp, in

November 1952, was the seven-cent Canada goose; as a model, he used the carcass of a dead bird that the great ornithologist Jack Miner had found in a field and sent to him. Again, the coin was a big hit, and more commissions followed. He was happiest working with images of animals, but was also asked to design the stamp commemorating the coronation of Queen Elizabeth II. That experience, however, was dispiriting; Hahn didn't like the way his drawing was translated into engraving and was disappointed with the finished product. He was, as his colleagues knew, ever the perfectionist.

So Emanuel Hahn enjoyed a long, productive, and varied career, but he owed much of his success to a set of circumstances that came together when he was a young man just beginning his life as a professional sculptor. Though the First World War brought much pain to the Hahn family, it also brought Emanuel great opportunities that otherwise might not have come his way.

AS AN ART FORM, sculpture had been in the doldrums before 1914. For decades, making a living at it was so difficult that the Royal Canadian Academy waived the membership dues for sculptors, on the assumption that they couldn't afford the expense. Hamilton MacCarthy, one of the few people to make a comfortable living at sculpture, complained that there was hardly any interest in the art form in Canada and noted that Toronto had surprisingly little public sculpture for a city of its size and importance. A few other big names, including Walter Allward and Louis-Philippe Hébert, joined MacCarthy in doing well from private and public commissions, but the general feeling was that, of all the arts, sculpture was considered the least important in Canadian society.

The First World War changed all that. What began as a short, sharp confrontation that many young men feared would be over before they had a chance to get into the action, instead degenerated into a slogging match in the trenches of the Western Front. Canada's first test came in April 1915, when the 1st Division battled through gas clouds north of the Belgian town of Ypres, stemming the German advance and just possibly saving the war. Canadians reacted with a mixture of sadness at the deaths of so many young men and pride that they had held the line when others faltered, but if they thought the bloodletting would end there, they were very much mistaken. Over the next three years, successive waves of Canadian volunteers, and eventually conscripts, were thrown into the maelstrom at places of which few people had ever heard but none of that generation would ever forget: Mount Sorrel, Courcelette, Vimy Ridge, Passchendaele. In August 1918, Canada's battle-hardened battalions, now recognized as the shock troops of the Allied armies, led the offensive that broke the back of the German Army, beginning a hundred-day push that took them all the way to Mons, in Belgium, in November 1918. There, suddenly and even surprisingly to those at the front, the war came to an end with an armistice agreement that would eventually be replaced by the peace treaty of July 1919.

By that time, the majority of Canada's soldiers had returned home, to try to pick up where they had left off years earlier. But of the more than 600,000 men and women who served in uniform, nearly 60,000 never came back. In homes across the country, their loved ones went through the pieces that remained: some photographs, perhaps a small package of letters lovingly saved, a mass-produced message of sympathy from the King, and vivid memories of a life cut short. But each casualty had one other thing: a name. The photographs and letters might one day crumble to dust, the King's condolences might get mislaid, but the name could be etched in stone on a memorial on the main street. It could be carved there for all to see, to remind future generations of the heroes who left this town when their country called, and gave all that they had to give. The commemorative impulse took hold in Canada as soon as word of the first battle deaths came back in 1915. It began with simple scrolls—they can still be seen in churches across the country—but by war's end communities began thinking of something more solid and enduring. Soon, every community worth its salt was in the market for an architect or sculptor to execute a war memorial. A few wanted buildings or parks that would be used on a daily basis; like the planners of the Confederation Memorial Program, they believed that the best form of tribute was one that would enrich the life of the community every day. But most communities were like the builders of Canada's nineteenth-century towers. They wanted something that would be a memorial and nothing else—a cairn or a stone cross, a sculpted soldier or an empty tomb—its only purpose to memorialize the dead in a form that was dignified and expressive.

The huge demand for war memorials gave Hahn a real crack at monumental sculpture and brought his work, if not his name, to prominence. The coming of war in August 1914 had been a trying time for him. Anti-German sentiment ran strong in Canada, and few staunch patriots felt charitable toward anyone with a German-sounding name. After twenty years of trying to fit into Toronto's Anglo-Saxon society, the Hahns suddenly found themselves right back where they had started, as immigrants facing thinly veiled hostility. Being ostracized socially and professionally just when his reputation as an established artist seemed assured was a bitter pill for Emanuel. But he channelled his emotions into his work, particularly two pieces that tried to come to terms with the conflict: *War the Despoiler* (1915), in which war is represented by a horrific reptilian beast that devours its victims, and *Fate* (1918), portraying a male figure stretched over a rock face that transforms into a human form to support him. Both works are provocative and daring, and were not really in keeping with the traditional patriotic rhetoric about the Great War.

Nor were they likely to appeal to communities shopping around for war memorials, a consideration that would come to have an impact on Hahn's creative output. By 1918, he was the chief designer for the Thomson Monument Company of Toronto, one of the largest makers of commemorative monuments in Canada. Thomson advertised widely in Canadian magazines and newspapers, and could provide memorials of every size and description, from modest obelisks to replicas of the Cenotaph in London, England, to bronze or stone figures. They had, quite literally, something for every taste and budget, but nothing with the ambivalence toward the war that had been implicit in *Fate* and *War the Despoiler.*

That doesn't mean that Hahn's commemorative work suffered by comparison with his earlier small pieces. On the contrary, even though as a salaried employee Hahn's name was rarely attached to his work in Thomson's advertising, the quality of his designs was unmistakable. He was as comfortable with allegorical designs as he was with realism. One symbolic design, entitled *Fetters Sundered,* was selected by the town of

Alvinston in southwestern Ontario and by Malvern Collegiate Institute in Toronto. As the program to the school's unveiling ceremony described it,

> [T]he Memorial takes the form of an ideal statue, expressing the spirit of Canadians in the Great War. Carved in imperishable granite the statue represents a stalwart youth whose right hand grasps a Crusader's sword, while the left holds aloft a broken chain, symbol of the struggle to which our young men gave their lives. Freedom has been won after a tremendous effort, which has left its trace on the boy's countenance. The attitude is not that of boastful triumph, but of grateful victory; reverently is his face raised to heaven in thankfulness. Firmly planted on the rock this virile figure well exhibits the confident determined spirit of young Canadian manhood, eager not to spare itself in resisting the attempt to impose the shackles of militarism.

At the other end of the spectrum were Hahn's highly realistic memorials, like the charging infantryman he executed for the town of St-Lambert, Quebec. Hahn called it *Going Over the Top,* and it freezes the soldier at the moment of emerging from a trench to charge across No Man's Land. A model was shown at the Ontario Society of Artists' 1924 exhibition, and the press praised it as a refreshing contrast to the "miserable examples of statuary" that had appeared on city streets in the years after the war. If *Going Over the Top* was all action and energy, *Tommy in His Greatcoat* was peaceful, calm, and reflective. The overcoat-shrouded soldier stands on uneven ground, leaning on his rifle and helmet and looking reflectively downwards. The statue was shown in 1923 at the Canadian National Exhibition and was eventually purchased by memorial committees in Lindsay, Ontario, and Moncton, New Brunswick.

TWO DESIGNS STAND OUT in Hahn's body of war memorials: one that is nowhere and one that is everywhere. As a sculptor of considerable talent, Hahn entered most of the competitions to erect war memorials in Canada in the 1920s, particularly those involving more prestigious contracts. In those cases, sculptors and architects would usually be given a number of basic guidelines stating the form, location, and cost of the memorial desired, and then would submit sketches; for some of the bigger competitions, two or three finalists would be asked to work up maquettes, or scale models, often done in clay. Typically, the judging was done by an expert panel of artists, sculptors, and architects, but it was usually up to the city's war memorial committee, drawn from local social and business elites, to decide whether the judges' decision would be accepted.

The commission for the memorial in Winnipeg would have been quite a plum, and Hahn promptly submitted a design when the competition opened in September 1925. A few days before Christmas, the panel of expert judges issued its decision on the forty-eight entries. The winning design was #33, a stark cenotaph flanked by draped figures representing Service and Sacrifice. The judges regarded the memorial to be "of great dignity and picturesque effect.... The sentiment is simply and directly expressed in a manner about which no doubt can be felt and no questions need to be asked. Great prominence is given to the tragic aspect to war, apt to be forgotten in times of peace. This monument is designed to express this aspect to those to whom the Great War will have become history rather than a memory." The name attached to #33 was Emanuel Hahn.

Manitobans got their first look at Hahn's design on Christmas Eve 1925, through a photo in the *Free Press,* and at first there was general satisfaction. But soon the rumblings began. Hahn, after all, was a German name—should a German really be designing a war memorial? Within weeks, the opposition had begun to gather. The Grand Army of United Veterans passed a resolution demanding that the memorial be done by someone who was British, and preferably Canadian; they objected most strenuously to the awarding of a contract to a man "of enemy and alien birth." There were even charges that the members of the war memorial committee were not loyal British subjects because they had awarded the prize to a German.

To try to get to the bottom of things, the Manitoba *Free Press* did a little digging into the sculptor's past, eventually publishing the findings in an editorial entitled "Who is Mr Hahn?" The editorial stressed that neither his father nor his father's brother had ever served in the German army and that his brother-in-law had served in the Canadian artillery through the war. It also emphasized that Hahn himself had never joined any of the German patriotic clubs or societies that had flourished in Toronto before 1914 and that he had already executed a number of important monumental commissions, including more than a few war memorials. In short, assured the *Free Press,* Winnipeggers need have no fear about the credentials of their new sculptor.

The article did little to calm the troubled waters, though, and eventually the chair of the memorial committee, R.D. Waugh (better known in the province as the head of the Manitoba Liquor Control Commission), was forced to pledge that no contract would be let until every individual and group had a chance to air its concerns. At a noisy meeting convened by Waugh, Hahn found few defenders. One by one, representatives of civic groups—the Imperial Order of Daughters of the Empire, the Travellers Association, the Amputations Association, the Great War Veterans Association, the Real Estate Exchange, the Kiwanis Club—got up to denounce the sculptor, his design, and the decision of the expert judges. According to a newspaper report of the meeting, "[O]ne man of prominence swears that if the monument is erected he will spit on it, on this memorial erected to the dead he reveres."

But the strongest opponent was Arthur Parker, secretary of the Winnipeg Board of Trade. He argued that Hahn was competent to design anything but a war memorial because he was naturalized and not British or Canadian born. "[N]aturalization of an individual does not make him Canadian in the true sense of the word," Parker announced. "He may be naturalized, but he does not come on an equal footing in any sense." Having Hahn design a war memorial, Parker said, was like having the tribute to a murder victim designed by a cousin of the murderer. The problem, in Parker's eyes, was that naturalization did not overcome the stigma of foreignness. Hahn was born a German, he would always be a German, and for that reason, he was not capable of working in anything but a Germanic style. "It could not be overlooked that there was German inspiration in this monument," Parker said. "The design itself was of German character and typified the German idea of war and was not British at all."

Against these arguments, Hahn's supporters could only call for rationality. Waugh simply noted that closing the competition to people of non-British birth would have disqualified the sculptors of Winnipeg's two other main memorials, Marguerite Taylor, a French-born sculptor who executed the city's Next of Kin Memorial, on the grounds of the provincial legislative building, and American James Frazer, who designed the Bank of Montreal's memorial at the corner of Portage and Main. In any case, Waugh observed astutely, it was no longer about the design itself; the debate had become one about who was to be recognized as Canadian. Another observer remarked wryly that he had immigrated to Canada from England on a ship called *The City of Berlin* and wondered, tongue only partly in cheek, if he would be denied rights of citizenship on those grounds.

Through letters from friends in Winnipeg, Hahn was fully aware of the debate as it played out in public meeting and newspaper column. He found the entire episode terribly painful, for it forced him to relive the prejudice that he and his family had suffered during the First World War. He even offered to withdraw his design, in hopes of saving the city further embarrassment. Waugh refused to consider that, but the outcome of the debate was never really in doubt. Bowing to public pressure, the war memorial committee decided to accept the judges' decision and award Hahn the first prize of $1000 but rejected his design and reopened the competition.

So, the entire process began again: a new competition was announced, with new terms designed to forestall the problems created in the first competition; a new panel of assessors was appointed, again experts drawn from the local cultural community; and a new slate of entries was reviewed. Just after Remembrance Day 1927, the results were announced. This time, the winner was a figure of heroic proportions. In the words of the design's creator, "[A] long low base of granite rises from the ground, from the very soil of Canada, its line sweeping forward at a gentle angle. At the front it ends abruptly forming an invulnerable wall. Standing firmly on this is the heroic figure of Canadian Youth. He is not aggressive; he is protective. He holds behind him, clasped in his hand, a great branch of maple, symbol of the far-flung Dominion he has been aroused to guard." The judges praised the new winner for being "remarkable in its originality and, by its heroic proportions bound to arrest the attention of the passer-by. It avoids the similarity of so many war memorials already erected…. The rugged execution of the dominant figure is outstanding, breathing as it were the spirit of the West with its strength and confidence, at the same time a memory of the past, emblematic of the spirit of those who answered their country's call."

This time, the winner was a young woman named Elizabeth Wyn Wood. Unlike Hahn, Wood came from solid British stock; born near Orillia, Ontario, where her father operated a dry goods and clothing store, she could trace her family's roots in Canada back to the 1830s. She had attended an Anglican boarding school in Toronto, studied art in Toronto, and by 1927 was an exceptionally promising young sculptor. A decade later, she would create the last of Canada's great First World War memorials, a remarkable monument unveiled in Welland, Ontario, in 1939, but for the moment, she basked in her first big success. When she was announced as the winner, congratulations poured in from all sides. One enthusiastic letter came from Eva Jones, a member of the Winnipeg War Memorial Committee, who praised the design and was particularly pleased that the competition had been won by a woman. Then at the end of her letter came the question that Wood must have been waiting for: "[W]e are curious to know if you are of Canadian or English birth." Wood was indeed of Canadian birth, but what hadn't yet come out was the name of her husband—Emanuel Hahn.

Wood had studied under Hahn at the Ontario College of Art after the war, and they had married in 1926. Creatively as well as personally, they made a wonderful match. Their styles were compatible but quite distinct, and although suggestions and encouragement passed between them (in 1927, they rented adjacent studios on Adelaide Street in Toronto), they worked separately on commissions. But that was not how some people in Winnipeg saw things. On the 15th of November the *Free Press* published a small picture of Wood that was noteworthy for its caption. It didn't say "Elizabeth Wood, noted Canadian sculptor" or "Elizabeth Wood, accomplished Canadian artist" but "Elizabeth Wood, wife of Emanuel Hahn." This tiny newspaper item captured the character of the debate—Wood was to be allowed no identity outside of her husband's. This was made clear in another newspaper column, which argued that her design was "essentially Teutonic in conception; it may be artistic but it is not typical of how we British people viewed the war, and the effects of the war." This, of course, was exactly the same criticism that had been levelled at Hahn's design and suggests the concept of shared guilt: because Wood was married to Hahn, she had lost the ability or the inclination to create a so-called British design and could only work in a Teutonic style. Her century-old British-Canadian roots no longer mattered, for she had surrendered them when she married Hahn. She became not a Canadian-born sculptor, but the wife of a German-born sculptor.

On 2 December 1927, the memorial committee met to consider the decision of the judges. This time, R.D. Waugh, who had so strongly defended Hahn's design, was leading the charge. He said that the design was "absolutely inappropriate for the purposes we have in view.... We are not looking for fine statues ... we are looking for something that will touch the hearts of the people." Wood's few supporters at the meeting did their best. Major David Duncan, an ex-soldier of the 43rd Battalion who stood out as Wood's stoutest defender, tried to cut through Waugh's rhetoric. It's not really about the design, he argued; it's about the ethnicity of Wood's husband. But few people were prepared to listen to reason. In the end, the committee decided to accept the judges' decision and declare Wood the winner of the competition, but it would not offer her the contract.

Wood learned by a letter on 16 December 1927 that, because her design "did not meet with general approval," the committee was unable to offer her the commission. The judges were outraged, and each of them wrote to her to express their indignation. Donald A. Ross referred to one critic, a former officer of the Canadian Expeditionary Force, who dismissed her submission on the grounds that swords (like the one Wood's figure was holding) weren't used in the war. "What is the use of trying to convert a mind like that?" he wrote resignedly. Another supporter was disgusted at the entire affair, arguing that Wood's design "fairly breathed youth and illustrated the cause that was preached at every recruiting meeting—protecting the home, the flag, and the Maple Leaf." He went on to refer to the Golden Boy, the classically inspired figure that stands atop the Manitoba legislature building, and said it was lucky there was no committee when Golden Boy was done or he'd be wearing "overalls and a cow's breakfast."

In the end, the contract for Winnipeg's war memorial was awarded to Gilbert Parfitt, a local craftsman who had the advantage of being the president of the Manitoba Society of Architects and being on retainer with the provincial government. His cenotaph, which now stands within sight of the soaring dome of the legislature building, is spare and austere—impressive from an architectural point of view, but lacking the dramatic elements that so distinguished the designs proposed by Hahn and Wood. It is certainly not, to borrow Waugh's words, "a fine statue."

IF THE WINNIPEG MEMORIAL was Hahn's most famous design that never made it into stone, he at least had the satisfaction of knowing that another of his works became the single most replicated war memorial sculpture in Canada. Among the cenotaphs, cairns, stone slabs, and obelisks that filled the advertising brochures of Canada's monument makers, one uncredited design from the Thomson Monument Company's catalogue stood out: the figure of a young soldier looking down at a battlefield cross beside him. He has the fine features of a Greek god, and a hank of thick, wavy hair falls over his forehead. His hand rests tenderly on the cross, and at his feet is a broken chain, symbolizing the defeat of tyranny. A healthy growth of poppies climbs up the base of the cross, which is inscribed IN FLANDERS FIELDS. The echoes of John McCrae's famous poem are inescapable, and the entire effect is of peaceful repose, a hint of sadness mixed with a feeling of pride.

Emanuel Hahn modelled the figure from life. That was his usual preference, but he also knew that in that work he had to achieve the kind of authenticity that war memorial committees demanded; more than one sculptor was driven to distraction by well-meaning citizens who badgered them with suggestions of how to make their stone soldier more accurate. So, Hahn brought a young man into his Toronto studio, outfitted him in an old infantry uniform, and worked with the model to find the pose he was seeking. The next step was to build a metal frame, or armature, in that pose (the figure was to be larger than life size, so the metal skeleton stood head and shoulders above the model), and then Hahn began to cover the frame with clay to bring the figure to life. As he worked to finish the sculpture, Hahn kept the uniform and rifle on hand to make sure he got the details right.

Hahn clearly did get the details, and everything else for that matter, just right. He captured the feelings of Canadians toward their dead soldiers so well that war memorial committees across the country began to send their orders for the figure into Thomson's Toronto office. At first glance, this seems a bit odd—surely a war memorial should be homegrown, or at least specially designed for one community alone. It wasn't something to be ordered from a catalogue, like a dining room suite or a manure spreader. In fact, the practice of catalogue shopping for memorials served a variety of purposes. For one, it allowed a small community with limited financial resources to purchase a work of superior quality; commissioning one directly from the artist would probably have been well beyond the means of most towns. There was also a deeper message. The very fact that the figure could be copied meant that the losses of distant communities would be connected. A British Columbian could see an echo of her own town's memorial in a New Brunswick village and thus could feel a sense of unity in tragedy—the memorial would remind the village that the war had touched all Canadians, that no part of the country had escaped its reach. At the same time, each memorial was slightly different—stone or bronze, a low base or a high one, varying inscriptions on the plaque, the landscaping touches, and of course a different list of names. These variations gave the catalogue memorial a local flavour that made each standing soldier uniquely part of his community.

All across Canada, towns and villages made the Hahn figure their own. The first may have been the city of Fort William, Ontario (now Thunder Bay), where the Women's Patriotic Society raised $8000 to purchase Hahn's design in grey marble and erect it on the grounds of city hall. The unveiling, on 19 October 1921, was timed to coincide with the national convention of the Great War Veterans Association, the forerunner of the Royal Canadian Legion, so the crowd on that bright Wednesday afternoon was bolstered by ex-soldiers from across Canada who adjourned the convention for a couple of hours to make the trip over from Port Arthur. The mayor's proclamation of a half-day holiday for the occasion didn't hurt attendance any either. In fact, the crowd was so big that special tickets had to be issued to control access to the area closest to the memorial.

Performing the unveiling was Robert Manion, the local member of Parliament who had won a Military Cross for bravery at the Battle of Vimy Ridge. In 1938, Manion would go on to join the legion of now-forgotten leaders of the federal Conservative Party, but on this day his comments focused on the sacrifices of the war. As a battalion medical officer, he had seen a lifetime's worth of broken and battered bodies on the battlefields of France and Flanders, but he asked the townspeople to reflect on the meaning of those deaths rather than the physical realities. He concluded by reminding them of their three duties: to remember the dead; to provide for the survivors; and "to bring about a world disarmament, so that a real parliament of men, a real federation of the world, would be effected."

The following summer on a sweltering June afternoon, some two thousand people gathered in Russell, Manitoba, to unveil Hahn's memorial, which the town had ordered in Vermont granite. Shortly before noon, local veterans, schoolchildren, the town band, and members of various community groups formed up at the Canadian Pacific Railway station and paraded along the main street to the monument. There, relatives of the dead were seated in untidy rows of kitchen chairs, benches, and camp stools (a notice in the Russell *Banner* had asked townspeople to loan chairs for the occasion) to hear speeches by the Reverence J.E. Secker, who had ministered to the people of Russell during the war, and Manitoba's lieu-tenant-governor, Sir James Aikens. Like Manion, Aikens called upon the spectators to live up to the ideals for which the dead had given their lives and spoke directly to the children, reminding them to take a lesson from the memorial as they passed by each day. The most moving moment came at the end of the ceremony, when Major A.M. Pratt, the principal of the local public school, read out the names of the eighty-three men and women from the district who died while in uniform. As each name was read, a different child tenderly deposited a small bunch of flowers at the base of the memorial.

On the Labour Day weekend in 1922, the ceremony was re-enacted in Hanover, a small mill town in western Ontario. The local chapter of the Imperial Order of Daughters of the Empire (IODE) had been the driving force behind the town's philanthropic efforts on behalf of soldiers during the war, and the chapter took it upon itself to organize the memorial committee as well. The IODE mounted a series of fundraising campaigns, collected nearly $5000, and placed an order with the Thomson Company for one of Hahn's soldiers, carved in granite. On that beautiful Sunday in September, more than three thousand people gathered around the public library to watch Ontario's lieutenant-governor, Harry Cockshutt, release the flag that shrouded the monument. He asked the townspeople to carry on the work of the fallen and to do so in a spirit of cooperation and mutual aid: "There is no place for selfish people—everyone should live in harmony in one great community." A stir of hushed conversation swept the crowd as the Union Jack fell away, and in an account of the unveiling published a week later, the Hanover *Post* declared that it liked what it saw—to the twenty-five local men whose names were carved on the monument's base, "the splendid memorial with its rugged appearance, and yet a touch of loveliness shown in the soldier's figure, is a worthy tribute."

One could go on describing the ceremonies that revealed Hahn's mourning soldier to the towns whose dead he represented—Cornwall, Bolton, Petrolia, and Milton in Ontario; Unity, Saskatchewan; Gaspé, Quebec; Westville, Nova Scotia; Fernie, British Columbia. In each community could be found the same gathering of veterans, bereaved relatives, schoolchildren, and civic leaders; the same heartfelt renditions of "O God Our Help in Ages Past" and "O Canada"; the same recitation of the names of men and women who would no longer walk the town streets; the same kinds of speeches—echoes of Manion's call to peace, Aikens's reminder to the youth of Russell, Cockshutt's plea for selflessness. And in each town, the flag fluttered to the ground to reveal the work of Emanuel Hahn.

One more unveiling bears mentioning. A community that knew the meaning of tragedy better than most was Springhill, Nova Scotia—the coal mines that ran deep under the town made sure of that. The annual toll to rock bursts, floods, explosions, and collapses was etched on the local miners' memorial, as was the single worst event in the town's history, a terrible day in February 1891 when 125 miners died in an explosion that shattered slopes Number One and Two of the Cumberland Mine. With the First World War, Springhill was again thrown into the old routine of mourning and commemoration. In the war's aftermath, the townspeople raised almost $5000 to purchase a version of Hahn's figure in Italian Carrara marble. A stonemason in nearby Amherst handled the construction of the memorial, which weighed a total of 59 tons, including the cement for the foundation, the dressed stone for the base, and the statue itself. The honour of unveiling the memorial on a warm day in August 1929 fell to Annie Goldrich of Springhill. She had watched four of her sons march away to war, but only Oscar had returned. Walter died at Mount Sorrel in June 1916, a burst of shellfire cutting him to pieces. Arthur lived just a few months longer; in October 1916 he went into the inferno that was the Battle of Courcelette and never came out. Stanley— well, Annie surely hoped that her youngest was safe with the forestry corps, well behind the front lines, and he was for a time, though just a month from the war's end, Stanley fell victim to the Spanish flu.

We do not know whether Annie Goldrich drew any comfort from the memorial, but the local newspaper, the Springhill *Record,* was moved by the imagery that Hahn had created: "It represents a Canadian soldier standing at the head of the grave of a comrade. The soldier's left hand rests upon the little wooden cross, his steel hat slung carelessly over his shoulder, his tunic open at the throat. A pose so characteristic of the soldier in a moment of quietness on the Western Front as he gazes upon the grave of a pal. The expression which the sculptor has carved into that face of stone is one which the soldier in us can understand but no words of ours can describe; it is wonderful."

Nothing in Emanuel Hahn's personal papers speaks of the Springhill unveiling, but he must have known how well his pensive soldier captured the conflicted emotions of a nation that had lost so much. As the *Record* suggested, pride and sorrow mingled in the sculpted soldier, but both were overwhelmed by a sense of loss. The figure, because he represented no one soldier, could be every soldier—he was Augustin Belanger of Fort William, Arthur Zimmerman of Hanover, Stanley Goldrich of Springhill, even, in the days before gender inclusivity, Margaret Lowe of Russell. He was every young person who marched away to war and never came back.

Though this iconic figure is surely his best known memorial, sadly Hahn's name is rarely connected to it. Apparently only one of them, in Westville, Nova Scotia, bears his signature, and his own daughter lived in Fort William for years before discovering that her father had designed the city's memorial. When Hahn died in February 1957, few obituaries mentioned the war memorials he created. Many of those monuments have been catalogued and described in various publications and on internet sites, but again, one looks long and hard to find any mention of the sculptor whose vision was behind the design. Emanuel Hahn deserves better not just because he was certainly one of Canada's finest sculptors, but because he created a lasting memorial that, when unveiled across Canada in towns large and small, brought people together and symbolized the common grief of a young nation. In a long career that left its mark on Canada in so many ways, Hahn's moving monument of the young lad standing over the grave of a comrade is one of his most striking achievements.

EPILOGUE

How do we define a nation-builder? A century ago, most people firmly believed that such an honour could go only to an illustrious figure (usually male)—a politician, a captain of industry, a general—who stood at the helm through times of trial or whose genius built the infrastructure of a modern society. In either case, a nation-builder was a larger-than-life figure that, by deed and example, generated or nurtured the kind of patriotic feeling that was supposedly characteristic of a true nation and that drew people together into a community that was more than the sum of its parts.

In the stories of these twelve far-reaching projects that helped to build the Canada we know, we have met a good number of Great Men in the Victorian mould—of that there is no question. There were the visionary leaders, such as Saskatchewan premier T. Walter Scott and federal cabinet minister Maurice Lamontagne, who had the political power to see their ideas through. There were the designers of inspiring edifices—the Francis Rattenburys and Edward Maxwells—whose creative vision came through in their architectural plans, and the legendary builders such as James Hodges and John By, who left their lasting mark in stone or steel.

I have tried to show, however, that nations are not built only, or perhaps even primarily, by such individuals. George Wilcox, who brought mail delivery to rural Canada, was a nation-builder, although he never considered himself anything but a simple farmer. Ellen Fairclough was a nation-builder, for it was she who pushed for performing arts centres as a way both to mark Canada's centennial and to celebrate its culture. So, too, was Emanuel Hahn, whose war memorials came to express the shared grief of a young country after war. It's unlikely that any of them will ever make it onto a list of Great Canadians, but that's precisely why we should never forget their efforts.

And we should not stop there. Adam Beck might be called the father of rural electrification in Ontario, but he didn't travel the province's back concessions, planting the poles and stringing the wire. William Thomas designed Brock's Monument, but he didn't risk his life assembling the stonework nearly 200 feet above the heights at Queenston. If nation-building calls for people with vision and political will, it also calls for people with strong backs and arms.

So the next time you drive past a work crew on the Trans-Canada Highway, remember that decades ago, a similar crew was toiling to build that highway. If you see a grain elevator standing alone on the prairies, look beyond the peeling paint and rotting wood to see what the structure once represented. Next time you speak to a telephone operator, remember that the job isn't much different from that once done by the thousands of women who ran telephone switchboards in the early 1900s across rural Canada. If you cross the Victoria Bridge, think for a moment of Edward Burke, a young labourer who was crushed by a falling timber at the bridge site in 1859, and the dozens of other workers who died during the bridge's construction. And remember that the success of any nation-building project depends on great people, but it depends even more on people, plain and simple.

FURTHER READING

M uch of the research for *Building Canada* was done using archival materials, contemporary newspapers and magazines, the debates of the House of Commons, and government reports. Although I omitted endnotes for the ease of the reader, I am happy to provide specific citations for any points of detail. There are also fine books covering many of these topics. I have listed below those that I found most helpful and encourage anyone to delve into them for more detail. Many of the books published in the nineteenth century are available online, at **www.canadiana.org**, an excellent website assembled by the Canadian Institute for Historical Microreproduction. Finally, for biographical information on many of the individuals in these stories, consult the indispensable *Dictionary of Canadian Biography*, now also available online at **www.biographi.ca**.

Handshakes across the Water

Each of these bridges has been the subject of at least one study. The Union Bridge is covered in Lucien Brault's *Links between Two Cities: Historic Bridges between Ottawa and Hull* (Ottawa/Hull: Cities of Ottawa and Hull, 1989), and Nick and Helma Mika's *Bytown: The Early Days of Ottawa* (Belleville: Mika Publishing, 1982). Not to be missed is John Mactaggart's own account, published in *Three Years in Canada: An Account of the Actual State of the Country in 1826–7–8* (London: H. Colburn, 1829). For more information on the Victoria Bridge, the report by engineer James Hodges, *Construction of the Great Victoria Bridge in Canada* (London: John Weale, 1860), is authoritative, while an exhibition guide by Stanley Triggs, Brian Young, Conrad Graham, and Gilles Lauzon, *Le Pont Victoria: Un lien vital / Victoria Bridge: The Vital Link* (Montreal: McCord Museum of Canadian History, 1992), provides more detail on the bridge and its impact on Montreal. For capturing the spirit of the time, Michel Choquette's National Film Board documentary *Victoria Bridge: The 8th Wonder of the World* is excellent. The best work on the Quebec Bridge is undoubtedly William D. Middleton's superb *The Bridge at Quebec* (Bloomington: Indiana University Press, 2001). The voluminous government reports on the disaster (*Report of the Select*

Committee Appointed to Investigate the Conditions and Guarantees under which the Dominion Government Paid Moneys to the Quebec Bridge Company [Ottawa: King's Printer, 1908] and *Royal Commission Quebec Bridge Inquiry Report,* two volumes [Ottawa: King's Printer, 1908]) also make illuminating reading. If you can find a copy, the souvenir booklet *The Quebec Bridge Carrying the Transcontinental Line of the Canadian Government Railways over the St. Lawrence River near the City of Quebec, Canada,* published in 1918, is a fascinating record. Copthorne Macdonald's *Bridging the Strait: The Story of the Confederation Bridge Project* (Toronto: Dundurn Press, 1997) is a celebratory account of the construction of that bridge, while Lorraine Begley's edited volume *Crossing That Bridge: A Critical Look at the Prince Edward Island Fixed Link* (Charlottetown: Ragweed Press, 1993) gives the other side of the story. The chapter's title is taken from L.J. Doucet's account of the Canso Causeway, *The Road to the Isle: The World's Deepest Causeway* (Fredericton: University Press of New Brunswick, 1955). For the strange story of one link that never got built, see Desmond Morton's article "The Newfoundland–Labrador Causeway: An Idea Whose Time Did Not Come," in *Aspects: A Publication of the Newfoundland Historical Society* 7/4 (December 1975): 17–19.

A Unity Based on Road and Wheel

The authoritative account of the construction of the Trans-Canada Highway is David Monaghan's fine study *Canada's "New Main Street": The Trans-Canada Highway as Idea and Reality, 1912–1956* (Ottawa: Canadian Science and Technology Museum, 2002). For a beautiful photographic journey along the highway, see Wes Rataushk's *Silver Highway: A Celebration of the Trans-Canada Highway* (Markham, ON: Fitzhenry and Whiteside, 1988). Marcus van Steen gives a sense of the inherent engineering difficulties in his article "The Trans-Canada Highway Makes Road-Building History North of Lake Superior," in *Canadian Geographical Journal* 65/5 (November 1962): 175–81. Thomas Wilby published his own account of his 1912 motor trip (*A Motor Tour through Canada* [London: John Lane, 1913]), although it is not easy to find; a fascinating complement is John Nicol's *The All-Red Route: From Halifax to Victoria in a 1912 Reo* (Toronto: McArthur & Company, 1999), the story of an attempt to retrace Wilby's path. For an account of a more modest trip, see John Mavor's "Auto Trip across the Prairie" in *Alberta History* 30/2 (1982): 37–8. George Glazebrook's *A History of Transportation in Canada* (Toronto: Ryerson Press, 1938) and Edwin C. Guillet's *The Story of Canadian Roads* (Toronto: University of Toronto Press, 1967) both provide valuable background information, as does Larry McNally's chapter on "Roads, Streets, and Highways," in Norman R. Ball's *Building Canada: A History of Public Works* (Toronto: University of Toronto Press, 1988), and *Rail, Road and River* (Toronto: Macmillan, 1937), by University of

Saskatchewan economics professor W.W. Swanson. For a comparison with another great road-building project, see Robert M. Stamp's *QEW: Canada's First Superhighway* (Erin, ON: Boston Mills Press, 1987). A great many books deal with Canada's early automotive history. One that I found particularly helpful is G.W. Taylor's *The Automobile Saga of British Columbia, 1864–1914* (Victoria: Morriss Publishing, 1984).

A Vast Aerial Highway

As there is no published history of the trans-Canada airway, I relied heavily on government documents. There is, however, some fascinating material in T.M. McGrath's *History of Canadian Airports* (Toronto: Lugus, 1992) and in Ian MacLachlan and Bruce MacKay's article "Lethbridge and the Trans-Canada Airway" in *Alberta History* (summer 2003): 2–13. My own book, *High Flight: Aviation and the Canadian Imagination* (Toronto: Penguin, 2002), discusses the airway, as well as contemporary views of its impact on the country. Readers with access to a large library should dig out some old magazine articles on the subject, like Lawrence Burpee's "The Trans-Canada Airway" in *Canadian Geographical Journal* 7/2 (August 1933): 65–74; and J. Fergus Grant's "Trans-Canada Airway," in *Canadian Geographical Journal* 14/2 (February 1937): 99–117.

In Every Way Worthy of the Province

Two good places to begin are a pictorial article, "Our Provincial and Territorial Legislative Buildings," in *Canadian Geographical Journal* (December 1983–January 1984), and Diana Bodnar's "The Prairie Legislative Buildings," in *Prairie Forum* 5/2 (1980): 143–56. Most of Canada's provincial legislatures have been the subject of excellent histories, including Elizabeth Eve's *Province House, Halifax, Nova Scotia* (Halifax: Government of Nova Scotia, 1997); Luc Noppen and Gaston Deschênes's *Québec's Parliament Building: Witness to History* (Quebec City: Assemblée Nationale, 1986); Eric Arthur's *From Front Street to Queen's Park: The Story of Ontario's Parliament Buildings* (Toronto: McClelland and Stewart, 1979); Marilyn Baker's *Manitoba's Third Legislative Building: Symbol in Stone. The Art and Politics of a Public Building* (Winnipeg: Hyperion Press, 1986); Hubert Mayes's "Through the Architect's Eyes: F.W. Simon Surveys His Masterwork— The Manitoba Legislative Building," in *Manitoba History* 38 (Fall–Winter 1999–2000): 30–34; Lewis Thomas's "The Saskatchewan Legislative Building and Its Predecessors," in *Journal of the Royal Architectural Institute of Canada* 32/7 (July 1955); and Gordon Barnhart's *Building for the Future: A Photo Journal of Saskatchewan's Legislative Building* (Regina: Canadian Plains Research Center, 2002). For other legislatures, I have pieced together background from a variety of accounts. Brief outlines of the history of Newfoundland's new legislature can be found in Michael Francis Harrington's "The Eleven-Storey Mountain: A New Capitol for Newfoundland," in *Atlantic Advocate* (January 1959): 34–7; and Gordon F. Pushie's "Confederation Building: A New Concept in Government Administrative Quarters," also in *Atlantic Advocate* (June 1960): 27–34. For the Fredericton building, see Robert Power and Colin Smith's "Renovating the New Brunswick Legislative Building," in *Canadian Parliamentary Review* 13/2 (Summer 1990): 8–10. There are also some fine biographies of the individuals and cities involved with these buildings: D.R. Babcock's *Alexander Cameron Rutherford: A Gentleman of Strathcona* (Calgary: University of Calgary Press, 1989); Gordon Barnhart's *"Peace, Progress and Prosperity": A Biography of Saskatchewan's First Premier, T. Walter Scott* (Regina: Canadian Plains Research Center, 2000); J. William Brennan's *Regina before Yesterday: A Visual History, 1882 to 1945* (Regina: City of Regina, 1978); Earl Drake's *Regina: The Queen City* (Toronto: McClelland and Stewart, 1955); and Irene Rogers's *Charlottetown: The Life in Its Buildings* (Charlottetown: PEI Museum and Heritage Foundation, 1983). Douglas Owram's *The Formation of Alberta: A Documentary History* (Calgary: Historical Society of Alberta, 1979) contains some amusing details about the struggle over the provincial capital.

In Character with a Northern Country

An excellent place to start is the work of architectural historian Harold Kalman: *The Railway Hotels and the Development of the Château Style in Canada* (Victoria: University of Victoria Maltwood Museum, 1968); and his two-volume set *A History of Canadian Architecture* (Don Mills: Oxford University Press Canada, 1995). For other opinions on the "Canadian style," see Abraham Rogatnik's "Canadian Castles: The Phenomena of the Railway Hotel" in *Architectural Review,* May 1967, 364–72; and Christopher Thomas's "'Canadian Castles'? The Question of National Styles in Architecture Revisited," *Journal of Canadian Studies* 32/1 (Spring 1997): 5–27. The style's translation into government architecture is well covered by Janet Wright in *Crown Assets: The Architecture of the Department of Public Works, 1867–1967* (Toronto: University of Toronto Press, 1997). For individual architects, readers should consult *The Architecture of Edward and W.S. Maxwell* (Montreal: Montreal Museum of Fine Arts, 1991); Anthony A. Barrett and Rhodri Windsor Liscombe's *Francis Rattenbury and British Columbia: Architecture and Challenge in the Imperial Age* (Vancouver: UBC Press, 1983); and Terry Reksten's *Rattenbury* (Victoria: Sono Nis Press, 1978). Many of the hotels have also spawned "biographies." A general collection is Barbara Chisholm's *Castles of the North: Canada's Grand Hotels* (Toronto: Lynx Images, 2001), but there are also a number of books on the Château Frontenac: Joan Elson Morgan's *Castle of*

Quebec (Toronto: J.M. Dent, 1949); Rosemary Pitcher's *Château Frontenac* (Toronto: McGraw–Hill Ryerson, 1971); and France Gagnon Pratte and Éric Petter's *The Château Frontenac: One Hundred Years in the Life of a Legendary Hotel* (Quebec City: Éditions Continuité, 1993). Joan Rankin's *Meet Me at the Château: A Legacy of Memory* (Toronto: Natural Heritage Books, 1990) is a personal history of the Château Laurier, while Terry Reksten's *The Empress Hotel: In the Grand Style* (Vancouver: Douglas & McIntyre, 1997) and Bart Robinson's *Banff Springs: The Story of a Hotel* (Banff: Summerthought, 1973) are excellent histories. For the story of the railway's tourism arm, see E.J. Hart's *The Selling of Canada: The CPR and the Beginnings of Canadian Tourism* (Banff: Altitude Publishing, 1983). John Eagle's *The Canadian Pacific Railway and the Development of Western Canada, 1896–1914* (Montreal: McGill–Queen's University Press, 1989) and W. Kaye Lamb's *History of the Canadian Pacific Railway* (New York: Macmillan, 1977) are also fine general histories of the company.

Making War on Cultural Poverty

The best account of the Massey Commission and the Confederation Memorial Program is Paul Litt's *The Muses, the Masses, and the Massey Commission* (Toronto: University of Toronto Press, 1992). Peter Akroyd's *The Anniversary Compulsion: Canada's Centennial Celebration* (Toronto: Dundurn Press, 1992) describes the centennial celebrations themselves, including the program. Books on the individual centres are few and far between, although many of them provide potted histories on their websites. Frank MacKinnon's *Honour the Founders! Enjoy the Arts: Canada's Confederation Memorial in Charlottetown* (Charlottetown: Fathers of Confederations Trust, 1990) is excellent, as is his earlier article "Confederation Conference Centennial," in *Canadian Geographical Journal* 69 (August 1964): 42–3. The centre in St. John's is discussed briefly in Paul O'Neill's *The Oldest City: The Story of St. John's, Newfoundland* (Portugal Cove: Boulder Publications, 2003). *Canada's National Arts Centre: Restoring the Vision* (Ottawa: NAC, 2001) makes interesting reading. The most revealing memoir, by a man who was deeply involved in both the Charlottetown Centre and the St. Lawrence Centre in Toronto, is Mavor Moore's *Reinventing Myself: Memoirs* (Toronto: Stoddart, 1994).

A Moveable Post Office

Any reading of the history of rural mail delivery should begin with George Wilcox's own account, *History of Rural Mail in Canada* (Ottawa: Canada Post, 1975), originally printed in 1918. An excellent companion piece is Brian Osborne and Robert Pike's article "Lowering 'The Walls of Oblivion': The Revolution in Postal Communications in Central Canada, 1851–1911," in *Canadian Papers in*

Rural History, vol. 4, ed. Donald H. Akenson (Ganonoque, ON: Langdale Press, 1984): 200–25. The historians and archivists at the Canadian Postal Museum have also written three excellent and well-illustrated books that relate to the subject: Chantal Amyot, Bianca Gendreau, and John Willis, *Special Delivery: Canada's Postal Heritage* (Hull: Canadian Museum of Civilization, 2000); Chantal Amyot and John Willis, *Country Post: Rural Postal Service in Canada, 1880 to 1945* (Ottawa: Canadian Museum of Civilization, 2003); and Jane E. Harrison, *Until Next Year: Letter Writing and the Mails in Canada, 1640–1830* (Hull: Canadian Museum of Civilization, 1997). A.W. Currie's "The Post Office since 1867" in the *Canadian Journal of Economics and Political Science* 24/2 (May 1958): 241–50 is a handy if brief survey. Readers interested in more detail on the origins of postal service in the regions should see Alfred Stanley Deaville's *The Colonial Postal Systems and Postage Stamps of Vancouver Island and British Columbia, 1849–1871: A Sketch of the Origin and Early Development of the Postal Service on the Pacific Seaboard of British North America* (Victoria: King's Printer, 1928); C.M. Jephcott, V.G. Greene, and John H.M. Young's *The Postal History of Nova Scotia and New Brunswick, 1754–1867* (Toronto: Sissons Publications, 1964); J.J. MacDonald's *The Nova Scotia Post: Its Offices, Masters and Marks, 1700–1867* (Toronto: Unitrade Press, 1985); or Winthrop S. Boggs's two-volume *The Postage Stamps and Postal History of Canada: A Handbook for Philatelists* (Kalamazoo: Chambers Publishing, 1945). For information on the more recent history of rural mail delivery, see Robert M. Campbell, *The Politics of the Post: Canada's Postal System from Public Service to Privatization* (Toronto: Broadview Press, 1994).

Calling Rural Canada

A number of fine books deal with the general history of telephones in Canada. I found Robert Collins's *A Voice from Afar: The History of Telecommunications in Canada* (Toronto: McGraw–Hill Ryerson, 1977); E.B. Ogle's *Long Distance Please: The Story of the TransCanada Telephone System* (Toronto: Collins, 1979); and Robert Babe's *Telecommunications in Canada: Technology, Industry, and Government* (Toronto: University of Toronto Press, 1990) particularly informative. As well, many books deal with telephone history in specific provinces: Walter Auld's *Voices of the Island: History of the Telephone on Prince Edward Island* (Halifax: Nimbus Publishing, 1985); Thomas Grindlay's *The Independent Telephone Industry in Ontario: A History* (Toronto: Ontario Telephone Service Commission, 1975); Gilbert Muir's "A History of the Telephone in Manitoba," in *Manitoba Historical Society Transactions,* series 3 (1964–65); James Mavor's *Government Telephones: The Experience of Manitoba, Canada* (Toronto: MacLean Publishing, 1917); Ronald Love's *SaskTel: The Biography of a Crown Corporation and the Development of Telecommunications in Saskatchewan* (Regina: SaskTel,

2003); J. Earl Williams's "Origin and Development of Public Telephones in Alberta," in *Alberta Historical Review* 11/2 (Spring 1963): 8–12; Tony Cashman's *Singing Wires: The Telephone in Alberta* (Edmonton: Alberta Government Telephones, 1972); J.D. Baker, "Development, Construction and Maintenance of Rural and Toll Lines in Alberta," in Peter S. Grant, ed., *Telephone Operation and Development in Canada, 1921–1971* (Toronto: University of Toronto, 1974): 1–11. Two published histories of individual rural telephone companies include Anne Duke Judd's *Bruce Municipal Telephone System: A Long Line of History, 1910–1994* (Tiverton, ON: BMTS, 1994) and Cecil Reaney's *A History of the Metcalfe Rural Telephone Company, 1909 to 1967* (Vernon: Osgoode, ON, Township Historical Society and Museum, 2001). Little has been written specifically on the social impact of telephones in rural areas, but see Robert M. Pike's "A Chequered Progress: Farmers and the Telephone in Canada, 1905–1951," in *Journal of Canadian Studies* 33/3 (Autumn 1998): 5–30. Pike also wrote *Adopting the Telephone: The Social Diffusion and Use of the Telephone in Urban Central Canada, 1876 to 1914* (Kingston: Queen's University, 1987) and, with Vincent Mosco, *From Luxury to Necessity and Back Again?: Canadian Consumers and the Pricing of Telephone Services in Historical and Comparative Perspectives* (Kingston: Queen's University, 1987). R.C. Fetherstonhaugh's *Charles Fleetford Sise, 1834–1918: A Biography* (Montreal: Gazette, 1944) and William Patten's *Pioneering the Telephone in Canada* (Montreal: private, 1926) are comprehensive, if self-serving, histories published with the blessing of the old Bell Telephone Company of Canada. Finally, mention should be made of two fine scholarly studies that touch on rural telephony: Christopher Armstrong and H.V. Nelles's *Monopoly's Moment: The Organization and Regulation of Canadian Utilities, 1830–1930* (Philadelphia: Temple University Press, 1986) and Michèle Martin's *"Hello, Central?": Gender, Technology, and Culture in the Formation of Telephone Systems* (Montreal: McGill–Queen's University Press, 1991).

Switches Control Everything but the Children

By far the best account of rural electrification is Keith Fleming's *Power at Cost: Ontario Hydro and Rural Electrification, 1911–1958* (Montreal: McGill–Queen's University Press, 1992). It can be supplemented by a number of contemporary studies: E.B. Biggar's *Hydro-Electric Development in Ontario: A History of Water-Power Administration under the Hydro-Electric Power Commission of Ontario* (Toronto: Biggar Press, 1920); R.F. Bucknam's *An Economic Study of Farm Electrification in New York, with a Discussion of Rural Electrification in the Provinces of Quebec and Ontario, Canada* (Ithaca, NY: Cornell University Agricultural Experiment Station, 1929); and the government-published *The Hydro-Electric Power Commission of Ontario: Its Origins, Administration and*

Achievements (Toronto, 1928). The histories of other provincial and municipal hydroelectric utility companies are also worth reading: M. Baker, J. Miller Pitt, and R.D. Pitt's *The Illustrated History of Newfoundland Light and Power* (St. John's: Creative Publishers, 1990); A. Kenneth Bell's *Getting the Lights: The Coming of Electricity to Prince Edward Island* (Charlottetown: PEI Museum and Heritage Foundation, 1989); W.E. Hawkins's *Electrifying Calgary: A Century of Public and Private Power* (Calgary: University of Calgary Press, 1987); D.S.G. Ross's "History of the Electrical Industry in Manitoba," in *Manitoba Historical Society Transactions,* series 3, 1963–64; Clinton White's *Power for a Province: A History of Saskatchewan Power* (Regina: Canadian Plains Research Center, 1976); and Jeremy Mouat's *The Business of Power: Hydro-Electricity in Southeastern British Columbia, 1897–1997* (Victoria: Sono Nis Press, 1997). Among the government reports, the most significant are *A Farm Electrification Program: Report of the Manitoba Electrification Enquiry Commission 1942* (Winnipeg: King's Printer, 1943); *Report of the Saskatchewan Reconstruction Council* (Regina: King's Printer, 1944); and *Royal Commission on Agriculture and Rural Life: Report No. 11 Farm Electrification* (Regina: King's Printer, 1957). The diaries of Laura Kaulback Slauenwhite can be found in Margaret Conrad, Toni Laidlaw, and Donna Smyth's *No Place Like Home: Diaries and Letters of Nova Scotia Women, 1771–1938* (Halifax: Formac Publishing, 1988), while the chapter's title is taken from Monda Halpern's wonderful book *And On That Farm He Had a Wife: Ontario Farm Women and Feminism* (Montreal: McGill–Queen's University Press, 2001).

Castles of the New World

Grain elevators have been a magnet for photographers and writers since they began disappearing from the landscape. Some of the most effective tributes are Hans Dommasch's *Prairie Giants* (Saskatoon: Western Producer Books, 1986); Elizabeth McLachlan's *Gone but Not Forgotten: Tales of Disappearing Grain Elevators* (Edmonton: NeWest Press, 2004); and Greg McDonnell's *Wheat Kings: Vanishing Landmarks of the Canadian Prairies* (Erin, ON: Boston Mills Press, 1998). The first elevator romantic, however, was Walter Herbert, with his article "Castles of the New World" in *Canadian Geographical Journal* 6/5 (May 1933): 241–55. John Everitt of Brandon University has written widely on the subject; among his articles are "A 'Tragic Muddle' and a 'Cooperative Success': An Account of Two Elevator Experiments in Manitoba, 1960–1928," in *Manitoba History* 18 (Fall 1989): 12–24; "The Line Elevator in Alberta," parts 1 and 2, in *Alberta History* 40/4 (Fall 1992) and 41/1 (Winter 1993); and, with Deryck Holdsworth, "Bank Branches and Elevators: Expressions of Big Corporations in Small Prairie Towns," in *Prairie Forum* 13/2 (Fall 1988): 173–190. Charles Anderson's *Grain: The Entrepreneurs* (Winnipeg: Watson and Dwyer, 1991) is an excellent general survey of the industry, as are D.A. MacGibbon's *The Canadian Grain Trade* (Toronto: Macmillan, 1932); Harald Patton's *Grain Growers' Cooperation in Western Canada* (New York: AMS Press, 1969 [1928]); and C.F. Wilson's *A Century of Canadian Grain: Government Policy to 1951* (Saskatoon: Western Producer Prairie Books, 1978). For a technical study of grain elevators written in their heyday, see W.C. Clark, "The Country Elevator in the Canadian West," in *Bulletin of the Departments of History and Political and Economic Science in Queen's University* 20 (July 1916). A good account of one of the biggest grain dealers is *The Grain Growers Record: An Abridged History, 1906–1943* (Winnipeg: United Grain Growers, 1944). Karen Nicholson surveys the debate over the survival of elevators in "Small Farmers, Big Business, and the Battle Over the Prairie Sentinels," in *Manitoba History* 45 (Spring 2003): 12–19.

Towers of Power

Like the tale of the trans-Canada airway, the story of these six towers had to be pieced together from a range of sources. Alan Gordon's *Making Public Pasts: The Contested Terrains of Montreal's Public Memories, 1891–1930* (Montreal: McGill–Queen's University Press, 2001) discusses Nelson's Column in Montreal, while the information on Nelson's experiences in Canada comes from Tom Pocock's *The Young Nelson in the Americas* (London: Collins, 1980). For the Wolfe and Montcalm monument, the starting point is the account on the website **www.collections.ic.gc.ca/quebec/monuments/wolfe_mont**. Robert Malcolmson has written a fine book on commemorating Brock, *Burying General Brock: A History of Brock's Monuments* (Niagara-on-the-Lake, ON: Friends of Fort George, 1996). There is also much of interest in Glenn McArthur and Annie Szamosi's biography *William Thomas, Architect, 1799–1860* (Ottawa: Archives of Canadian Art, 1996). An indispensable account of these early towers is David Bentley's wonderful essay "Monumental Tensions: Commemoration of British Political and Military Heroes in Canada," in his edited volume *Mnemographia Canadensis: Essays on Memory, Community and Environment in Canada* (London, ON: Canadian Poetry Press, 1999), vol. 1, 23–45.

For information on the newer towers, I had to rely primarily on newspaper and magazine accounts, although some books provided valuable background: Grant MacEwan's *Calgary Cavalcade: From Fort to Fortune* (Saskatoon: Western Producer Book Service, 1975) on the context of the Husky Tower; Donald MacKay's *The People's Railway: A History of Canadian National* (Vancouver: Douglas & McIntyre, 1992) for the corporate history behind the CN Tower; and Norman R. Ball, *"Mind, Heart, and Vision": Professional Engineering in Canada 1887 to 1987* (Ottawa: National Museum of Science and Technology, 1987) for the engineering challenges in building the tower. Malachy Grant's talk to the Empire Club, "The CN Tower," in *The Empire Club of Canada Speeches, 1975–1976* (Toronto: The Empire Club Foundation, 1976): 147–58, is a worthwhile addition to the literature.

Carved in Imperishable Granite

The most complete biography of Emanuel Hahn is Victoria Baker's exhibit guide, *Emanuel Hahn and Elizabeth Wyn Wood: Tradition and Innovation in Canadian Sculpture* (Ottawa: National Gallery of Canada, 1997). The story of the Winnipeg Cenotaph was told first in James Gray's article "The Battle of the Winnipeg Cenotaph" in *Canadian Forum* (November 1934): 60–4. He updated it for his later book, *The Roar of the Twenties* (Toronto: Macmillan, 1975). The standard survey of Canadian war memorials remains Robert Shipley's *To Mark Our Place: A History of Canadian War Memorials* (Toronto: NC Press, 1987). For a more general account of Canada's memory of the Great War, including war memorials, see my own book, *Death So Noble: Memory, Meaning and the First World War* (Vancouver: UBC Press, 1997).

PHOTO CAPTIONS AND CREDITS

1. **Handshakes Across the Water**
   The *Duchess of Atholl* steaming under the Quebec Bridge, 1934 / Library and Archives Canada / PA-044740.

2. **A Unity Based on Road and Wheel**
   Digging a cut along the Trans-Canada Highway, Tea Lake, Ontario, ca. 1925 / Archives of Ontario RG2-71 VB-42.

3. **A Vast Aerial Highway**
   Workers clear deadfall from the landing strip at Salmo, British Columbia, May 1933 / Library and Archives Canada / PA-035072.

4. **In Every Way Worthy of the Province**
   The Provincial Legislature, Regina / Jonathan F. Vance, photographer.

5. **In Character with a Northern Country**
   Tourists admire the Banff Springs Hotel, October 1929 / William R. Oliver, photographer / Library and Archives Canada / PA-058085.

6. **Making War on Cultural Poverty**
   The Confederation Centre of the Arts in Charlottetown, formerly the Fathers of Confederation Memorial Building / Barrett & MacKay, photographer / The Confederation Centre of the Arts.

7. **A Moveable Post Office**
   The first rural mail delivery, between Hamilton and Ancaster, October 1908 / Library and Archives Canada / C-027791.

8. **Calling Rural Canada**
   The switchboard of the rural telephone system in Medora, Manitoba, ca. 1915 / Archives of Manitoba / N17016.

9. **Switches Control Everything but the Children**
   Surveying the miracle of rural electrification / *A Farm Electrification Program: Report of the Manitoba Electrification Enquiry Commission 1942* (Winnipeg: King's Printer, 1943).

10. **Castles of the New World**
    Lining up at the grain elevators in Vulcan, Alberta, 1920s / Canadian Government Motion Picture Bureau, photographer / Library and Archives Canada / PA-802183.

11. **Towers of Power**
    The York Pioneers celebrating at the Brock Monument, from *Canadian Illustrated News,* vol. 4, 7 September 1872, p. 10 / Library and Archives Canada / C-058782.

12. **Carved in Imperishable Granite**
    Emanuel Hahn's war memorial in Milton, Ontario / J. Peter Vance, photographer.

INDEX